Essentials of the Java™ Programming Language

A Hands-On Guide

Monica Pawlan

ADDISON-WESLEY

An imprint of Addison Wesley Longman, Inc.

Reading, Massachusetts • Harlow, England • Menlo Park, California
Berkeley, California • Don Mills, Ontario • Sydney
Bonn • Amsterdam • Tokyo • Mexico City

The publisher offers discounts on this book when ordered in quantity for special sales. For more information, please contact:

Pearson Education Corporate Sales Division
One Lake Street
Upper Saddle River, NJ 07458
(800) 382-3419

Library of Congress Cataloging-in Publication Data

Pawlan, Monica
    Essentials of the Java programming language: a hands-on guide/Monica Pawlan,
        p.   cm.
    Includes bibliographical references and index.
    ISBN 0-201-70720-9 (alk. paper)
    1. Java (Computer program language) I. Title

    QA76.73.J38 P39 2000
    005.13'3--dc21   00-025260

ISBN 0-201-70720-9

Text printed on recycled and acid-free paper.

1 2 3 4 5 6 7 8 9 10-MA-04 03 02 01 00

First printing, May 2000

Contents

Preface   **xiii**

LESSON 1
Compiling and Running a Simple Program   **1**
Covered in This Lesson   1
A Word About the Java Platform   2
Setting Up Your Computer   3
Writing a Program   3
Compiling the Program   3
Interpreting and Running the Program   4
Code Comments   5
    Double Slashes   5
    C-Style Comments   5
    Doc Comments   5
API Documentation   6
Setting the CLASSPATH Environment Variable on a Windows Platform   6
Exercises   6
More Information   7

LESSON 2
Building Applications   **9**
Covered in This Lesson   9
Application Structure and Elements   9
Fields and Methods   12
Constructors   14
To Summarize   16
Exercises   16
More Information   16

Lesson 3
Building Applets   17
Covered in This Lesson   17
Application to Applet   17
Run the Applet   19
Applet Structure and Elements   19
    Extending a Class   20
    Behavior   21
    Appearance   22
Packages   23
Exercises   24
More Information   24

Lesson 4
Building a User Interface   25
Covered in This Lesson   25
Project Swing APIs   26
Import Statements   26
Class Declaration   28
Instance Variables   29
Constructor   29
Action Listening   31
Event Handling   32
main Method   32
Exercises: Applets Revisited   33
Summary   35
More Information   35

Lesson 5
Building Servlets   37
Covered in This Lesson   37
About the Example   38
HTML Form   38
Servlet Code   40
    Class and Method Declarations   41
    Method Implementation   42
JavaServer Pages Technology   43
    HTML Form   43
    JSP Page   44
Exercises   45
More Information   46

LESSON 6
File Access and Permissions 47
Covered in This Lesson 47
File Access by Applications 48
Constructor and Instance Variable Changes 49
Method Changes 49
System Properties 52
File.separatorChar 52
Exception Handling 52
File Access by Applets 55
Granting Applets Permission 57
    Creating a Policy File 57
    Running an Applet with a Policy File 57
Restricting Applications 58
File Access by Servlets 59
Exercises 59
More Information 60
Code for This Lesson 61
    FileIO Program 61
    FileIOAppl Program 63
    FileIOServlet Program 65
    AppendIO Program 66

LESSON 7
Database Access and Permissions 69
Covered in This Lesson 69
Database Setup 70
Create Database Table 70
Database Access by Applications 70
    Establishing a Database Connection 71
    Final and Private Variables 72
    Writing and Reading Data 73
Database Access by Applets 74
    JDBC Driver 75
    JDBC-ODBC Bridge with ODBC Driver 76
Database Access by Servlets 78
Exercises 79
More Information 79
Code for This Lesson 79
    Dba Program 79
    DbaAppl Program 82

DbaOdbAppl Program   84
DbaServlet Program   86

LESSON 8
Remote Method Invocation   **89**
Covered in This Lesson   90
About the Example   90
   Program Behavior   90
   File Summary   90
   Compile the Example   92
   Start the RMI Registry   93
   Start the Server   95
   Run the RMIClient1 Program   96
   Run the RMIClient2 Program   97
RemoteServer Class   98
Send Interface   99
RMIClient1 Class   99
   actionPerformed Method   99
   main Method   100
RMIClient2 Class   100
   actionPerformed Method   101
   main Method   101
Exercises   102
More Information   102
Code for This Lesson   102
   RMIClient1 Program   102
   RMIClient2 Program   104
   RemoteServer Program   105
   Send Interface   106

LESSON 9
Socket Communications   **107**
Covered in This Lesson   107
What Are Sockets and Threads?   108
About the Examples   108
   Client-Side Behavior   109
   Server-Side Behavior   109
   Compile and Run   110
Example 1: Single-Threaded Server Example   110
   Server-Side Program   110
   Client-Side Program   111

Example 2: Multithreaded Server Example   113
Exercises   116
More Information   116
Code for This Lesson   116
    SocketClient Program   116
    SocketServer Program   118
    SocketThrdServer Program   120

LESSON 10
User Interfaces Revisited   123
Covered in This Lesson   123
About the Example   124
    Fruit Order Client (RMIClient1)   124
    Server Program   125
    View Order Client (RMIClient2)   125
    Compile and Run the Example   126
Fruit Order (RMIClient1) Code   128
    Instance Variables   128
    Constructor   129
    Event Handling   131
    Cursor Focus   133
    Converting Strings to Numbers and Back   134
Server Program Code   135
    Send Interface   135
    RemoteServer Class   135
View Order Client (RMIClient2) Code   136
Exercises   138
    Calculations and Pressing Return   138
    Nonnumber Errors   138
    Extra Credit   138
More Information   139
Code for This Lesson   139
    RMIClient1 Program   139
    RMIClient2 Program   143
    RMIClient1 Improved Program   147

LESSON 11
Developing the Example   153
Covered in This Lesson   153

Tracking Orders   153
    sendOrder Method   154
    getOrder Method   154
    Other Changes to Server Code   155
Maintaining and Displaying a Customer List   157
    About Collections   157
    Creating a Set   158
    Accessing Data in a Set   159
    Displaying Data in a Dialog Box   160
Exercises   161
More Information   162
Code for This Lesson   162
    RemoteServer Program   162
    RMIClient2   164

LESSON 12
Internationalization   169
Covered in This Lesson   169
Identify Culturally Dependent Data   169
Create Keyword and Value Pair Files   171
    German Translations   173
    French Translations   174
Internationalize Application Text   175
    Instance Variables   175
    main Method   175
    Constructor   177
    actionPerformed Method   178
Internationalize Numbers   178
Compile and Run the Application   179
    Compile   179
    Start the RMI Registry   180
    Start the Server   180
    Start the RMIClient1 Program in German   180
    Start the RMIClient2 Program in French   181
Exercises   181
More Information   182
Code for This Lesson   183
    RMIClient1   183
    RMIClient2   187

LESSON 13
Packages and JAR File Format   **193**
Covered in This Lesson   193
Setting up Class Packages   193
    Create the Directories   194
    Declare the Packages   195
    Make Classes and Fields Accessible   195
    Change Client Code to Find the Properties Files   196
Compile and Run the Example   196
    Compile   197
    Start the RMI Registry   197
    Start the Server   198
    Start the RMIGermanApp Program   198
    Start the RMIClient2 Program in French   198
Using JAR Files to Deploy   199
    Server Set of Files   199
    Fruit Order Set of Files (RMIClient1)   200
    View Order Set of Files   202
Exercises   202
More Information   203

LESSON 14
Object-Oriented Programming   **205**
Covered in This Lesson   205
Object-Oriented Programming Defined   206
    Classes   206
    Objects   207
    Well-Defined Boundaries and Cooperation   207
Inheritance and Polymorphism   209
Data Access Levels   211
    Classes   212
    Fields and Methods   212
    Global Variables and Methods   213
Your Own Classes   213
    Well-Defined Boundaries and Cooperation   214
    Inheritance   214
    Access Levels   215
Exercises   215
More Information   216

APPENDIX A
Cryptography   **217**
Covered in This Lesson   217
About the Example   218
Compiling and Running the Example   220
Source Code   220
   Sealing the Symmetric Key   221
   Encrypting the Symmetric Key with the RSA Algorithm   229
Exercises   237
More Information   237

APPENDIX B
Code Listings   **239**
Covered in This Lesson   239
Application Code   239
   RMIClient1   240
   RMIClient2   245
   DataOrder   249
   Send   249
   RemoteServer   250
   RMIFrenchApp   251
   RMIGermanApp   256
   RMIEnglishApp   260
Cryptography Example   265
   Sealing the Symmetric Key: RMIClient1 Program   265
   Sealing the Symmetric Key: RMIClient2 Program   271
   Encrypting the Symmetric Key with the RSA Algorithm:
     RMIClient1 Program   276
   Encrypting the Symmetric Key with the RSA Algorithm:
     RMIClient2 Program   283

Further Reading   **289**

Index   **291**

Preface

If you are new to programming in the Java™ language and have some experience with other languages, this tutorial could be for you. It walks you through how to use the Java® 2 Platform software to develop a basic network application that uses common Java 2 Platform features. This tutorial is not comprehensive, but instead it takes you on a straight and uncomplicated path through the more common features available in the Java platform. This tutorial is a learning tool and should be viewed as a stepping-stone for persons who find the currently available materials a little too overwhelming to start with.

To reduce your learning curve, this tutorial begins with a simple program in Lesson 1, develops the program by adding new features in every lesson, and leaves you with a general electronic-commerce application and a basic understanding of object-oriented programming concepts in Lesson 14. Unlike other, more reference-style texts that give you a lot of definitions and concepts at the beginning, this tutorial takes a practical approach. New features and concepts are described when they are added to the example application, and the end of each lesson points to texts where you can get more information.

Please note the final application is for instructional purposes only and would need more work to make it production worthy. By the time you finish this tutorial, you should have enough knowledge to go on comfortably to other Java programming language learning materials currently on the market and continue your studies.

If you have no programming experience at all, you might still find this tutorial helpful; but you also might want to take an introductory programming course before you proceed.

Lessons 1 through 8 explain how applications, applets, and servlets/JavaServer Pages™ technology are similar and different, how to build a basic user interface that handles simple user input, how to read data from and write data to files and databases, and how to send and receive data over the network.

Lessons 9 through 14 are somewhat more complex and build on the material presented in the first eight lessons. These lessons walk you through socket communications, building a user interface using more components, grouping multiple data elements as one unit (collections), saving data between program invocations (serialization), and internationalizing a program. Lesson 14 concludes the series with basic object-oriented programming concepts.

This tutorial covers object-oriented concepts at the end, after you have had practical experience with the language so you can relate the object-oriented concepts to your experiences. This should make learning the concepts a little easier. Remember, this tutorial is a learning tool, and the intention is that you gain enough experience and information here to go on comfortably to other more comprehensive and in-depth texts to continue your studies.

Appendix A provides a version of the enterprise example that uses encryption and decryption technology to pass a credit card number over the network. This material is in an appendix because the encryption and decryption software is currently available only in the United States and Canada.

Appendix B presents the complete and final application code for this tutorial.

NOTE   JavaBeans™ technology, which lets you create portable program components that follow simple naming and design conventions, is not covered here. While creating a simple JavaBean component is easy, understanding JavaBeans features requires knowledge of such things as properties, serialization, events, and inheritance. When you finish these lessons, you should have the knowledge you need to continue your studies with a good text on JavaBeans technology.

Acknowledgments

Many Java Developer Connection^{SM} (JDC) members contributed comments and suggestions to this material when the first eight lessons appeared on the JDC Web site in March and April of 1999, and the last eight lessons appeared the following July. With these suggestions and many others received from the review team at Addison-Wesley, the material has evolved into an introduction to Java programming language features for persons new to the platform and unfamiliar with the terminology. In particular, I'd like to thank Anton Stiglic (Zero Knowledge), John C. 'Buck' Field, Jonathan Hughes, C. B. Dasgupta, Paul Brinkley, J. D. Baker, Bob Bell, Matt Fahrner, Howard Harkness, Orson Alvarez, and Joshua Engel.

I also relied on the help of coworkers, friends, and family for whose help I am very grateful. In that light I would like to thank both my friend and coworker, Mary Aline, for providing the French translations for Lesson 12, Internationalization (page 165) and my best friend and husband Jeffrey Pawlan (WA6KBL), who worked with Wolf Geihe (DJ4OA) in Germany to provide the German translations for that same chapter. And I do not want to forget Stephanie Wilde, our contract editor at the JDC, who helped with copyediting the early versions of this material posted to the JDC Web site, and Dana Nourie, our JDC HTML editor, who in her quest to learn the Java programming language provided unending enthusiasm for this work and contributed to the section on how to set the CLASSPATH environment variable on the Windows platform (page 6).

Special thanks go to Alan Jacobs and Orson Alvarez, who went through the example code and text making a number of excellent suggestions to improve them, and to Calvin Austin, whose helpful suggestions at the outset made the earlier lessons more understandable and accessible to novice programmers. Finally, thanks to Danesh Forouhari who made some excellent suggestions to improve the graphics and who encouraged me to include a short section on JavaServer Pages technology.

Finally, I want to acknowledge various individual reviewers within Sun Microsystems, Inc., whose expert knowledge in their respective areas was an invaluable asset to completing the examples: Rama Roberts (object-oriented programming), Dale Green (internationalization), Alan Sommerer (JAR file format and packages), Jan Luehe (cryptography), Joshua Bloch (collections), and Tony Squier (databases).

Compiling and Running a Simple Program

IF you are new to the Java™ programming language, you are probably wondering what all the talk is about. You might have heard of applets, applications, and servlets/JavaServer Pages technology, but are not sure what they are or when you would want to write an applet as opposed to writing an application or a servlet. Maybe you are just curious about the basic set of application programming interfaces (APIs) available in the platform and do not want to read a lot of pages to find out what is available.

This short tutorial gives you a hands-on introduction to the Java programming language. It starts with compiling and running the simple program presented in this lesson; adds new features in each successive lesson; explains the differences and similarities between applets, applications, and servlets/JavaServer Pages technology; covers new terminology and concepts along the way; and introduces APIs commonly used in general programs.

Covered in This Lesson

- A Word about the Java Platform
- Setting Up Your Computer
- Writing a Program
- Compiling the Program
- Interpreting and Running the Program
- Code Comments
- API Documentation
- Setting the CLASSPATH Environment on a Windows Platform

- Exercises
- More Information

A Word about the Java Platform

Before you can write and compile programs, you need to understand what the Java platform is and to set your computer up to run the programs. The Java platform consists of the Java application programming interfaces (APIs) and the Java virtual machine (Java VM).

Java APIs are libraries of compiled code that you can use in your programs. They let you add ready-made and customizable functionality to save you programming time. The simple program in this lesson uses a Java API to print a line of text to the console. The printing capability is provided in the API, ready for you to use; you supply the text to be printed.

Figure 1-1 shows the Java platform architecture. The Java VM sits on top of your native operating system. Your program sits on top of the Java VM and calls compiled code from the API libraries that live within the Java VM.

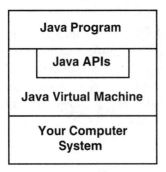

Figure 1-1   Java Platform Architecture

Programs written in the Java programming language are run (or interpreted) by another program called the Java VM. If you have used Visual Basic or another interpreted language, this concept is probably familiar to you. Rather than running directly on the native operating system, the program is interpreted by the Java VM for the native operating system. This means that any computer system with a Java VM installed can run programs written in the Java programming language, regardless of the computer system on which the applications were originally developed. For example, a program developed on a personal computer (PC) with the Windows NT operating system should run equally well without modification on a Sun Ultra workstation with the Solaris operating system, and vice versa.

Setting Up Your Computer

Before you can write and run the simple program in this lesson, you need to install the Java platform on your computer system. The Java platform is available free of charge from the java.sun.com Web site (`http://java.sun.com/products/jdk/1.2`). You can choose between the Java®2 Platform software for Windows 95/98/NT, the Solaris™ Operating Environment, or Linux. The download page contains the information you need to install and configure the Java platform for writing and running programs. You can find free downloads for other platforms by searching the Web.

NOTE Make sure you have the Java platform installed and configured for your system before you try to write and run the simple program presented next.

Writing a Program

The easiest way to write a simple program is with a text editor. So, using the text editor of your choice, create a text file with the following text, and be sure to name the text file `ExampleProgram.java`. Programs written in the Java programming language are case sensitive, so pay particular attention to the capitalization. This simple program prints "I'm a Simple Program" to the command line. Its structure and elements are described in the next lesson.

```
//A Very Simple Example
class ExampleProgram {
  public static void main(String[] args){
     System.out.println("I'm a Simple Program");
  }
}
```

Compiling the Program

A program written in the Java programming language has to be converted to a form the Java VM can understand so any computer with a Java VM can interpret and run the program. Compiling means taking the programmer-readable text in your program file (also called source code) and converting it to byte codes, platform-independent instructions for the Java VM.

The Java compiler is invoked at the command line on Unix and DOS shell prompts as follows:

```
javac ExampleProgram.java
```

> **NOTE**   Part of the configuration process for setting up the Java platform is set-
> ting the classpath. The classpath can be set either by using the -classpath
> option with the javac compiler command and java interpreter command or by
> setting the CLASSPATH environment variable. Make sure you have set the class-
> path to point to the current directory so the compiler and interpreter commands
> can find the ExampleProgram class. See the section <u>Setting the CLASSPATH</u>
> <u>Environment Variable on a Windows Platform</u> (page 6) for more information.

Interpreting and Running the Program

Once your program successfully compiles into Java byte codes, you can inter-pret and run applications on any Java VM or interpret and run applets in any Web browser with a Java VM, such as Netscape or Internet Explorer, built in. Interpreting and running means invoking the Java VM byte code interpreter which converts the Java byte codes to platform-dependent machine codes so your computer can understand and run the program.

The Java interpreter is invoked at the command line on Unix and DOS shell operating systems as follows:

```
java ExampleProgram
```

At the command line, you should see

```
I'm a Simple Program
```

Figure 1-2 shows how the entire sequence looks in a window.

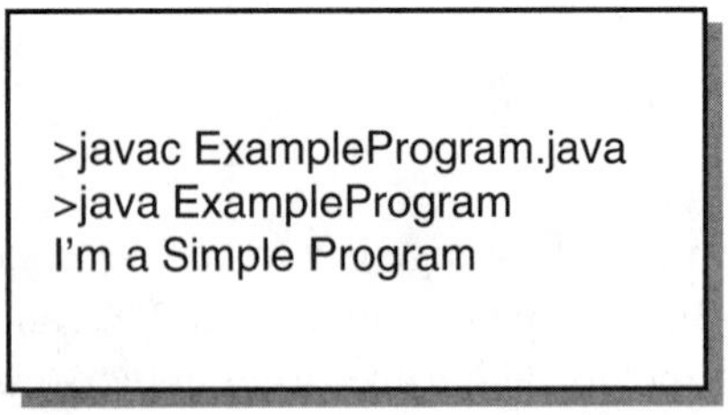

```
>javac ExampleProgram.java
>java ExampleProgram
I'm a Simple Program
```

Figure 1-2   Compiling and Interpreting a Simple Program

Code Comments

Code comments are placed in source files to describe what is happening in the code to someone who might be reading the file, to comment-out lines of code, to isolate the source of a problem for debugging purposes, or to generate API documentation. To these ends, the Java programming language supports three kinds of comments: double slashes, C-style, and doc comments.

Double Slashes

Double slashes (//) are used in the C++ programming language; they tell the compiler to treat everything from the slashes to the end of the line as text.

```
//A Very Simple Example
class ExampleProgram {
  public static void main(String[] args){
     System.out.println("I'm a Simple Program");
  }
}
```

C-Style Comments

Instead of double slashes, you can use C-style comments (/* */) to enclose one or more lines of code to be treated as text.

```
/* These are C-style comments */
class ExampleProgram {
  public static void main(String[] args){
    System.out.println("I'm a Simple Program");
  }
}
```

Doc Comments

To generate documentation for your program, use doc comments (/** */) to enclose lines of text for the javadoc tool to find. The javadoc tool locates the doc comments embedded in source files and uses those comments to generate API documentation.

```
/** This class displays a text string on the the console. */
class ExampleProgram {
   public static void main(String[] args){
     System.out.println("I'm a Simple Program");
   }
 }
```

With one simple class, there is no reason to generate API documentation. API documentation makes sense when you have an application made up of a number of complex classes that need documentation. The tool generates HyperText Markup Language (HTML) files (Web pages) that describe the class structures and contain the text enclosed by the doc comments.

API Documentation

The Java platform installation includes API documentation, which describes the APIs available for you to use in your programs. By default, the files are stored in a doc directory beneath the directory in which you installed the platform. For example, if the platform is installed in /usr/local/java/jdk1.2, the API documentation is in /usr/local/java/jdk1.2/doc/api.

Setting the CLASSPATH Environment Variable on a Windows Platform

To set the CLASSPATH environment variable on the Windows platform, open the AUTOEXEC.BAT file in your root directory in a text editor, or type sysedit in Run from the Start button and insert the following. The following example assumes C is the main drive and the one on which the JDK is installed:

```
SET PATH=%PATH%;%JAVAHOME%\BIN
PATH=C:\WINDOWS;C:\WINDOWS\COMMAND;C:\JDK\BIN;
SET CLASSPATH=.;C:\jdk\lib\tools.jar,%CLASSPATH%
```

Write the SET CLASSPATH command on one line, save the file, and close the editor. To force these settings to take place, open an MS-DOS window and type autoexec.bat, or restart your computer.

Exercises

1. What is the name of the program that runs (or interprets) programs written in the Java programming language?

2. Name the interpreter command, and explain what it does.

3. Name the compiler command, and explain what it does.

More Information

See the Java 2 SDK Tools Web page for more information on setting the classpath and using the javac and java commands.

```
http://java.sun.com/products/jdk/1.2/docs/tooldocs/
    tools.html
```

See "Common Compiler and Interpreter Problems" in *The Java™ Tutorial, Second Edition* [Cam98] for troubleshooting help.

The javadoc home page has more information on the javadoc command and its output.

```
http://java.sun.com/products/jdk/javadoc/index.html
```

You can also view the API Documentation for the Java 2 Platform on the java.sun.com site.

```
http://java.sun.com/products/jdk/1.2/docs/api/index.html
```

Building Applications

ALL applications, applets, and servlets written in the Java programming language have essentially the same structure and share many common elements. They also have some differences. This lesson describes the structure and elements common to applications. Lesson 3, Building Applets (page 17), describes the structure and elements common to applets, and Lesson 5, Building Servlets (page 37), describes the structure and elements common to servlets.

Covered in This Lesson

- Application Structure and Elements
- Fields and Methods
- Constructors
- To Summarize
- Exercises
- More Information

Application Structure and Elements

An application is created from classes. A class defines class fields to store the data and class **methods** to work on the data. A **class** is similar to a struct in the C and C++ languages in that it can store related data of different types. However, the big difference between a class and a `struct` is that a class also defines methods to work on its data, whereas C functions or C++ member functions are separate from the `struct` that defines the data.

As shown in Figure 2-1, a very simple class might store a string of text, define one method to set the string, and define another method to get the string and print it to the console. Methods that get and set the data are called **accessor** methods.

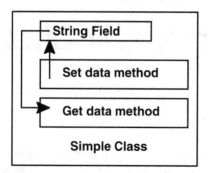

Figure 2-1   Simple Class with One Field and Accessor Methods

Figure 2-2 shows a `main` method. Every application needs one class with a `main` method. The class with the `main` method is the entry point for the program and is the class name passed to the `java` interpreter command to run the application. The code in the `main` method executes first when the program starts.

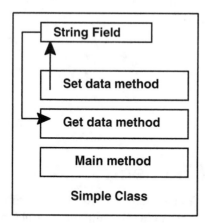

Figure 2-2   Main Method

Here, again, is the `ExampleProgram.java` code from the section <u>Writing a Program</u> (page 3). It has no fields or accessor methods, but because it is the only class in the program, it has a `main` method.

```
class ExampleProgram {
    public static void main(String[] args){
        System.out.println("I'm a Simple Program");
    }
}
```

In the above code, the public static void keywords mean that the Java virtual machine (Java VM) interpreter can call the program's main method to start the program (public) without creating an instance of the class (static). The program does not return data to the Java VM interpreter (void) when it ends.

An instance of a class has data members and methods as defined by that class. While the class describes the data and the methods to work on the data, a class instance acquires and works on the data. Figure 2-3 shows three instances of the StoreData class by the following names: FirstInstance, SecondInstance, and ThirdInstance. While class instances share the same definition (class), they are separate from each other in that each instance can acquire and work on different data.

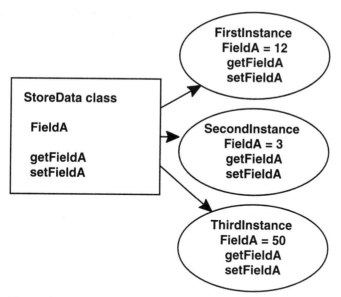

Figure 2-3   Class Instances

It is not always necessary to create a class instance to call methods and access fields in a class. An instance of the ExampleProgram class is never created because it has no fields to access and only the one static main method to call. The ExampleProgram main method just calls System.out.printIn. The java.lang.System class, among other things, provides functionality to send text to the terminal window where the program was started. It has all static fields and methods. The static out field in the System class is type Print-Stream, which is a class that provides various forms of print methods, including the printIn method.

The Java platform lets a program call a method in a class without creating an instance of that class, as long as the method being called is static. So, just as the Java VM interpreter command can call the static main method in the ExampleProgram class without creating an instance of the ExampleProgram class, the ExampleProgram class can call the static println method in the System class without creating an instance of the System class.

As you explore the Java programming language, you will come across library classes such as System, Math, or Color that contain all or some static methods and fields, and you might find that static methods and fields can make sense when you write your own classes. For example, the Color class provides ready access to common colors such as red, blue, and magenta through its static fields, and you can get custom colors by creating a Color class instance and passing specific values to the Color class constructor. For more information on constructors, see the section Constructors (page 14).

The following section uses a series of easy examples that build on the ExampleProgram class to help you further understand the relationships between and the rules for using static and nonstatic fields and methods.

Fields and Methods

The LessonTwoA.java program alters the simple example to store the text string in a static field called text. The text field is static so its data can be accessed directly by the static call to out.printIn without creating an instance of the LessonTwoA class.

```
class LessonTwoA {
//Static field added
  static String text = "I'm a Simple Program";

  public static void main(String[] args){
    System.out.println(text);
  }
}
```

The LessonTwoB.java and LessonTwoC.java programs add a getText method to the program to retrieve and print the text. The LessonTwoB program accesses the nonstatic text field with the nonstatic getText method. Nonstatic methods and fields are called **instance methods** and **fields**. This

FIELDS AND METHODS   **13**

approach requires that an instance of the `LessonTwoB` class be created in the `main` method.

To keep things interesting, this example also includes a `static` text field and a nonstatic instance method (`getStaticText`) to retrieve it. A nonstatic method can access both `static` and nonstatic fields.

```
class LessonTwoB {
//Static and non-static fields
   String text = "I'm a Simple Program";
   static String text2 = "I'm static text";

//Methods to access data in fields
   String getText(){ return text; }
   String getStaticText(){return text2;}

   public static void main(String[] args){
     LessonTwoB progInstance = new LessonTwoB();
     String retrievedText = progInstance.getText();
     String retrievedStaticText =
       progInstance.getStaticText();
     System.out.println(retrievedText);
     System.out.println(retrievedStaticText);
   }
}
```

The `LessonTwoC` program accesses the `static` text field with the `static` `getText` method. Static methods and fields are called **class methods** and **fields**. This approach allows the program to call the `static` `getText` method directly without creating an instance of the `LessonTwoC` class.

```
class LessonTwoC {
   static String text = "I'm a Simple Program";
//Accessor method
   static String getText(){
    return text;
   }
   public static void main(String[] args){
     String retrievedText = getText();
     System.out.println(retrievedText);
   }
}
```

So as you can see from the examples just given, class methods can operate only on class fields, but instance methods can operate on class and instance fields. You might wonder what the difference means: In short, there is only one copy of the data stored or set in a class field, but each instance has its own copy of the data stored or set in an instance field.

Figure 2-4 shows three class instances with one static field and one instance field. At runtime, there is one copy of the value for `static FieldA`, and each instance points to the one copy. When `setFieldA(50)` is called on the first instance, the value of the one copy changes from 36 to 50, and all three instances point to the new value. However, when setFieldB(25) is called on the first instance, the value for `non-static FieldB` changes from 0 to 25 for the first instance only because each instance has its own copy of FieldB.

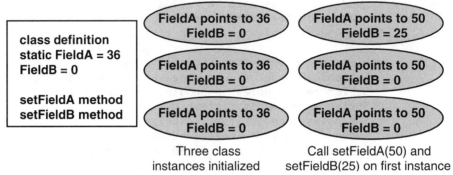

Three class   Call setFieldA(50) and
instances initialized   setFieldB(25) on first instance

Figure 2-4   Static Fields

Constructors

Classes have the special method, called a `constructor`, shown in Figure 2-5. The `constructor` is called when a class instance is created and always has the same name as the class and no return type. Constructors are used to create new class instances and to initialize their fields.

If you do not write your own constructor, the compiler adds an empty constructor, called the default constructor, and initializes all noninitialized fields and variables to zero. A constructor that you write might or might not have parameters, depending on whether the class provides its own initialization data or gets it from the calling method.

The `LessonTwoD` program converts the `LessonTwoB` program to use a constructor without parameters to initialize the text string field:

```
class LessonTwoD{
  String text;
```

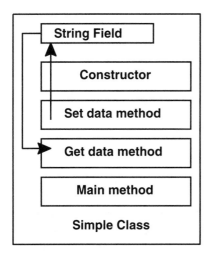

Figure 2-5 Constructor

```
//Constructor
  LessonTwoD(){
    text = "I'm a Simple Program";
  }

  String getText(){
    return text;
  }

  public static void main(String[] args){
    LessonTwoD progInst = new LessonTwoD();
    String retrievedText = progInst.getText();
    System.out.println(retrievedText);
  }
}
```

The LessonTwoE program passes the string to be printed to the constructor as a parameter:

```
class LessonTwoE{
  String text;

//Constructor
  LessonTwoE(String message){
    text = message;
  }
```

```
    String getText(){
      return text;
    }

  public static void main(String[] args){
    LessonTwoE progInst = new LessonTwoE(
      "I'm a simple program");
    String retrievedText = progInst.getText();
    System.out.println(retrievedText);
    }
  }
```

To Summarize

A simple program that prints a short text string to the console would probably do everything in the main method and do away with the constructor, text field, and getText method. This lesson used a very simple program to show you the structure and elements in a basic program written in the Java language.

Exercises

1. An application must have one class with which kind of method?

2. What is the difference between class and instance fields?

3. What are accessor methods?

More Information

See "Understanding Instance and Class Members" in *The Java™ Tutorial, Second Edition* [Cam98] for a thorough discussion of this topic.

Building Applets

L IKE applications, applets are created from classes. However, applets do not have a `main` method as an entry point, but they do have several methods to control specific aspects of applet execution. Applications run in the Java VM installed on a computer system, but applets run in the Java VM installed in a Web browser. You can also run an applet in a special tool, `appletviewer`, for testing applets.

This lesson converts one of the applications from Lesson 2, Building Applications (page 9), to an applet, describes the structure and elements common to applets, and shows you how to use the `appletviewer` tool.

Covered in This Lesson

- Application to Applet
- Run the Applet
- Applet Structure and Elements
- Packages
- Exercises
- More Information

Application to Applet

The following code is the applet equivalent to the `LessonTwoB` example (page 13) from Lesson 2, Building Applications. Figure 3-1 shows how the running applet looks. The structure and elements of the applet code are covered in the section <u>Applet Structure and Elements</u> (page 19).

Figure 3-1   A Simple Applet

```
import java.applet.Applet;
import java.awt.Graphics;
import java.awt.Color;

//Make applet class public
public class SimpleApplet extends Applet{
  String text = "I'm a simple applet";

  public void init() {
    text = "I'm a simple applet";
    setBackground(Color.cyan);
  }

  public void start() {
    System.out.println("starting...");
  }

  public void stop() {
    System.out.println("stopping...");
  }

  public void destroy() {
    System.out.println("preparing to unload...");
  }

  public void paint(Graphics g){
    System.out.println("Paint");
    g.setColor(Color.blue);
    g.drawRect(0, 0, getSize().width -1,
      getSize().height -1);
    g.setColor(Color.red);
```

```
      g.drawString(text, 15, 25);
   }
}
```

The `SimpleApplet class` is declared `public` so the program that runs the applet (a browser or the `appletviewer` tool), which is not local to the program, can access it.

Run the Applet

To see the applet in action, you need an HTML file with the Applet tag. The Applet tag references the compiled `SimpleApplet.class` which, in this example, is in the same directory with the HTML file.

```
<HTML>
<BODY>
<APPLET CODE=SimpleApplet.class WIDTH=200 HEIGHT=100>
</APPLET>
</BODY>
</HTML>
```

The easiest way to run the applet is with the `appletviewer` tool as follows, where `simpleApplet.html` is a file that contains the above HTML code:

```
appletviewer simpleApplet.html
```

NOTE To run an applet written with Java 2 APIs in a browser, the browser must be enabled for the Java 2 Platform. If your browser is not enabled for the Java 2 Platform, you have to use the `appletviewer` tool to run the applet or install Java Plug-in (`http://java.sun.com/products/plugin/index.html`). Java Plug-in lets you run applets on Web pages under the 1.2 version of the Java VM instead of the Web browser's default Java VM.

Applet Structure and Elements

The Java API `Applet` class has what you need to design the appearance and manage the behavior of an applet. The `Applet` class provides a graphical user interface (GUI) component called a `Panel` and a number of methods. To create an applet, extend the `Applet` class and implement the appearance and behavior you want.

The applet's appearance is created by drawing onto the `Panel` or adding other GUI components such as push buttons, scrollbars, or text areas to the `Panel`. The applet's behavior is defined by implementing its methods.

Extending a Class

Most classes of any complexity extend other classes. To extend another class means to take the data and behavior from the parent class and add more data and/or behavior to the child class. In the C++ language, this is called **subclassing**.

The class being extended is the parent class, and the class doing the extending is the child class. Another way to say this is the child class inherits the fields and methods of its parent or chain of parents. Child classes either call or override their inherited methods. The Java programming language allows only single inheritance where a child class is limited to one parent.

Figure 3-2 shows how the SimpleApplet class extends the Applet class, which extends the Panel class, which extends the Container class. The Container class extends the Object class, which is the parent of all Java classes.

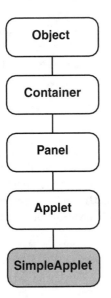

Figure 3-2   Extending the Applet Class

The Applet class provides the init, start, stop, destroy, and paint methods that you saw in the example applet code. The SimpleApplet class must override these methods to do what the SimpleApplet class needs them to do because the Applet class provides no functionality for these methods.

The Component class, however, does provide functionality for the setBackground method, which is called in the init method. The call to setBackground is an example of calling a method inherited from a parent class instead of overriding a method inherited from a parent class.

You might wonder why the Java language provides methods without implementations. It is to provide conventions for everyone to use for consistency across Java APIs. If everyone wrote his or her own method to start an applet, for example, but gave it a different name such as begin or go, the applet code would not be interoperable with other programs, tools, and browsers, or portable across multiple platforms. For example, both Netscape and Internet Explorer know how to look for the init and start methods.

Behavior

An applet is controlled by the software that runs it. Usually, the underlying software is a browser, but it can also be the appletviewer tool as you saw in the earlier example. The underlying software controls the applet by calling the methods the applet inherits from the Applet class. You do not have to implement all of these methods, only the ones you need.

The init Method

The init method is called when the applet is first created and loaded by the underlying software. This method performs one-time operations that the applet needs to function, such as creating the user interface or setting the font. In the following example, the init method initializes the text string and sets the background color:

```
public void init() {
  text = "I'm a simple applet";
  setBackground(Color.cyan);
}
```

The start Method

The start method is called when the applet is visited, such as when the user goes to a Web page with an applet on it. The example prints a string to the console to tell you the applet is starting. In a more complex applet, the start method would do things, such as begin animation or play sounds, required at the start of the applet.

```
public void start() {
  System.out.println("starting...");
}
```

After the `start` method executes, the platform calls the `paint` method to draw
to the applet's Panel. A **thread** is a single, sequential flow of control within the
applet, and every applet is made up of multiple threads. `Applet` drawing methods are always called from a dedicated drawing and event-handling thread.
You will find more information on threads in Lesson 9, Socket Communications (page 107).

The stop and destroy Methods

The `stop` method stops the applet when the applet is no longer on the screen,
such as when the user goes to another Web page. The example prints a string to
the console to tell you the applet is stopping. In a more complex applet, this
method should do things like stop animation or sounds. The `destroy` method
is called when the browser exits. Your applet should implement this method to
do any needed final cleanup:

```
public void stop() {
   System.out.println("stopping...");
}

public void destroy() {
   System.out.println("preparing to unload...");
}
```

Appearance

The `Applet` class is a `Panel` component that inherits a `paint` method from its
parent `Container` class. To draw on the applet's `Panel`, implement the `paint`
method to do the drawing. The `Graphics` object passed to the `paint` method
defines a **graphics context** for drawing on the `Panel`. The `Graphics` object
has methods for graphical operations, such as setting drawing colors, and
drawing graphics, images, and text. The `paint` method for the `SimpleApplet`
draws the *I'm a simple applet* string in red inside a blue rectangle.

```
public void paint(Graphics g){
   System.out.println("Paint");

//Set drawing color to blue
   g.setColor(Color.blue);

 //Specify the x, y, width and height for a rectangle
   g.drawRect(0, 0,
   getSize().width -1,
   getSize().height -1);
```

```
//Set drawing color to red
  g.setColor(Color.red);

//Draw the text string at the (15, 25) x-y location
  g.drawString(text, 15, 25);
}
```

Packages

The applet code also has at the top three `import` statements that explicitly import the `Applet`, `Graphics`, and `Color` classes in the `java.applet` and `java.awt` API library packages for use in the applet. Applications of any size and all applets access ready-made Java API classes organized into packages located elsewhere on the local or networked system. This is true whether the Java API classes come in the Java platform download from a third-party or are classes you write yourself and store in a directory separate from the program.

There are two ways to access these ready-made libraries: `import` statements, which you saw in the code for the section <u>Application to Applet</u> (page 17) and full package names. This code rewrites the example applet to use full package names instead of `import` statements. A compiled class in one package can have the same name as a compiled class in another package: the package name differentiates the two classes. For example `java.lang.String` and `mypackage.String` reference two completely different classes.

```
public class SimpleApplet extends java.applet.Applet{
  String text = "I'm a simple applet";

  public void init() {
    text = "I'm a simple applet";
    setBackground(java.awt.Color.cyan);
  }
  public void start() {
    System.out.println("starting...");
  }
  public void stop() {
    System.out.println("stopping...");
  }
  public void destroy() {
    System.out.println("preparing to unload...");
  }

  public void paint(java.awt.Graphics g){
    System.out.println("Paint");
    g.setColor(Color.blue);
```

```
    g.drawRect(0, 0,
    getSize().width -1,
    getSize().height -1);
    g.setColor(java.awt.Color.red);
    g.drawString(text, 15, 25);
  }
}
```

NOTE   The examples in Lessons 1 and 2 did not need a package declaration to call the `System.out.println` Java API class because the `System` class is in the `java.lang` package and all classes in that package are included by default.

Exercises

1. What are some differences between applications and applets?

2. Name the applet methods that control the applet's behavior.

3. Describe two ways to access API library classes organized into packages from your programs.

More Information

You can find more information on applets in "Writing Applets" in *The Java™ Tutorial, Second Edition* [Cam98].

You might also find this book helpful: *Developing Professional Java™ Applets* [Hop96] by K. C. Hopson, Stephen E. Ingram, and Patrick Chan.

Building a User Interface

T<small>HIS</small> lesson adds a user interface to the `LessonTwoD` application on page 15. The user interface is built with the Java Foundation Classes (JFC) Project Swing (Project Swing) APIs. Project Swing APIs provide a wide range of classes for building friendly and sophisticated graphical user interfaces and handling action events from user inputs such as mouse clicks and keyboard presses.

This is a very basic introduction to Project Swing that is developed more in Lesson 10, User Interfaces Revisited (page 123). You will find pointers to more in-depth material on Project Swing at the end of this lesson.

Covered in This Lesson

- Project Swing APIs
- Import Statements
- Class Declaration
- Instance Variables
- Constructor
- Action Listening
- Event Handling
- `main` Method
- Exercises: Applets Revisited
- Summary
- More Information

Project Swing APIs

The Project Swing APIs provide a full array of building blocks (components) for creating interesting, sophisticated, and friendly user interfaces. You can choose from basic controls such as buttons and checkboxes, components that contain other components such as frames and panels, and information displays such as labels and text areas.

When you build a user interface, you place basic components and information displays inside container components, and if the user interface has many elements, you can place container components within other container components. Ultimately, all applets and applications have top-level containers to hold all their user interface components.

An applet's top-level container is a browser window, and an application's top-level container is a frame. A frame component is a window that provides a title, banner, and methods to manage the appearance and behavior of the window. An applet relies on the browser for this type of functionality. Figure 4-1 shows an applet's top-level panel nested in a browser window and an application's top-level panel nested in a frame. While an applet can have only one top-level panel, an application can have many.

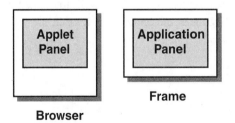

Figure 4-1   Top-Level Browser and Top-Level Frame

The Project Swing code for this lesson builds the simple application shown in Figure 4-2. The frame on the left appears when you start the application, and the frame on the right appears when you click the button. Click again to go back to the original frame on the left.

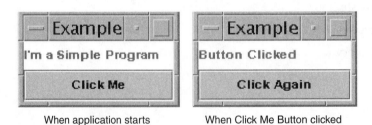

Figure 4-2   Project Swing Application

Import Statements

The import statements in the SwingUI.java code that follows indicate which Java API packages and classes the program uses. The first two lines import specific classes in the Abstract Window Toolkit (AWT) package, and the third line imports the event package within the awt package. You could replace these lines with one line—import java.awt.*—to import the entire awt package instead.

Your code will be clearer to someone else reading it if you import only the classes and packages you need and no others. However, if you use a lot of classes in one package, it is probably easier to import an entire package including its subpackages, as shown by the fourth import javax.swing statement.

```java
import java.awt.Color;
import java.awt.BorderLayout;
import java.awt.event.*;
import javax.swing.*;

//Class Declaration
class SwingUI extends JFrame implements ActionListener {

//Instance variables
   JLabel text, clicked;
   JButton button, clickButton;
   JPanel panel;
   private boolean _clickMeMode = true;

//Constructor
   SwingUI(){ //Begin Constructor
     text = new JLabel("I'm a Simple Program");
     button = new JButton("Click Me");
     button.addActionListener(this);
     panel = new JPanel();
     panel.setLayout(new BorderLayout());
     panel.setBackground(Color.white);
     getContentPane().add(panel);
     panel.add(BorderLayout.CENTER, text);
     panel.add(BorderLayout.SOUTH, button);
   } //End Constructor
```

```
//Event handling
public void actionPerformed(ActionEvent event){
  Object source = event.getSource();
   if (source == button) {
      if (_clickMeMode) {
         text.setText("Button Clicked");
         button.setText("Click Again");
         _clickMeMode = false;
      } else {
         text.setText("I'm a Simple Program");
         button.setText("Click Me");
         _clickMeMode = true;
      }
   }
}


//main method
public static void main(String[] args){
    SwingUI frame = new SwingUI();
    frame.setTitle("Example");
    WindowListener l = new WindowAdapter() {
      public void windowClosing(WindowEvent e) {
         System.exit(0);
      }
    };
    frame.addWindowListener(l);
    frame.pack();
    frame.setVisible(true);
  }
}
```

NOTE   The Abstract Window Toolkit (AWT) is an API library that provides classes for building a user interface and handling action events. However, Project Swing extends the AWT with a full set of GUI components and services, pluggable look and feel capabilities, and assistive technology support. Project Swing components include Java language versions of the AWT components such as buttons and labels and a rich set of higher-level components such as list boxes and tabbed panes. Given the enhanced functionality and capabilities in the Project Swing class libraries, this tutorial focuses on the Project Swing APIs.

Class Declaration

The class declaration indicates the top-level frame for the application's user interface. In this example, the SwingUI class extends a JFrame class that implements the ActionListener interface. The Project Swing JFrame class extends the Frame class, which is part of the AWT APIs. Project Swing component classes have the same name as their AWT counterparts prefixed with the letter J.

```
class SwingUI extends JFrame implements ActionListener{
```

The `ActionListener` interface provides an interface for handling action events, and like all other interfaces in the Java programming language, defines a set of methods but does not implement their behavior. Instead, you provide the interface method implementations for the class that implements the interface.

The Java platform lets a class extend only one class, but lets it implement any number of interfaces. In this example, the `SwingUI` class extends the `JFrame` class and implements the `ActionListener` interface.

When a program class implements an interface, it must provide behavior for all methods defined in that interface. The `ActionListener` interface has only one method, the `actionPerformed` method. So the `SwingUI` class must implement the `actionPerformed` method, which is covered in the section Event Handling (page 32).

Instance Variables

The next lines in the `SwingUI` class declare the Project Swing component classes that the `SwingUI` class uses. These are instance variables (or fields) that can be accessed by any method in the instantiated class. In the example, they are built in the `SwingUI` constructor and accessed in the `actionPerformed` method implementation.

The `private boolean` variable is an instance variable that is accessible only to the `SwingUI` class and is used in the `actionPerformed` method to find out whether the `button` has been clicked. You will find more information on data access levels in Lesson 14, Object-Oriented Programming (page 205).

```
JLabel text;
JButton button;
JPanel panel;
//Start out waiting to be clicked
private boolean _clickMeMode = true;
```

Constructor

The constructor creates the user interface components, adds the components to the `JPanel` object, adds the panel to the frame, and makes the `JButton` components action listeners, all of which is covered in the section Action Listening (page 31). The `JFrame` object is created in the `main` method when the program starts.

```
SwingUI(){
  text = new JLabel("I'm a Simple Program");
  button = new JButton("Click Me");

 //Add button as an event listener
  button.addActionListener(this);

//Create panel
  panel = new JPanel();

//Specify layout manager and background color
  panel.setLayout(new BorderLayout());
  panel.setBackground(Color.white);

//Add label and button to panel
  getContentPane().add(panel);
  panel.add(BorderLayout.CENTER, text);
  panel.add(BorderLayout.SOUTH, button);
}
```

When the JPanel object is created, the layout manager and the background color are specified. The layout manager in use determines how user interface components are arranged in the display area. The code uses the BorderLayout layout manager, which arranges user interface components in the five areas shown in Figure 4-3.

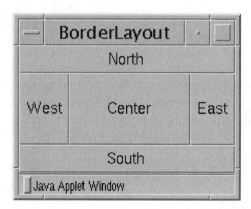

Figure 4-3   Border Layout

To add a component to the layout, specify the area using the static fields provided in the BorderLayout class for this purpose: BorderLayout. NORTH, BorderLayout.SOUTH, BorderLayout.EAST, BorderLayout.WEST, and BorderLayout.CENTER.

This next code segment adds components to the panel in the center and south regions of the border layout. Components are not added directly to a JFrame, but rather to its content pane. Because the layout manager controls the layout of components, it is set on the content pane where the components reside. A content pane provides functionality that allows different types of components to work together in Project Swing. The call to the getContentPane method of the JFrame class adds the panel to the JFrame container.

```
//Create panel
  panel = new JPanel();

//Specify layout manager and background color
  panel.setLayout(new BorderLayout());
  panel.setBackground(Color.white);

//Add label and button to panel
  getContentPane().add(panel);
  panel.add(BorderLayout.CENTER, text);
  panel.add(BorderLayout.SOUTH, button);
}
```

Action Listening

To handle action events, you have to implement the ActionListener interface and add the action listener to the JButton components. In the following example the action listener is the SwingUI object because its class implements the ActionListener interface.

In this example this means that the SwingUI object listens for action events. When a button click action event occurs, the Java platform services pass the button click action to the actionPerformed method implemented in the SwingUI class. The actionPerformed implementation described in the section Event Handling (page 32) handles the action event.

Component classes have the appropriate add methods to add action listeners to them. The JButton class has an addActionListener method, and the parameter passed to addActionListener is this, meaning that the SwingUI action listener is added to the button and the Java platform services pass button-generated actions to the actionPerformed method in the SwingUI class.

```
  button = new JButton("Click Me");
//Add button as an event listener
  button.addActionListener(this);
```

Event Handling.

The `actionPerformed` method is passed an event object that represents the action event that occurred. Next, it uses an `if` statement to find out if the `button` component fired the action event, and it tests the `_clickMeMode` variable to find out if the button component is waiting to be clicked or has already been clicked.

If the `button` component is in a waiting to be clicked state, the label and button text are changed to reflect that the button was just clicked. If the `button` component is in an already clicked state, the label and button text are changed to invite another click.

```java
public void actionPerformed(ActionEvent event) {
    Object source = event.getSource();
        if (source == button){
            if (_clickMeMode) {
                text.setText("Button Clicked");
                button.setText("Click Again");
                _clickMeMode = false;
            } else {
                text.setText("I'm a Simple Program");
                button.setText("Click Me");
                _clickMeMode = true;
            }
        }
}
```

main Method

The `main` method creates the top-level `frame`, sets the title, and includes code that lets the user close the window using the `frame` menu.

```java
public static void main(String[] args) {
//Create top-level frame
    SwingUI frame = new SwingUI();
    frame.setTitle("Example");
//This code lets you close the window
    WindowListener l = new WindowAdapter() {
        public void windowClosing(WindowEvent e) {
            System.exit(0);
        }
    };
    frame.addWindowListener(l);
//This code lets you see the frame
    frame.pack();
    frame.setVisible(true);
 }
}
```

The code for closing the window shows an easy way to add event handling functionality to a program. If the event listener interface you need provides more functionality than the program actually uses, you can use an adapter class.

The Java APIs provide adapter classes for all listener interfaces with more than one method. This way, you can use the adapter class instead of the listener interface and implement only the methods you need. In the example, the `WindowListener` interface has seven methods, and this program needs only the `windowClosing` method. Therefore it makes sense to use the `Window-Adapter` class instead of the `WindowListener` interface.

This next code segment extends the `WindowAdapter` class and overrides the `windowClosing` method. The `new` keyword creates an anonymous instance of the extended inner class. It is anonymous because you are not assigning a name to the class and you cannot create another instance of the class without executing the code again. It is an inner class because the extended class definition is nested within the `SwingUI` class.

This approach takes only a few lines of code, while implementing the `Window-Listener` interface would require six empty method implementations. Be sure to add the `WindowAdapter` object to the `frame` object so the `frame` object will listen for window events.

```
    WindowListener l = new WindowAdapter() {
//The instantiation of object l is extended
//to include this code:
    public void windowClosing(WindowEvent e) {
        System.exit(0);
    }
};
    frame.addWindowListener(l);
```

Exercises: Applets Revisited

Using what you learned in Lesson 3, Building Applets (page 17), and in this lesson, convert the example code for this lesson into the applet shown in Figure 4-4. A solution using the `JApplet` class follows.

You could also use the `Applet` class, which was the class used in Lesson 3, Building Applets (page 17). The `JApplet` class is the Project Swing class equivalent for creating applets, and the applet code for this exercise is almost identical except the `JApplet` class requires calls to `getContentPane()` for setting the layout and color and for adding components to the panel, which you do not need if you use the `Applet` class.

Figure 4-4   Applet Version of Application

```java
import java.awt.Color;
import java.awt.BorderLayout;
import java.awt.event.*;
import javax.swing.*;

public class ApptoAppl extends JApplet
  implements ActionListener {
    JLabel text;
    JButton button;
    JPanel panel;
    private boolean _clickMeMode = true;

    public void init() {
      getContentPane().setLayout(new BorderLayout());
      getContentPane().setBackground(Color.white);
      text = new JLabel("I'm a Simple Program");
      button = new JButton("Click Me");
      button.addActionListener(this);
      getContentPane().add(BorderLayout.CENTER, text);
      getContentPane().add(BorderLayout.SOUTH, button);
    }

  public void start() {
      System.out.println("Applet starting.");
    }

public void stop(){
  System.out.println("Applet stopping.");
}
public void destroy(){
  System.out.println("Destroy method called.");
}
```

```
public void actionPerformed(ActionEvent event) {
  Object source = event.getSource();
  if (source == button){
    if (_clickMeMode) {
      text.setText("Button Clicked");
      button.setText("Click Again");
      _clickMeMode = false;
    } else{
      text.setText("I'm a Simple Program");
      button.setText("Click Me");
      _clickMeMode = true;
    }
  }
 }
}
```

Summary

The differences between the applet and application versions of the example are as follows:

- The applet class is `public` so another program such as `appletviewer` can access it.

- The applet class extends `Applet`; the application class extends `JFrame`.

- The applet version has no `main` method.

- The application constructor is replaced in the applet by `start` and `init` methods.

- GUI components are added directly to the `Applet`; in the case of an application, GUI components are added to the content pane of its `JFrame` object.

More Information

For more information on Project Swing and event handling, see *The JFC Swing Tutorial: A Guide to Constructing GUIs* [Wal99].

To find out about other available layout managers, see the JDC article "Exploring the AWT Layout Managers" at `/developer/technicalArticles/GUI/AWTLayoutMgr/index.html`.

The inner classes specification provides more information on inner classes.

```
http://java.sun.com/products/jdk/1.1/docs/guide/
    innerclasses/spec/innerclasses.doc3.html#13592
```

Building Servlets

Lıᴋᴇ applications and applets, servlets are created from classes, but servlets are different from applications and applets in that the purpose of a servlet is to extend a server program to enhance its functionality. One very common use for servlets is to extend a Web server by providing dynamic Web content.

Servlets are easy to write. All you need is the Java 2 Platform software and the JavaServer Web Development Kit (JSWDK). You can download a free copy of the JSWDK from the `java.sun.com` Web site.

This lesson shows you how to create a very simple browser-based HTML form that invokes a basic servlet to process user data entered onto the form, and concludes with showing you how to convert the servlet to use JavaServer Pages™ (JSP) technology. The example is the servlet version of the applet and application in Lesson 4, Building a User Interface (page 25).

The intent in this lesson is to show you how applets, applications, servlets, and JSP pages are similar yet different. If you want to know more about servlets than is covered here, you can find pointers to more in-depth material at the end of this lesson.

Covered in This Lesson

- About the Example
- HTML Form
- Servlet Code
- JavaServer Pages Technology

- Exercises
- More Information

About the Example

Web servers respond to browser requests using the HyperText Transfer Protocol (HTTP). HTTP is the protocol for moving hypertext files across the Internet; HTML documents contain text that has been marked up for interpretation by an HTML browser such as Netscape.

A browser accepts user input through an HTML form. The simple form used in this lesson has one text input field for the user to enter text and a Submit button. When the user clicks the Submit button, the simple servlet is invoked to process the user input. In this example, the simple servlet returns an HTML page that displays the text entered by the user.

Figure 5-1 shows the flow of data between the browser and the servlet for this example.

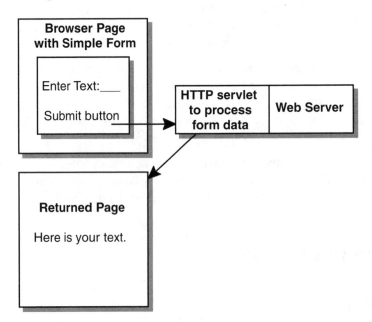

Figure 5-1   Returning an HTML Page

HTML Form

The HTML form is embedded in an HTML file. The form shown in Figure 5-2 is created by the HTML code that follows it.

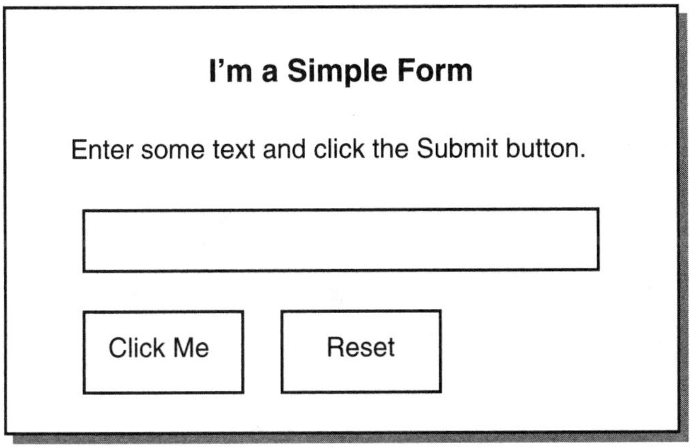

I'm a Simple Form

Enter some text and click the Submit button.

Click Me   Reset

Figure 5-2 Simple HTML Form

The HTML form has an ACTION parameter where you specify the location of the servlet.

```
<HTML>
<HEAD>
<TITLE>Example</TITLE>
</HEAD>
<BODY BGCOLOR="WHITE"><BR>
<H2>I'm a Simple Form</H2>
Enter some text and click the Submit button.<BR>
<FORM METHOD="POST" ACTION="/servlet/ExampServlet">
<INPUT TYPE="TEXT" NAME="DATA" SIZE=30>
<P>
<INPUT TYPE="SUBMIT" VALUE="Click Me">
<INPUT TYPE="RESET">
</FORM>
</BODY>
</HTML>
```

When the user clicks the Click Me button on the form, the servlet gets the entered text and returns an HTML page with the text. The HTML page that is returned to the browser by the ExampServlet servlet assumes the user entered *Four score and seven years ago* (see Figure 5-3). The servlet code to retrieve the user's input and generate this HTML page is described on page 40.

NOTE   To run the example, you have to put the servlet and HTML files in the correct directories for the Web server you are using. For example, with Java WebServer 1.1.1, you put the servlet in ~/JavaWebServer1.1.1/servlets and the HTML file in the ~/JavaWebServer1.1.1/public_html directories.

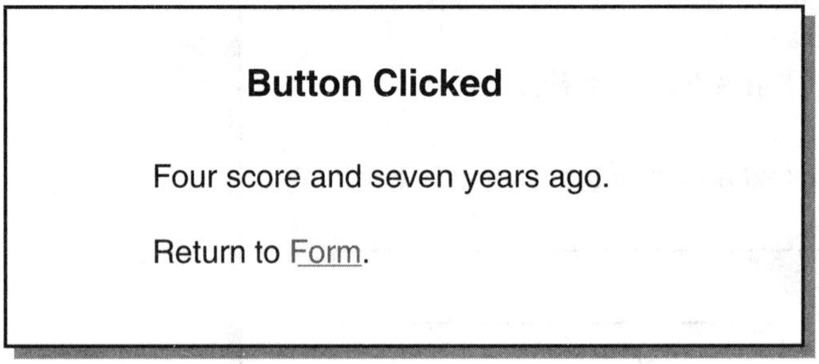

Button Clicked

Four score and seven years ago.

Return to Form.

Figure 5-3   HTML Page Returned to Browser

Servlet Code

The ExampServlet program builds an HTML page to return to the user. This means the servlet code does not use any Project Swing or AWT components or have action event handling code. For this simple servlet, you only need to import these packages:

- java.io for system input and output. The HttpServlet class uses the IOException class in this package to signal that an input or output exception of some kind has occurred.

- javax.servlet, which contains generic (protocol-independent) servlet classes. The HttpServlet class uses the ServletException class in this package to indicate a servlet problem.

- javax.servlet.http, which contains HTTP servlet classes. The HttpServlet class is in this package.

```java
import java.io.*;
import javax.servlet.*;
import javax.servlet.http.*;

public class ExampServlet extends HttpServlet {
  public void doPost(HttpServletRequest request,
                     HttpServletResponse response,
                     throws ServletException, IOException {

    response.setContentType("text/html");
    PrintWriter out = response.getWriter();
    out.println("<body bgcolor=FFFFFF>");
    out.println("<h2>Button Clicked<h2>");
    String data = request.getParameter("data");
```

```
      if(data != null && data.length() > 0){
        out.println(data);
      } else {
        out.println("No text entered.");
      }
        out.println("<P>Return to <A HREF=../exampServlet.htm>
                    Form</A>");
        out.close();
    }
  }
```

Class and Method Declarations

All HTML servlet classes extend the HttpServlet abstract class. The HttpServlet class simplifies writing HTTP servlets by providing a framework for handling the HTTP protocol. Because HttpServlet is abstract, your servlet class must extend it and override at least one of its methods. An abstract class is a class that contains unimplemented methods and cannot be instantiated itself. You extend the abstract class and implement the methods you need so all HTTP servlets use a common framework to handle the HTTP protocol.

```
public class ExampServlet extends HttpServlet {
   public void doPost(HttpServletRequest request,
                      HttpServletResponse response)
                throws ServletException, IOException{
```

The ExampServlet class is declared public so the Web server that runs the servlet, which is not local to the servlet, can access it.

The ExampServlet class defines a doPost method with the same name, return type, and parameter list as the doPost method in the HttpServlet class. By defining doPost this way, the ExampServlet class overrides and implements the doPost method in the HttpServlet class.

The doPost method performs the HTTP POST operation, which is the type of operation specified in the HTML form used for this example. The other possibility is the HTTP GET operation, in which case you would implement the doGet method instead.

In short, GET requests might pass parameters to a Uniform Resource Locator (URL) by appending them to the URL. POST requests might pass additional data to a URL by directly sending it to the server separately from the URL. POST requests cannot be bookmarked or e-mailed and do not change the URL of the response. GET requests can be bookmarked and e-mailed and add information to the URL of the response.

NOTE A Uniform Resource Locator (URL) is an address for a resource on the network.

The parameter list for the doPost method takes a request and a response object. The browser sends a request to the servlet, and the servlet sends a response back to the browser. The doPost method implementation accesses information in the request object to find out who made the request, what form the request data is in, and which HTTP headers were sent. It uses the response object to create an HTML page in response to the browser's request. The doPost method throws an IOException, if there is an input or output problem when it handles the request, and a ServletException, if the request could not be handled. These exceptions are handled in the HttpServlet class.

Method Implementation

The first part of the doPost method uses the response object to create an HTML page. It first sets the response content type to be text/html and then gets a PrintWriter object for formatted text output, as follows:

```
response.setContentType("text/html");
PrintWriter out = response.getWriter();
out.println("<body bgcolor=#FFFFFF>");
out.println("<h2>Button Clicked</h2>");
```

The next line uses the request object to get the data from the text field on the form and store it in the data variable. The getparameter method gets the named parameter, returns null if the parameter is not set, and returns an empty string if the parameter has no value.

```
String data = request.getParameter("data");
```

The next part of the doPost method gets the data out of the data parameter and passes it to the response object to add to the HTML response page.

```
if(data != null && data.length() > 0){
  out.println(data);
}else {
  out.println("No text entered.");
}
```

The last part of the doPost method creates a link to take the user from the HTML response page back to the original form and then closes the response:

```
out.println("<P>Return to
  <A HREF=../exampServlet.html>Form</A>");
out.close();
}
```

JavaServer Pages Technology

JavaServer Pages is a web technology that lets you put segments of servlet code directly within a static HTML or eXtensible Markup Language (XML) page. When the JSP page is executed, the application server creates, compiles, loads, and runs a background servlet to execute the servlet code segments and return an HTML page.

A JSP page looks like an HTML or XML page with servlet code segments embedded between various forms of leading (<%) and closing (%>) JSP scriptlet tags. There are no HttpServlet methods such as doGet and doPost. Instead, the code that would normally be in those methods is embedded directly in the JSP page using scriptlet tags.

HTML Form

Converting the example for this lesson to use a JSP page instead of a servlet is easy. First, change the ACTION parameter in the HTML form to invoke the JSP page instead of the servlet as shown below. Note that the JSP page is not in the servlets directory, but in the same directory with the HTML page.

```
<HTML>
<BODY BGCOLOR="WHITE">
<TITLE>Example</TITLE>
<TABLE><TR><TD WIDTH="275">

<H2>I'm a Simple Form</H2>
Enter some text and click the Submit button.<BR>

<FORM METHOD="POST" ACTION="ExampJsp.jsp">
<INPUT TYPE="TEXT" NAME="data" SIZE=30>
<P>
<INPUT TYPE="SUBMIT" VALUE="Click Me">
<INPUT TYPE="RESET">
</FORM>
</TD></TR></TABLE>
</BODY>
</HTML>
```

Second, create the JSP page as described next.

JSP Page

The following JSP page (ExampJSP.jsp) is equivalent to ExampServlet. It starts with the usual HTML, HEAD, TITLE, and BODY tags and concludes with closing the BODY and HTML tags. In between are two types of JSP tags: directives and scriptlets.

JSP directives are instructions processed by the JSP engine when the JSP page is translated to a servlet. The directives used in this example tell the JSP engine to include certain packages and classes. Directives are enclosed by the <%@ and %> directive tags.

JSP scriptlets let you embed Java code segments into the JSP page. The embedded code is inserted directly into the servlet that executes when the page is requested. Scriptlets are enclosed in the <% and %> scriptlet tags.

A scriptlet can use the following predefined variables: request, response, out, and in. This means you can use these variables without declaring them. For example, the PrintWriter out = response.getWriter() line to create the out object is not needed here.

```
<HTML>
<HEAD>
<TITLE>Example JSP Page</TITLE>
</HEAD>

<BODY>
<%@ page import="java.io.*" %>
<%@ page import="javax.servlet.*" %>
<%@ page import="javax.servlet.http.*" %>

<%
    response.setContentType("text/html");
    out.println("<body bgcolor=FFFFFF>");
    out.println("<h2>Button Clicked<h2>");
    String data = request.getParameter("data");

    if(data != null && data.length() > 0){
      out.println(data);
    } else {
      out.println("No text entered.");
    }
      out.println(
        "<P>Return to <A HREF=../exampJsp.html>Form</A>");
      out.close();
%>
</BODY>
</HTML>
```

Other JSP tags you can use are comments (<%-- comment %>), declarations
(<%! String data %>), expressions (<%= expression %>), and JSP-specific
tags. This is the JSP page converted to use the comment and declaration tags.

```
<HTML>
<HEAD>
<TITLE>Example JSP Page</TITLE>
</HEAD>

<%-- Import Statements --%>
<%@ page import="java.io.*" %>
<%@ page import="javax.servlet.*" %>
<%@ page import="javax.servlet.http.*" %>

<%-- Declaration --%>
<%! String data; %>

<%
    response.setContentType("text/html");
    out.println("<body bgcolor=FFFFFF>");
    out.println("<h2>Button Clicked<h2>");
    data = request.getParameter("data");

    if(data != null && data.length() > 0){
      out.println(data);
    } else {
      out.println("No text entered.");
    }
      out.println(
        "<P>Return to <A HREF=../exampJsp.html>Form</A>");
      out.close();
%>
</BODY>
</HTML>
```

Exercises

1. What is the function of a servlet?

2. What does the request object do?

3. What does the response object do?

4. How is a JSP page different from a servlet?

More Information

You can find more information on servlets in "Servlets" in *The Java*™ *Tutorial Continued* [Cam99].

You can find more information on Java WebServer on the `www.sun.com` Web site.
`http://www.sun.com/software/jwebserver/index.html`

Get a free copy of the JavaServer Development Kit (JSDK) from the `java.sun.com` Web site.
`http://java.sun.com/products/servlet/index.html`

You might also find this book helpful: *Java*™ *Servlet Programming* [Hun98] by Jason Hunter and William Crawford. It includes information on JavaServer Pages technology.

File Access and Permissions

So far, you have learned how to retrieve and handle a short text string entered from the keyboard into a simple graphical user interface (GUI) or HTML form. Programs also retrieve, handle, and store data in files and databases.

This lesson expands the applet, application, and servlet examples from the previous lessons to perform basic file access using the APIs in the `java.io` package. The lesson also shows you how to grant applets and servlets permission to access specific files and how to restrict an application so it has access to specific files only. In Lesson 7, Database Access and Permissions (page 69), you learn how to perform similar operations on a database.

Covered in This Lesson

- File Access by Applications
- Constructor and Instance Variable Changes
- Method Changes
- System Properties
- `File.separatorChar`
- Exception Handling
- File Access by Applets
- Granting Applets Permission
- Restricting Applications
- File Access by Servlets
- Exercises

- More Information
- Code for This Lesson

File Access by Applications

The Java 2 Platform software provides a rich range of classes for reading character data (alphanumeric) or byte data (a unit consisting of a combination of eight 1's and 0's) into a program and writing character or byte data out to an external file, storage device, or program. The source or destination might be on the local computer system where the program is running or anywhere on the network.

This section shows you how to read data from and write data to a file on the local computer system.

- Reading: A program opens an input stream on the file and reads the data in serially (in the order it was written to the file).
- Writing: A program opens an output stream on the file and writes the data out serially.

This first example converts the `SwingUI.java` example from Lesson 4, Building a User Interface (page 25), to accept user input through a text field and save it to a file.

The window on the left appears when you start the `FileIO` application. When you click the button, whatever is entered into the text field is saved to a file. After that, the file is opened and read, and its text is displayed in the window on the right. Click again and you are back to the original window with a blank text field ready for more input (see Figure 6-1).

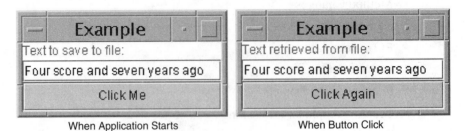

When Application Starts   When Button Click

Figure 6-1   File Access by Applications

The conversion from the `SwingUI` program for Lesson 4 to the `FileIO` program for this lesson primarily involves the `constructor` and the `action-Performed` method as described here. The entire program appears on page 61.

Constructor and Instance Variable Changes

The constructor instantiates the textField with a value of 30. This value tells the Java platform the number of columns to use to calculate the preferred width of the text field object. Lower values result in a narrower display; likewise, higher values result in a wider display.

Next, the text label object is added to the North section of the BorderLayout, and the textField object is added to the Center section, as follows:

```
//Instance variable for text field
   JTextField textField;

//Constructor
 FileIO(){
   text = new JLabel("Text to save to file:");
   button = new JButton("Click Me");
   button.addActionListener(this);

//Text field instantiation
   textField = new JTextField(30);
   panel = new JPanel();
   panel.setLayout(new BorderLayout());
   panel.setBackground(Color.white);
   getContentPane().add(panel);

//Adjustments to layout to add text field
   panel.add(BorderLayout.NORTH, text);
   panel.add(BorderLayout.CENTER, textField);
   panel.add(BorderLayout.SOUTH, button);
 }
```

Method Changes

The actionPerformed method uses the FileInputStream and FileOutput-Stream classes to read data from and write data to a file. These classes handle data in byte streams, as opposed to character streams, which are used in the applet example. A more detailed explanation of the changes to the method implementation follows the code.

```
public void actionPerformed( ActionEvent event){
  Object source = event.getSource();
  if(source == button){
     String s = null;
//Variable to display text read from file
   if (_clickMeMode){
       FileInputStream in=null;
```

```
        FileOutputStream out=null;
      try {
//Code to write to file
        String text = textField.getText();
        byte b[] = text.getBytes();
        String outputFileName = System.getProperty ("user.home",
                              File.separatorChar + "home" +
                              File.separatorChar + "zelda") +
                              File.separatorChar + "text.txt";
        out = new FileOutputStream(outputFileName);
        out.write(b);
//Clear text field
        textField.setText("");
//Code to read from file
        String inputFileName = System.getProperty ("user.home",
                              File.separatorChar + "home" +
                              File.separatorChar + "zelda") +
                              File.separatorChar + "text.txt";
        File inputFile = new File(inputFileName);
        in = new FileInputStream(inputFile);
        byte bt[] = new byte[(int)inputFile.length()];
        in.read(bt);
        String s = new String(bt);
    } catch(java.io.IOException e){
        System.out.println("Cannot access text.txt");
    } finally {
      try {
        in.close();
        out.close();
      } catch(java.io.IOException e) {
        System.out.println("Cannot close");
      }
    }
    //Clear text field
      textField.setText("");
    //Display text read from file
    text.setText("Text retrieved from file:");
    textField.setText(s);
    button.setText("Click Again");
    _clickMeMode = false;
  } else {
//Save text to file
    text.setText("Text to save to file:");
```

```
        textField.setText("");
        button.setText("Click Me");
        _clickMeMode = true;
      }
    }
  }
```

To write the user text to a file, the text is retrieved from the textField and converted to a byte array.

```
        String text = textField.getText();
        byte b[] = text.getBytes();
```

Next, a FileOutputStream object is created to open an output stream on the text.txt file.

```
String outputFileName = System.getProperty("user.home",
                        File.separatorChar + "home" +
                        File.separatorChar + "zelda") +
                        File.separatorChar + "text.txt";
out = new FileOutputStream(outputFileName);
```

The FileOutputStream object writes the byte array to the text.txt file.

```
    out.write(b);
```

The code to open a file for reading is similar. To read text from a file, a File object is created and used to create a FileInputStream object.

```
String inputFileName = System.getProperty("user.home",
                       File.separatorChar + "home" +
                       File.separatorChar + "zelda") +
                       File.separatorChar + "text.txt";
File inputFile = new File(inputFileName);
in = new FileInputStream(inputFile);
```

Next, a byte array that is the same length as the file into which the text is stored is created:

```
byte bt[] = new byte[(int)inputFile.length()];
in.read(bt);
```

Finally, the byte array is used to construct a String object, which contains the retrieved text displayed in the textField component.

```
String s = new String(bt);
textField.setText(s);
```

NOTE   You might think you could simplify this code by not creating the `File` object and just passing the `inputFileName String` object directly to the `FileInputStream` constructor. The problem is the `FileInputStream` object reads a byte stream, and a byte stream is created to a specified size. In this example, the byte stream needs to be the same size as the file, and that size varies depending on the text written to the file. The `File` class has a length method that lets you get this value so the byte stream can be created to the correct size each time.

System Properties

The code in the previous section used a call to `System.getProperty` to create the pathname to the file in the user's home directory. The `System` class maintains a set of properties that define attributes of the current working environment. When the Java platform starts, system properties are initialized with information about the runtime environment, including the current user, the Java platform version, and the character used to separate components of a file name (`File.separatorChar`).

The call to `System.getProperty` uses the keyword `user.home` to get the user's home directory and supplies the default value `File.separatorChar +` "home" `+ File.separatorChar +` "zelda" in case no value is found for this key.

File.separatorChar

The code shown in the section <u>Method Changes</u> (page 49) used the `java.io.File.separatorChar` variable to construct the directory pathname. This variable is initialized to contain the file separator value stored in the `file.separator` system property; it gives you a way to construct platform-independent pathnames. For example, the pathnames `/home/zelda/text.txt` for Unix and `\home\zelda\text.txt` for Windows are written as `File.separatorChar +` "home" `+ File.separatorChar +` "zelda" `+ File.separatorChar +` "text.txt" in a platform-independent construction.

Exception Handling

The Java programming language includes classes that represent conditions that can be thrown by a program during execution. Throwable classes can be divided into error and exception conditions; they descend from the java. lang.Exception and java.lang.Error classes shown in Figure 6-2. An Exception subclass indicates a throwable exception that a reasonable application might want to catch, and an Error subclass indicates a serious throwable error that a reasonable application should not try to catch.

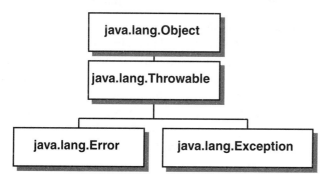

Figure 6-2   Exception Classes

All exceptions except java.lang.RuntimeException and its subclasses are called checked exceptions. The Java platform requires that a method catch or specify all checked exceptions that can be thrown within the scope of a method. If a checked exception is not caught or specified, the compiler throws an error.

In the FileIO example, the actionPerformed method has file input and output code that could throw a java.lang.IOException checked exception in the event the file cannot be created for the write operation or opened for the read operation. To handle these possible exception situations, the file input and output code in the actionPerformed method is enclosed in a try and catch block.

```
try {
  //Write to file
  //Read from file
} catch (java.lang.IOException e) {
  //Do something if read or write fails
}
```

If a method does not catch a checked exception, it must specify that it can throw the checked exception because a checked exception that can be thrown by a method is really part of the method's public interface. Callers of the method must know about the checked exceptions a method might throw so they can take appropriate actions to handle the exception.

While it is true that checked exceptions must be either caught or specified, sometimes you do not have a choice. For example, the `actionPerformed` method already has a public interface definition that cannot be changed to specify the `java.io.IOException`. If you add a throws clause to the `action-Performed` method, you will get a compiler error. So in this case, the only thing you can do is catch and handle the checked exception.

However, methods you define yourself can either specify exceptions or catch and handle them. Following is an example of a user-defined method that specifies an exception. In this case, the method implementation does not have to catch and handle `IllegalValueException`, but callers of this method must catch and handle `IllegalValueException`. The decision to throw an exception or catch and handle it in a user-defined method depends on the method behavior. Sometimes it makes more sense for the method to handle its own exceptions, and sometimes it makes more sense to give that responsibility to the callers.

```
public int aMethod(int number1, int number2) throws
IllegalValueException{
  //Body of method
}
```

Whenever you catch exceptions, you should handle them in a way that is friendly to your users. The exception and error classes have a `toString` method to print system error text and a `printStackTrace` method to print a stack trace, which can be very useful for debugging your application during development. It is probably better, however, to deploy the program with a more user-friendly approach to handling problems.

You can provide your own application-specific error text to print to the command line, or you can display a dialog box with application-specific error text. Using application-specific error text will also make it much easier to internationalize the application (page 169) later because you will have access to the text. The section <u>Displaying Data in a Dialog Box</u> (page 156) explains how to display a dialog box with the text you want.

```
//Do this during development
   } catch(java.io.IOException e) {
     System.out.println(e.toString());
     System.out.println(e.printStackTrace());
   }
//But deploy it like this
   } catch(java.io.IOException e){
     System.out.println("Cannot access text.txt");
   }
```

The example uses a `finally` block for closing the `in` and `out` objects. The `finally` block is the final step in a `try` and `catch` block and contains clean-up code for closing files or releasing other system resources. Statements in the `finally` block are executed no matter what happens in the `try` block. So, even if an error occurs in the `try` block, you can be sure the `Statement` and `ResultSet` objects will be closed to release the memory they were using.

```
} finally {
  try {
    in.close();
    out.close();
  } catch(java.io.IOException e) {
    System.out.println("Cannot close");
  }
}
```

File Access by Applets

The file access code for the `FileIOAppl` applet (page 63) is equivalent to the `FileIO` application, but it shows how to use the APIs for handling data in character streams instead of byte streams. You can use either approach in applets or applications. In this lesson, the choice to handle data in byte streams in the application and character streams in the applet is arbitrary. In your programs, base the decision on your specific application requirements.

The changes to instance variables and the `constructor` are identical to the application code, and the changes to the `actionPerformed` method are nearly identical with these exceptions:

- Writing: The `textField` text is retrieved and passed directly to the `out.write` call.

- Reading: A character array is created to store the data read in from the input stream.

NOTE See the section <u>Granting Applets Permission</u> (page 57) before running this applet.

```
public void actionPerformed(ActionEvent event){
  Object source = event.getSource();
  if (source == button){
//Variable to display text read from file
    String s = null;
```

```
        if (_clickMeMode){
          FileReader in = null;
          FileWriter out = null;
          try {
//Code to write to file
            String text = textField.getText();
            String outputFileName = System.getProperty("user.home",
                              File.separatorChar + "home" +
                              File.separatorChar + "zelda") +
                              File.separatorChar + "text.txt";
            out = new FileWriter(outputFileName);
            out.write(text);
//Code to read from file
            String inputFileName = System.getProperty("user.home",
                              File.separatorChar + "home" +
                              File.separatorChar + "zelda") +
                              File.separatorChar + "text.txt";
          File inputFile = new File(inputFileName);
          in = new FileReader(inputFile);
          char c[] = new char[(int)inputFile.length()];
          in.read(c);
          s = new String(c);
        } catch(java.io.IOException e) {
          System.out.println("Cannot access text.txt"
        } finally {
          try {
            in.close();
            out.close();
          } catch(java.io.IOException e) {
            System.out.println("Cannot close");
          }
        }
      //Clear text field
        textField.setText("");
      //Display text read from file
        text.setText("Text retrieved from file:");
        textField.setText(s);
        button.setText("Click Again");
        _clickMeMode = false;
      } else {
//Save text to file
        text.setText("Text to save to file:");
        button.setText("Click Me");
        _clickMeMode = true;
      }
    }
  }
```

Granting Applets Permission

If you tried to run the applet example in a directory other than your home directory, you undoubtedly saw errors when you clicked the Click Me button. This is because Java 2 platform security imposes restrictions on applets. An applet cannot access local system resources such as files without explicit permission. In terms of the example for this lesson, the applet cannot write to or read from the text.txt file without explicit permission.

Java 2 platform security is enforced by the default security manager, which disallows all potentially threatening access operations, unless the applet executes with a policy file that specifically grants the needed access. So for the FileUIAppl program to write to and read from the text.txt file, the applet has to execute with a policy file that grants the appropriate read and write access to the text.txt file.

Creating a Policy File

Policy tool is a Java 2 platform security tool for creating policy files. The policy file you need to run the applet follows. You can use the Policy tool to create it (type policytool at the command line), or copy the following text into an ASCII file. The advantage to using the Policy tool is that you can avoid typos and syntax errors that will make the policy file ineffective.

```
grant {
    permission java.util.PropertyPermission "user.home",
        "read";
    permission java.io.FilePermission
      "${user.home}/text.txt", "read,write";
};
```

Running an Applet with a Policy File

Assuming the policy file is named polfile and is in the same directory with an HTML file named fileIO.html that contains the HTML to run the FileIOAppl applet, you would run the applet in the appletviewer tool like this:

```
appletviewer -J-Djava.security.policy=polfile fileIO.html
```

NOTE If your browser is enabled for the Java 2 Platform or if you have Java Plug-in installed, you can run the applet from the browser if you put the policy file in your local home directory and rename it `java.policy` for Windows and `.java.policy` for Unix. You can get Java Plug-In from the `java.sun.com` Web site at this URL:

```
http://java.sun.com/products/plugin/index.html
```

Following is an HTML file to run the `FileIOAppl` applet:

```
<HTML>
<BODY>
<APPLET CODE=FileIOAppl.class WIDTH=200 HEIGHT=100>
</APPLET>
</BODY>
</HTML>
```

Restricting Applications

Normally, applications do not run under the default security manager, but you can launch an application with special command-line options and a policy file to achieve the same kind of restriction you get with applets. This is how to do it:

```
java -Djava.security.manager -Djava.security.policy=polfile
    FileIO
```

Because the application runs within the security manager, which disallows all access, the policy file needs two additional permissions to run the applet. The `accessEventQueue` permission lets the security manager access the event queue where action events are stored and loads the user interface components. The `showWindowWithoutWarningBanner` permission lets the application execute without displaying the banner warning that its window was created by another program (the security manager).

```
grant {
  permission java.awt.AWTPermission "accessEventQueue";
  permission java.awt.AWTPermission
    "showWindowWithoutWarningBanner";
  permission java.util.PropertyPermission "user.home",
    "read";
  permission java.io.FilePermission
    "${user.home}/text.txt", "read,write";
};
```

File Access by Servlets

Although servlets are invoked from a browser, they are under the security policy in force for the Web server under which they run. The `FileIOServlet` program (page 65) writes to and reads from the `text.txt` file without restriction under Java Web Server™ 1.1.1.

Figure 6-3 shows an HTML form that invokes `FileIOServlet` (top) and the HTML form returned by `FileIOServlet` (bottom).

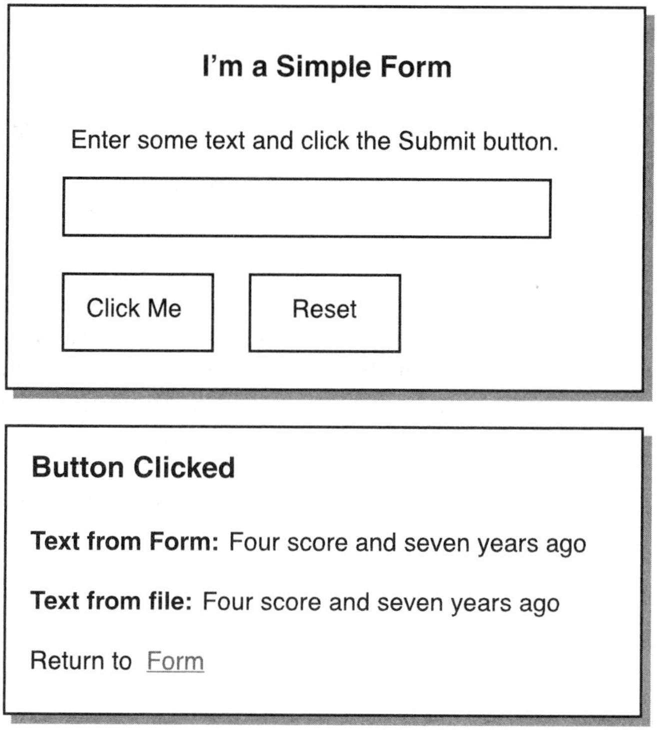

I'm a Simple Form

Enter some text and click the Submit button.

| Click Me | Reset |

Button Clicked

Text from Form: Four score and seven years ago

Text from file: Four score and seven years ago

Return to Form

Figure 6-3   File I/O and Servlets

Exercises

1. **Error Handling.** If you want to make the code for this lesson more user friendly, you could separate the write and read operations and provide two `try` and `catch` blocks. The error text for the read operation could be `Cannot read text.txt`, and the error text for the write operation could be `Cannot write text.txt`. As an exercise, change the

code to handle the read and write operations separately. The `FileIO` class on page 61 shows the solution.

2. **Appending.** So far the examples have shown you how to read in and write out streams of data in their entirety. Often you might want to append data to an existing file or read in only certain amounts. Using the `RandomAccessFile` class, alter the `FileIO` class to append to the file. You can find information on the `RandomAccessFile` class at this URL:

```
http://java.sun.com/products/jdk/1.2/docs/api/java/io/
    RandomAccessFile.html
```

Give it a try before taking a look at the `AppendIO` class on page 66.

More Information

See "Reading and Writing (But No 'Rithmetic)" in *The Java™ Tutorial, Second Edition* [Cam98] for information on transferring data between programs and between a program and memory and performing operations such as buffering or character encoding on data as it is read or written.

You can learn more about component sizing in "Solving Common Layout Problems" and "Layout Management" in *The Java™ Tutorial, Second Edition* [Cam98].

You can find more information on error handling in "Handling Errors with Exceptions" in *The Java™ Tutorial, Second Edition* [Cam98].

See "Controlling Applets" in *The Java™ Tutorial, Second Edition* [Cam98] for more information on the Policy tool.

Code for This Lesson

- FileIO
- FileIOAppl
- FileIOServlet
- AppendIO

FileIO Program

```java
import java.awt.Color;
import java.awt.BorderLayout;
import java.awt.event.*;
import javax.swing.*;
import java.io.*;
import java.awt.Color;
class FileIO extends JFrame implements ActionListener {
    JLabel text;
    JButton button;
    JPanel panel;
    JTextField textField;
    private boolean _clickMeMode = true;

    FileIO() { //Begin Constructor
      text = new JLabel("Text to save to file:");
      button = new JButton("Click Me");
      button.addActionListener(this);
      textField = new JTextField(30);
      panel = new JPanel();
      panel.setLayout(new BorderLayout());
      panel.setBackground(Color.white);
      getContentPane().add(panel);
      panel.add(BorderLayout.NORTH, text);
      panel.add(BorderLayout.CENTER, textField);
      panel.add(BorderLayout.SOUTH, button);
    } //End Constructor

    public void actionPerformed(ActionEvent event){
      Object source = event.getSource();
//The equals operator (==) is one of the few operators
//allowed on an object in the Java programming language
      if (source == button) {
        String s = null;
        //Write to file
        if (_clickMeMode){
```

```
       FileInputStream in=null;
     FileOutputStream out=null;
     try {
      String text = textField.getText();
      byte b[] = text.getBytes();
      String outputFileName = System.getProperty("user.home",
                           File.separatorChar + "home" +
                           File.separatorChar + "zelda") +
                           File.separatorChar + "text.txt";
      out = new FileOutputStream(outputFileName);
      out.write(b);
     } catch(java.io.IOException e) {
       System.out.println("Cannot write to text.txt");
     }
//Read from file
     try {
      String inputFileName = System.getProperty("user.home",
                           File.separatorChar + "home" +
                           File.separatorChar + "zelda") +
                           File.separatorChar + "text.txt";
       File inputFile = new File(inputFileName);
       in = new FileInputStream(inputFile);
       byte bt[] = new byte[(int)inputFile.length()];
       in.read(bt);
       s = new String(bt);
     } catch(java.io.IOException e) {
       System.out.println("Cannot read from text.txt");
     } finally {
       try {
         in.close();
         out.close();
       } catch(java.io.IOException e) {
         System.out.println("Cannot close");
       }
     }
   //Clear text field
     textField.setText("");
   //Display text read from file
     text.setText("Text retrieved from file:");
     textField.setText(s);
     button.setText("Click Again");
     _clickMeMode = false;
   } else {
```

```
    //Save text to file
            text.setText("Text to save to file:");
            textField.setText("");
            button.setText("Click Me");
            _clickMeMode = true;
        }
     }
 }

  public static void main(String[] args){
    FileIO frame = new FileIO();
    frame.setTitle("Example");
    WindowListener l = new WindowAdapter() {
      public void windowClosing(WindowEvent e) {
        System.exit(0);
      }
    };
    frame.addWindowListener(l);
    frame.pack();
    frame.setVisible(true);
  }
}
```

FileIOAppl Program

```
import java.awt.Color;
import java.awt.BorderLayout;
import java.awt.event.*;
import javax.swing.*;
import java.io.*;

public class FileIOAppl extends JApplet  implements ActionListener {
    JLabel text;
    JButton button;
    JPanel panel;
    JTextField textField;
    private boolean _clickMeMode = true;

    public void init(){
      getContentPane().setLayout(new BorderLayout(1, 2));
      getContentPane().setBackground(Color.white);
      text = new JLabel("Text to save to file:");
      button = new JButton("Click Me");
      button.addActionListener(this);
      textField = new JTextField(30);
      getContentPane().add(BorderLayout.NORTH, text);
      getContentPane().add(BorderLayout.CENTER, textField);
```

```
        getContentPane().add(BorderLayout.SOUTH, button);
      }
    public void start() {
       System.out.println("Applet starting.");
}

    public void stop() {
       System.out.println("Applet stopping.");
    }

    public void destroy() {
       System.out.println("Destroy method called.");
    }

    public void actionPerformed(ActionEvent event){
       Object source = event.getSource();
       if (source == button) {
         String s = null;
//Variable to display text read from file
         if (_clickMeMode) {
           FileReader in=null;
           FileWriter out=null;
           try {
     //Code to write to file
             String text = textField.getText();
             String outputFileName = System.getProperty("user.home",
                              File.separatorChar + "home" +
                              File.separatorChar + "zelda") +
                              File.separatorChar + "text.txt";
             out = new FileWriter(outputFileName);
             out.write(text);

     //Code to read from file
             String inputFileName = System.getProperty("user.home",
                              File.separatorChar + "home" +
                              File.separatorChar + "zelda") +
                              File.separatorChar + "text.txt";
             File inputFile = new File(inputFileName);
             in = new FileReader(inputFile);
             char c[] = new char[(int)inputFile.length()];
             in.read(c);
             s = new String(c);
           } catch(java.io.IOException e) {
             System.out.println("Cannot access text.txt");
           } finally {
             try {
```

```
                            in.close();
                            out.close();
                        } catch(java.io.IOException e) {
                            System.out.println("Cannot close");
                        }
                    }
//Clear text field
                    textField.setText("");
//Display text read from file
                    text.setText("Text retrieved from file:");
                    textField.setText(s);
                    button.setText("Click Again");
                    _clickMeMode = false;
                } else {
//Save text to file
                    text.setText("Text to save to file:");
                    button.setText("Click Me");
                    textField.setText("");
                    _clickMeMode = true;
                }
            }
        }//end action performed method
}
```

FileIOServlet Program

```
import java.io.*;
import javax.servlet.*;
import javax.servlet.http.*;

public class FileIOServlet extends HttpServlet {
    public void doPost(HttpServletRequest request,
                       HttpServletResponse response)
                       throws ServletException, IOException
    {
        response.setContentType("text/html");
        PrintWriter out = response.getWriter();
        out.println("<body bgcolor=FFFFFF>");
        out.println("<h2>Button Clicked</h2>");
        String data = request.getParameter("data");
        FileReader fin = null;
        FileWriter fout = null;

        if (data != null && data.length() > 0) {
          out.println("<STRONG>Text from form:</STRONG>");
          out.println(data);
        } else {
          out.println("No text entered.");
```

```java
        }
        try {
//Code to write to file
            String outputFileName=
            System.getProperty("user.home",
            File.separatorChar + "home" +
            File.separatorChar + "monicap") +
            File.separatorChar + "text.txt";
            fout = new FileWriter(outputFileName);
            fout.write(data);
//Code to read from file
            String inputFileName =
                System.getProperty("user.home",
                File.separatorChar + "home" +
                File.separatorChar + "monicap") +
                File.separatorChar + "text.txt";
            File inputFile = new File(inputFileName);
            fin = new FileReader(inputFile);
            char c[] = new char[30];
            fin.read(c);
            String s = new String(c);
            out.println("<P><STRONG>Text from file:</STRONG>");
            out.println(s);
        } catch(java.io.IOException e) {
            System.out.println("Cannot access text.txt");
        } finally {
          try {
           fout.close();
           fin.close();
          } catch(java.io.IOException e) {
           System.out.println("Cannot close");
          }
        }
        out.println(
          "<P>Return to <A HREF=../simpleHTML.html>Form</A>");
        out.close();
    }
}
```

AppendIO Program

```java
import java.awt.Color;
import java.awt.BorderLayout;
import java.awt.event.*;
import javax.swing.*;
import java.io.*;
```

```
class AppendIO extends JFrame implements ActionListener {
  JLabel text;
  JButton button;
  JPanel panel;
  JTextField textField;
  private boolean _clickMeMode = true;

  AppendIO() { //Begin Constructor
    text = new JLabel("Text to save to file:");
    button = new JButton("Click Me");
    button.addActionListener(this);
    textField = new JTextField(30);
    panel = new JPanel();
    panel.setLayout(new BorderLayout());
    panel.setBackground(Color.white);
    getContentPane().add(panel);
    panel.add(BorderLayout.NORTH, text);
    panel.add(BorderLayout.CENTER, textField);
    panel.add(BorderLayout.SOUTH, button);
  } //End Constructor

  public void actionPerformed(ActionEvent event){
    Object source = event.getSource();
    if (source == button){
      String s = null;
      if (_clickMeMode){
      RandomAccessFile out = null;
      FileInputStream in = null
        try {
    //Write to file
          String text = textField.getText();
          byte b[] = text.getBytes();
          String outputFileName = System.getProperty("user.home",
                            File.separatorChar + "home" +
                            File.separatorChar + "zelda") +
                            File.separatorChar + "text.txt";
          File outputFile = new File(outputFileName);
          out = new RandomAccessFile(outputFile, "rw");
          out.seek(outputFile.length());
          out.write(b);

    //Write a new line (NL) to the file.
          out.writeByte('\n');
    //Read from file
          String inputFileName = System.getProperty("user.home",
                            File.separatorChar + "home" +
```

```
                                File.separatorChar + "zelda") +
                                File.separatorChar + "text2.txt";
          File inputFile = new File(inputFileName);
          in = new FileInputStream(inputFile);
          byte bt[] = new byte[(int)inputFile.length()];
          in.read(bt);
          s = new String(bt);
      } catch(java.io.IOException e) {
          System.out.println(e.toString());
      } finally {
          try {
            out.close();
            in.close();
          } catch(java.io.IOException e) {
            System.out.println("Cannot close");
          }
        }
//Clear text field
        textField.setText("");
//Display text read from file
        text.setText("Text retrieved from file:");
        textField.setText(s);
        button.setText("Click Again");
        _clickMeMode = false;
      } else {
//Save text to file
        text.setText("Text to save to file:");
        textField.setText("");
        button.setText("Click Me");
        _clickMeMode = true;
      }
    }
 }//end action performed method

 public static void main(String[] args) {
   JFrame frame = new AppendIO();
   frame.setTitle("Example");
   WindowListener l = new WindowAdapter() {
   public void windowClosing(WindowEvent e) {
       System.exit(0);
     }
   };
   frame.addWindowListener(l);
   frame.pack();
   frame.setVisible(true);
  }
}
```

Database Access and Permissions

THIS lesson converts the application, applet, and servlet examples from Lesson 6, File Access and Permissions (page 47), to write to and read from a database using JDBC™. JDBC is the Java database connectivity API available in the Java 2 Platform software.

The code for this lesson is very similar to the code you saw in Lesson 6, but additional steps beyond converting the file access code to database access code include setting up the environment, creating a database table, and connecting to the database. Creating a database table is a database administration task that is typically not part of your program code. However, establishing a database connection and accessing the database are part of your code.

As in Lesson 6, File Access and Permissions (page 47), the applet needs appropriate permissions to connect to the database. Which permissions it needs vary with the type of driver used to make the database connection. This lesson explains how to determine the permissions your program needs to run successfully.

Covered in This Lesson

- Database Setup
- Create Database Table
- Database Access by Applications
- Database Access by Applets
- Database Access by Servlets
- Exercises

- More Information
- Code for This Lesson

Database Setup

You need access to a database if you want to run the examples in this lesson. You can install a database on your machine, or perhaps you have access to a database at work. Either way, you also need a database driver and any relevant environment settings so your program can load the driver into memory and locate the database. The program will also need database login information in the form of a user name and password.

A database driver is software that lets a program establish a connection with a database. If you do not have the right driver for the database to which you want to connect, your program will be unable to establish the connection.

Drivers either come with the database, or they are available from the Web. If you install your own database, consult the documentation for the driver for information on installation and any other environment settings you need for your platform. If you are using a database at work, consult your database administrator for this information.

To show you three ways to establish a database connection, the application example uses the jdbc driver, the applet examples use the jdbc and jdbc.odbc drivers, and the servlet example uses the jdbc.odbc driver. All examples connect to an OracleOCI7.3.4 database. Connections to other databases will involve similar steps and code. Be sure to consult your documentation or system administrator if you need help connecting to the database.

Create Database Table

Once you have access to a database, create a table in it for the examples in this lesson. You need a table named dba with one text field for storing character data.

```
TABLE DBA (
        TEXT              varchar2(100),
        primary key (TEXT) )
```

Database Access by Applications

The application example converts the FileIO program from Lesson 6, File Access and Permissions (page 47), to write data to and read data from a database. The top window in Figure 7-1 appears when you start the Dba application, and the window beneath it appears when you click the Click Me button. The entire Dba source code appears on page 79.

When you click the Click Me button, whatever is entered into the text field is saved to the database table. After that, the data is retrieved from the database table and redisplayed in the window as shown in the bottom window. If you write data to the table more than once, the database table will have multiple rows, and you might have to enlarge the window to see all the data.

When Application Starts

After Writing Orange and Apple to Database

Figure 7-1   Database Access by Applications

Establishing a Database Connection

A database connection is established with the DriverManager and Connection classes available in the java.sql package. The JDBC DriverManager class can handle multiple database drivers and initiates all database communication. To load the driver and connect to the database, the application needs a Connection object and String objects that represent the _driver and _url.

The _url string is in the form of a Uniform Resource Locator (URL). It consists of the URL, Oracle subprotocol, and Oracle data source in the form jdbc:oracle:thin, plus username, password, machine, port, and protocol information.

```
private Connection c;
private final String _driver =
  "oracle.jdbc.driver.OracleDriver";
private final String _url =
  "jdbc:oracle:thin:username/password@developer:1521:ansid";
```

The actionPerformed method calls the Class.forName(_driver) method to load the driver and calls the DriverManager.getConnection method to establish the connection. The section Exception Handling (page 52) in Lesson 6, File Access and Permissions, describes try and catch blocks. The only thing different here is the block uses two catch statements because two different checked exceptions must be caught.

The call to Class.forName(_driver) throws java.lang.ClassNotFoundException, and the call to c = DriverManager.getConnection(_url) throws java.sql.SQLException. In the case of either error, the application tells the user what is wrong and exits because the program cannot operate in any meaningful way without a database driver or connection.

```
public void actionPerformed(ActionEvent event) {
  try {
//Load the driver
  Class.forName(_driver);
 //Establish database connection
  c = DriverManager.getConnection(_url);
 } catch (java.lang.ClassNotFoundException e) {
  System.out.println("Cannot find driver class");
  System.exit(1);
 } catch (java.sql.SQLException e) {
  System.out.println("Cannot get connection");
  System.exit(1);
 }
```

Final and Private Variables

The member variables used to establish the database connection shown earlier are declared private, and two of those variables are also declared final.

final: A final variable contains a constant value that can never change once it is initialized. In the example, the user name and password are final variables because you would not want to allow an instance of this or any other class to change the information.

private: A private variable can be accessed only by the class in which it is declared. No other class can read or change private variables. In the example, the database driver, the user name, and the password variables are private to prevent an outside class from accessing them and jeopardizing the database connection or from compromising the secret user name and password information.

Writing and Reading Data

In the write operation, a Statement object is created from the Connection. The Statement object has methods for executing SQL queries and updates. Next, a String object that contains the SQL update for the write operation is constructed and passed to the executeUpdate method of the Statement object.

```
Object source = event.getSource();
  if (source == button) {
    if (_clickMeMode) {
       JTextArea displayText = new JTextArea();
       Statement stmt = null;
       ResultSet results = null'
       try {
  //Code to write to database
          String theText = textField.getText();
          stmt = c.createStatement();
          String updateString =
            "INSERT INTO dba VALUES ('" + theText + "')";
          int count = stmt.executeUpdate(updateString);
```

SQL commands are String objects and therefore, follow the rules of String construction where the string is enclosed in double quotes ("") and variable data is appended with a plus sign (+). The variable theText is a text variable. Single quotes are prepended and appended to comply with SQL syntax.

In the read operation, a ResultSet object is created from the executeQuery method of the Statement object. The ResultSet contains the data returned by the query. The code iterates through the ResultSet, retrieves the data, and appends the data to the displayText text area.

```
//Code to read from database
    results = stmt.executeQuery( "SELECT TEXT FROM dba ");
    while(results.next()){
      String s = results.getString("TEXT");
      displayText.append(s + "\n");
    }
```

```
        } catch(java.sql.SQLException e) {
          System.out.println("Cannot create SQL statement");
        } finally {
          try {
            stmt.close();
            results.close();
          } catch(java.sql.SQLException e) {
            System.out.println("Cannot close");
          }
        }
      //Display text read from database
        text.setText("Text retrieved from database:");
        button.setText("Click Again");
        _clickMeMode = false;
      //Display text read from database
      } else {
        text.setText("Text to save to database:");
        textField.setText("");
        button.setText("Click Me");
        _clickMeMode = true;
      }
```

Database Access by Applets

The applet version of the example is like the application code described earlier except for the standard differences between applications and applets described in Lesson 3, Building Applets (page 17). The entire DbaAppl source code appears on page 79.

However, if you run the applet without a policy file, you get a stack trace indicating access denied errors. You learned about policy files and how to use one to launch an applet with the permissions it needs in Lesson 6, File Access and Permissions (page 47). In that lesson, you were given a policy file with the correct permissions and told how to use it to launch the applet. This lesson shows you how to read a stack trace to determine the permissions you need in a policy file.

To keep things interesting, this lesson has two versions of the database access applet: one uses the JDBC driver, and the other uses the JDBC-ODBC bridge with an Open DataBase Connectivity (ODBC) driver. Both applets do the same operations to the same database table using different drivers. Each applet has its own policy file with different permission lists, and each has different requirements for locating the database driver.

JDBC Driver

The JDBC driver is meant to be used in a program written exclusively in the Java programming language. It converts JDBC calls directly into the protocol used by the DBMS. This type of driver is available from the DBMS vendor and is usually packaged with the DBMS software.

Starting the Applet

To run successfully, the DbaAppl applet needs an available database driver and policy file. This section walks through the steps to get everything set up. Here is the HTML file for running the DbaAppl applet:

```
<HTML>
<BODY>
<APPLET CODE=DbaAppl.class WIDTH=200 HEIGHT=100>
</APPLET>
</BODY>
</HTML>
```

And here is how to start the applet with appletviewer:

```
appletviewer DbaApplet.html
```

Locating the Database Driver

Assuming the driver is not available to the DriverManager for some reason, the following error generates when you click the Click Me button:

```
cannot find driver
```

This error means the DriverManager looked for the JDBC driver in the directory where the applet HTML and class files are and could not find it. To correct this error, copy the driver to the directory where the applet files are, and, if the driver is bundled in a zip file, unzip the zip file so the applet can access the driver. Once you have the driver in place, launch the applet again:

```
appletviewer dbaApplet.html
```

Reading a Stack Trace

Assuming the driver is locally available to the applet and the DbaAppl applet is launched without a policy file, you get the following stack trace when you click the Click Me button.

```
java.security.AccessControlException: access denied
(java.net.SocketPermission developer resolve)
```

The first line in the stack trace tells you access is denied. This means the applet does not have the needed access permission. The second line means that to correct this condition you need a SocketPermission that gives the applet access to the machine where the database is located. For this example, that machine is named developer. If you run this example in your own environment, the machine name will be different.

You can use the Policy tool to create the policy file you need, or you can create it with an ASCII editor. This is the policy file with the permission indicated by the stack trace:

```
grant {
permission java.net.SocketPermission "developer", "resolve";
};
```

Run the applet again but this time with a policy file named DbaApplPol that has the above permission in it:

```
appletviewer -J-Djava.security.policy=DbaApplPol
   dbaApplet.html
```

You get a stack trace again, but this time it is a different error condition.

```
java.security.AccessControlException: access denied
(java.net.SocketPermission 129.144.176.176:1521 con-
nect,resolve)
```

Now you need a SocketPermission that allows access to the Internet Protocol (IP) address and port on the machine where the database is located. Following is the DbaApplPol policy file with the permission indicated by the stack trace added to it:

```
grant {
permission java.net.SocketPermission "developer", "resolve";
permission java.net.SocketPermission
   "129.144.176.176:1521", "connect,resolve";
};
```

Run the applet again. If you use the above policy file with the permissions indicated, it should work just fine:

```
appletviewer -J-Djava.security.policy=DbaApplPol
   dbaApplet.html
```

JDBC-ODBC Bridge with ODBC Driver

Open DataBase Connectivity (ODBC) is Microsoft's programming interface for accessing a large number of relational databases on numerous platforms. The JDBC-ODBC bridge is built into the Solaris and Windows versions of the Java platform so you can do two things:

1. Use ODBC from a program written in the Java language.

2. Load ODBC drivers as JDBC drivers. This example uses the JDBC-ODBC bridge to load an ODBC driver to connect to the database. The applet has no ODBC code, however.

The DriverManager uses environment settings to locate and load the database driver. This means the driver file does not have to be accessible locally.

Start the Applet

Following is an HTML file for running the DbaOdbAppl applet. The entire DbaOdbAppl source code appears on page 84.

```
<HTML>
<BODY>
<APPLET CODE=DbaOdbAppl.class    WIDTH=200    HEIGHT=100>
</APPLET>
</BODY>
</HTML>
```

And here is how to start the applet:

```
appletviewer dbaOdb.html
```

Reading a Stack Trace

If the DbaOdbAppl applet is launched without a policy file, the following stack trace is generated when the user clicks the Click Me button:

```
java.security.AccessControlException: access denied
(java.lang.RuntimePermission accessClassInPack-
age.sun.jdbc.odbc )
```

The first line in this stack trace tells you access is denied. This means the stack trace was generated because the applet tried to access a system resource without the proper permission. The second line means you need a RuntimePermission that gives the applet access to the sun.jdbc.odbc package, which provides the JDBC-ODBC bridge functionality to the Java VM.

You can use Policy tool to create the policy file you need, or you can create it with an ASCII editor. This is the policy file with the permission indicated by the stack trace:

```
grant {
  permission java.lang.RuntimePermission
    "accessClassInPackage.sun.jdbc.odbc";
};
```

Run the applet again but this time with a policy file named DbaOdbPol that has the above permission in it:

```
appletviewer -J-Djava.security.policy=DbaOdbPol dbaOdb.html
```

You get a stack trace again, but this time it is a different error condition.

```
java.security.AccessControlException: access denied
(java.lang.RuntimePermission file.encoding read)
```

The stack trace means the applet needs read permission to the encoded (binary) file. This is the DbaOdbPol policy file with the permission indicated by the stack trace added to it:

```
grant {
  permission java.lang.RuntimePermission
    "accessClassInPackage.sun.jdbc.odbc";
  permission java.util.PropertyPermission
    "file.encoding", "read";
};
```

Run the applet again. If you use the above policy file with the permissions indicated, it should work just fine.

```
appletviewer -J-Djava.security.policy=DbaOdbPol dbaOdb.html
```

NOTE   If you install Java Plug-In and run this applet from your browser, put the policy file in your home directory and rename it java.policy for Windows and .java.policy for Unix.

Database Access by Servlets

As you learned in Lesson 5, Building Servlets (page 37), servlets are under the security policy in force for the Web server under which they run. The DbaServlet servlet for this lesson executes without restriction under Java Web Server 1.1.1. The DbaServlet source code appears on page 86.

The Web server has to be configured to locate the database. Consult your Web server documentation or database administrator for help. With Java Web Server 1.1.1, the configuration setup involves editing the start-up scripts with such things as environment settings for loading the ODBC driver and locating and connecting to the database.

Exercises

1. What are `final` variables?

2. What does a `Statement` object do?

3. How can you determine which permissions an applet needs to access local system resources such as a database?

More Information

You can find more information on variable access settings in "Objects and Classes" in *The Java™ Tutorial, Second Edition* [Cam98].

You can find more information on policy permissions in "Security in JDK 1.2" in *The Java™ Tutorial, Second Edition* [Cam98].

Code for This Lesson

- Dba
- DbaAppl
- DbaOdbAppl
- DbaServlet

Dba Program

```
import java.awt.Color;
import java.awt.BorderLayout;
import java.awt.event.*;
import javax.swing.*;
import java.sql.*;
import java.net.*;
import java.util.*;
import java.io.*;

class Dba extends JFrame implements ActionListener {
    JLabel text;
    JButton button;
```

```
      JPanel panel;
      JTextField textField;
      private Connection c;
      private boolean _clickMeMode = true;

      private final String _driver =
        "oracle.jdbc.driver.OracleDriver";
      private final String _url =
        "jdbc:oracle:thin:username/password@developer:1521:ansid";
      Dba() { //Begin Constructor
        text = new JLabel("Text to save to database:");
        button = new JButton("Click Me");
        button.addActionListener(this);
        textField = new JTextField(20);
        panel = new JPanel();
        panel.setLayout(new BorderLayout());
        panel.setBackground(Color.white);
        getContentPane().add(panel);
        panel.add(BorderLayout.NORTH, text);
        panel.add(BorderLayout.CENTER, textField);
        panel.add(BorderLayout.SOUTH, button);
      } //End Constructor

      public void actionPerformed(ActionEvent event){
        try {
// Load the Driver
          Class.forName(_driver);
// Make Connection
          c = DriverManager.getConnection(_url);
        }
        catch (java.lang.ClassNotFoundException e) {
         System.out.println("Cannot find driver");
         System.exit(1);
        } catch (java.sql.SQLException e) {
          System.out.println("Cannot get connection");
          System.exit(1);
        }

      Object source = event.getSource();
      if (source == button){
        if (_clickMeMode){
          JTextArea displayText = new JTextArea();
          Statement stmt = null;
          ResultSet results = null;
          try{
      //Code to write to database
          String theText = textField.getText();
```

```
            stmt = c.createStatement();
            String updateString = "INSERT INTO dba VALUES ('" +
theText + "')";
            int count = stmt.executeUpdate(updateString);
      //Code to read from database
            results = stmt.executeQuery(
              "SELECT TEXT FROM dba ");
            while (results.next()) {
              String s = results.getString("TEXT");
              displayText.append(s + "\n");
            }
          } catch(java.sql.SQLException e) {
            System.out.println("Cannot create SQL statement");
          } finally {
            try {
              stmt.close();
              results.close();
            } catch(java.sql.SQLException e) {
              System.out.println("Cannot close");
            }
          }
        //Display text read from database
          text.setText("Text retrieved from database:");
          button.setText("Click Again");
          _clickMeMode = false;
//Display text read from database
        } else {
          text.setText("Text to save to database:");
          textField.setText("");
          button.setText("Click Me");
          _clickMeMode = true;
        }
      }
    }
    public static void main(String[] args) {
      Dba frame = new Dba();
      frame.setTitle("Example");
      WindowListener l = new WindowAdapter() {
        public void windowClosing(WindowEvent e) {
          System.exit(0);
        }
      };
      frame.addWindowListener(l);
      frame.pack();
      frame.setVisible(true);
    }
}
```

DbaAppl Program

```java
import java.awt.Color;
import java.awt.BorderLayout;
import java.awt.event.*;
import javax.swing.*;
import java.sql.*;
import java.net.*;
import java.io.*;

public class DbaAppl extends JApplet implements ActionLis-
tener {
   JLabel text;
   JButton button;
   JTextField textField;
   private Connection c;
   private boolean _clickMeMode = true;

   private final String _driver =
      "oracle.jdbc.driver.OracleDriver";
   private final String _url =
      "jdbc:oracle:thin:username/password@developer:1521:ansid";

   public void init() {
      getContentPane().setBackground(Color.white);
      text = new JLabel("Text to save to file:");
      button = new JButton("Click Me");
      button.addActionListener(this);
      textField = new JTextField(20);
      getContentPane().setLayout(new BorderLayout());
      getContentPane().add(BorderLayout.NORTH, text);
      getContentPane().add(BorderLayout.CENTER, textField);
      getContentPane().add(BorderLayout.SOUTH, button);
   }

   public void start() {
      System.out.println("Applet starting.");
   }

   public void stop() {
      System.out.println("Applet stopping.");
   }

   public void destroy() {
    System.out.println("Destroy method called.");
   }
```

```
       public void actionPerformed(ActionEvent event) {
         try{
            Class.forName (_driver);
            c = DriverManager.getConnection(_url);
          }catch (java.lang.ClassNotFoundException e){
           System.out.println("Cannot find driver class");
           System.exit(1);
          }catch (java.sql.SQLException e){
           System.out.println("Cannot get connection");
           System.exit(1);
          }

        Object source = event.getSource();
          if (_clickMeMode){
            JTextArea displayText = new JTextArea();
            Statement stmt = null;
            ResultSet results = null;
            try{
        //Code to write to database
              String theText = textField.getText();
              stmt = c.createStatement();
              String updateString = "INSERT INTO dba VALUES ('" +
    theText + "')";
              int count = stmt.executeUpdate(updateString);
        //Code to read from database
              results = stmt.executeQuery(
                "SELECT TEXT FROM dba ");
              while (results.next()) {
                String s = results.getString("TEXT");
                displayText.append(s + "\n");
              }
            } catch(java.sql.SQLException e) {
              System.out.println("Cannot create SQL statement");
            } finally {
              try {
                stmt.close();
                results.close();
              } catch(java.sql.SQLException e) {
                System.out.println("Cannot close");
              }
            }
    //Display text read from database
            text.setText("Text retrieved from file:");
            button.setText("Click Again");
            _clickMeMode = false;
    //Display text read from database
          } else {
            text.setText("Text to save to file:");
```

```
            textField.setText("");
            button.setText("Click Me");
            _clickMeMode = true;
          }
        }
      }
    }
```

DbaOdbAppl Program

```java
import java.awt.Color;
import java.awt.BorderLayout;
import java.awt.event.*;
import javax.swing.*;
import java.sql.*;
import java.net.*;
import java.io.*;

public class DbaOdbAppl extends JApplet implements Action-
Listener {
  JLabel text, clicked;
  JButton button, clickButton;
  JTextField textField;
  private boolean _clickMeMode = true;
  private Connection c;
  private final String _driver =
    "sun.jdbc.odbc.JdbcOdbcDriver";
  private final String _user = "username";
  private final String _pass = "password";
  private final String _url = "jdbc:odbc:jdc";

  public void init() {
    text = new JLabel("Text to save to file:");
    clicked = new JLabel("Text retrieved from file:");
    button = new JButton("Click Me");
    button.addActionListener(this);
    clickButton = new JButton("Click Again");
    clickButton.addActionListener(this);
    textField = new JTextField(20);
    getContentPane().setLayout(new BorderLayout());
    getContentPane().setBackground(Color.white);
    getContentPane().add(BorderLayout.NORTH, text);
    getContentPane().add(BorderLayout.CENTER, textField);
    getContentPane().add(BorderLayout.SOUTH, button);
  }

  public void start() {
  }
```

```java
    public void stop() {
        System.out.println("Applet stopping.");
    }

    public void destroy() {
        System.out.println("Destroy method called.");
    }

    public void actionPerformed(ActionEvent event) {
      try {
        Class.forName (_driver);
        c = DriverManager.getConnection(_url, _user, _pass);
      } catch (Exception e) {
        e.printStackTrace();
        System.exit(1);
      }

      Object source = event.getSource();
      if (source == button) {
        if (_clickMeMode) {
          JTextArea displayText = new JTextArea();
          Statement stmt = null;
          ResultSet results = null;
          try{
      //Code to write to database
            String theText = textField.getText();
            stmt = c.createStatement();
            String updateString = "INSERT INTO dba VALUES ('" +
                                theText + "')";
            int count = stmt.executeUpdate(updateString);
      //Code to read from database
            results = stmt.executeQuery(
              "SELECT TEXT FROM dba ");
            while (results.next()) {
              String s = results.getString("TEXT");
              displayText.append(s + "\n");
            }
          } catch(java.sql.SQLException e) {
            System.out.println("Cannot create SQL statement");
          } finally {
            try {
              stmt.close();
              results.close();
            } catch(java.sql.SQLException e) {
              System.out.println("Cannot close");
            }
          }
  //Display text read from database
        } else {
```

```
            text.setText("Text to save to file:");
            textField.setText("");
            button.setText("Click Me");
            _clickMeMode = true;
          }
        }
      }
    }
```

DbaServlet Program

```java
import java.io.*;
import javax.servlet.*;
import javax.servlet.http.*;
import java.sql.*;
import java.net.*;
import java.io.*;

public class DbaServlet extends HttpServlet {
  private Connection c;
  private static final String _driver = "sun.jdbc.odbc.Jdb-
cOdbcDriver";
  private static final String _user = "username";
  private static final String _pass = "password";
  private static final String _url = "jdbc:odbc:jdc";

  public void doPost(HttpServletRequest request,
                     HttpServletResponse response)
                     throws ServletException, IOException {

  response.setContentType("text/html");
  PrintWriter out = response.getWriter();
  out.println("<body bgcolor=FFFFFF>");
  out.println("<h2>Button Clicked</h2>");
  String data = request.getParameter("data");

  if (data != null && data.length() > 0) {
    out.println("<STRONG>Text from form:</STRONG>");
    out.println(data);
  } else {
    out.println("No text entered.");
  }

//Establish database connection
  try {
   Class.forName (_driver);
   c = DriverManager.getConnection(_url, _user,_pass);
  } catch (java.sql.SQLException e) {
```

```
          System.out.println("Cannot get connection");
          System.exit(1);
          } catch (java.lang.ClassNotFoundException e) {
          System.out.println("Driver class not found");
      }
    Statement stmt = null;
    ResultSet results = null;
    try {
      //Code to write to database
      stmt = c.createStatement();
      String updateString = "INSERT INTO dba VALUES ('" + data
+ "')";
      int count = stmt.executeUpdate(updateString);
      //Code to read from database
      results = stmt.executeQuery("SELECT TEXT FROM dba ");
      while (results.next()) {
        String s = results.getString("TEXT");
        out.println("<BR><STRONG>Text from database:</
STRONG>");
        out.println(s);
      }
    } catch(java.sql.SQLException e) {
      System.out.println("Cannot create SQL statement");
    } finally {
      try {
        stmt.close();
        results.close();
       } catch(java.sql.SQLException e) {
         System.out.println("Cannot close");
       }
    }
    out.println(
      "<P>Return to <A HREF=../dbaHTML.html>Form</A>");
    out.close();
  }
}
```

Remote Method Invocation

THE Java Remote Method Invocation (RMI) API enables client and server communications over a network. Typically, client programs send requests to a server program, and the server program responds to those requests.

A common example is sharing a word processing program over a network. The word processor is installed on a server, and anyone who wants to use it starts it from his or her machine by double clicking an icon on the desktop or typing at the command line. The invocation sends a request to a server program for access to the software, and the server program responds by making the software available to the requestor.

Figure 8-1 shows a publicly accessible remote server object that enables client and server communications. Clients can easily communicate directly with the server object and indirectly with each other through the server object using URLs and HTTP. This lesson explains how to use the RMI API to establish client and server communications.

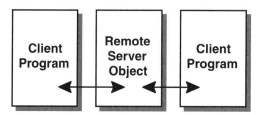

Figure 8-1   Client and Server Communications

> **NOTE** Enterprise JavaBeans™ technology is another Java API for remote communications. While writing a simple Enterprise Bean is easy, running it requires an application server and deployment tools. Because the Enterprise JavaBeans API is similar to RMI, you should be able to go on to a good text on Enterprise JavaBeans and continue your studies when you finish here.

Covered in This Lesson

- About the Example
- RemoteServer Class
- Send Interface
- RMIClient1 Class
- RMIClient2 Class
- Exercises
- More Information
- Code for This Lesson

About the Example

This lesson adapts the `FileIO` program from Lesson 6, File Access and Permissions (page 47), to use the RMI API.

Program Behavior

As shown in Figure 8-2, the `RMIClient1` program presents a simple user interface and prompts for text input. When you click the `Click Me` button, the text is sent to the remote server object; when you click the `Click Me` button on the `RMIClient2` program, the text is retrieved from the remote server object and displayed in the `RMIClient2` user interface.

As shown in Figure 8-3, if you start a second instance of `RMIClient1`, type in some text, and click its `Click Me` button, that text is sent to the remote server object where it can be retrieved by the `RMIClient2` program. To see the text sent by the second client, click the `RMIClient2 Click Me` button.

File Summary

The example program consists of the `RMIClient1` program, the remote server object and interface, and the `RMIClient2` program as illustrated in Figure 8-4.

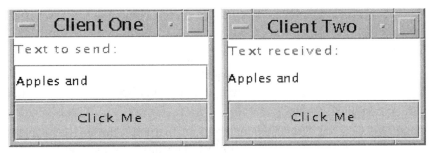

First Instance of Client 1

Figure 8-2   Sending Data over the Network

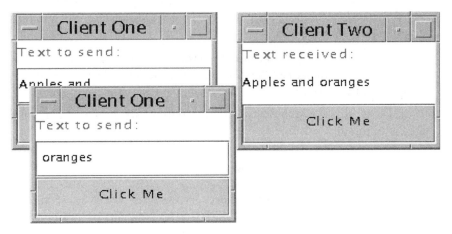

Figure 8-3   Two Instances of Client 1

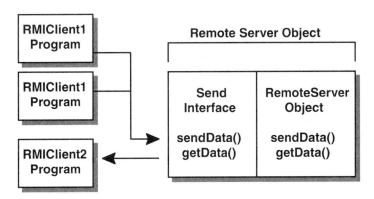

Figure 8-4   Simple RMI Application

The corresponding source code files for these executables are described in the bulleted list that follows.

- RMIClient1.java: Client program that calls the sendData method on the RemoteServer server object. The sendData method is made available to RMIClient1 through the Send interface. The entire source code is on page 102.

- RMIClient2.java: Client program that calls the getData method on the RemoteServer server object. The getData method is made available to RMIClient2 through the Send interface. The entire source code is on page 104.

- Send.java: Remote interface that declares the sendData and getData remote server methods. This interface makes the remote server object methods available to clients anywhere on the system. The entire source code is on page 106.

- RemoteServer.java: Remote server object that implements Send.java and the sendData and getData remote methods. The entire source code is on page 105.

In addition, this java.policy security policy file grants the permissions needed to run the example:

```
grant {
  permission java.net.SocketPermission "*:1024-65535",
     "connect,accept,resolve";
  permission java.net.SocketPermission  "*:80", "connect";
  permission java.awt.AWTPermission  "accessEventQueue";
  permission java.awt.AWTPermission
    "showWindowWithoutWarningBanner";
};
```

Compile the Example

The instructions assume development is in the zelda home directory. The server program is compiled in the home directory for user zelda but copied to the public_html directory for user zelda where it runs.

Unix:

```
cd /home/zelda/classes
javac Send.java
javac RemoteServer.java
javac RMIClient2.java
javac RMIClient1.java
rmic -d . RemoteServer
```

```
cp RemoteServer*.class /home/zelda/public_html/classes
cp Send.class /home/zelda/public_html/classes
```

Win32:

```
cd \home\zelda\classes
javac Send.java
javac RemoteServer.java
javac RMIClient2.java
javac RMIClient1.java
rmic -d . RemoteServer
copy RemoteServer*.class \home\zelda\public_html\classes
copy Send.class \home\zelda\public_html\classes
```

The first two javac commands compile the RemoteServer and Send class and interface. The next two javac commands compile the RMIClient2 and RMIClient1 classes.

The next line runs the rmic command on the RemoteServer server class. This command produces output class files of the form ClassName_Stub.class and ClassName_Skel.class. These output stub and skel classes let client programs communicate with the RemoteServer server object.

The first copy command moves the RemoteServer class file with its associated skel and stub class files to a publicly accessible location in the /home/zelda/public_html/classes directory on the server machine, so they can be publicly accessed and downloaded. They are placed in the public_html directory to be under the Web server running on the server machine because these files are accessed by client programs using URLs.

The second copy command moves the Send class file to the same location for the same reason. The RMIClient1 and RMIClient2 class files are not made publicly accessible; they communicate from their client machines using URLs to access and download the remote object files in the public_html directory.

- In Figure 8-5 you can see that RMIClient1 is invoked from a client-side directory and uses the server-side Web server and client-side Java VM to download the publicly accessible files.

- RMIClient2 is invoked from a client-side directory and uses the server-side Web server and client-side Java VM to download the publicly accessible files.

Start the RMI Registry

Before you start the client programs, you must start the RMI Registry, which is a server-side naming repository that allows remote clients to get a reference to the remote server object.

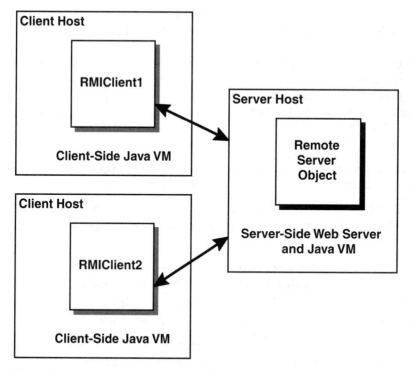

Figure 8-5   Downloading Publicly Accessible Files

Before you start the RMI Registry, make sure the shell or window in which you run the `rmiregistry` command does not have a `CLASSPATH` environment variable that points to the remote object classes. The `CLASSPATH` environment variable should not point to `stub` and `skel` classes anywhere on your system except where they are supposed to be. If the RMI Registry finds these classes in another location when it starts, it will not load them from the Java VM where the server is running, which will create problems when clients try to download the remote server classes.

The following commands unset the `CLASSPATH` and start the RMI Registry on the default 1099 port. You can specify a different port by adding the port number as follows where 4321 is a port number: `rmiregistry 4321`. If you specify a different port number, you must specify the same port number in your server-side code as well (page 98).

Unix:

```
cd /home/zelda/public_html/classes
unsetenv CLASSPATH
rmiregistry &
```

Win32:
```
cd \home\zelda\public_html\classes
set CLASSPATH= CLASSPATH
start rmiregistry
```

NOTE   You might want to set the CLASSPATH back to its original setting at this point.

Start the Server

To run the example programs, start the RemoteServer program first. If you start either RMIClient1 or RMIClient2 first, they will not be able to establish a connection with the server because the RemoteServer program is not running. In this example, the RemoteServer program is started from the /home/zelda/public_html/classes directory.

The lines beginning at java should be all on one line with spaces where the lines break. The properties specified with the -D option to the java interpreter command are program attributes that manage the behavior of the program for this invocation.

NOTE   In this example, the host machine is kq6py. To make this example work, substitute the host name with the name of your own machine.

Unix:
```
cd /home/zelda/public_html/classes
java -Djava.rmi.server.codebase=http://kq6py/~zelda/classes
    -Djava.rmi.server.hostname=kq6py.eng.sun.com
    -Djava.security.policy=java.policy RemoteServer
```

Win32:
```
cd \home\zelda\public_html\classes
java -Djava.rmi.server.codebase=
    file:c:\home\zelda\public_html\classes
    -Djava.rmi.server.hostname=kq6py.eng.sun.com
    -Djava.security.policy=java.policy RemoteServer
```

The commands to start the server use the following options:

- The `java.rmi.server.codebase` property specifies where the publicly accessible classes are located.

- The `java.rmi.server.hostname` property is the complete host name of the server where the publicly accessible classes reside.

- The `java.rmi.security.policy` property specifies the policy file with the permissions needed to run the remote server object and access the remote server classes for download.

- `RemoteServer` is the class to execute.

Run the RMIClient1 Program

In this example, `RMIClient1` is started from the `/home/zelda/classes` directory. The lines beginning at `java` should all be on one line with spaces where the lines break. Properties specified with the `-D` option to the `java` interpreter command are program attributes that manage the behavior of the program for this invocation.

NOTE   In this example, the host machine is kq6py. To make this example work, substitute the host name with the name of your own machine.

Unix:

```
cd /home/zelda/classes
java -Djava.rmi.server.codebase=http://kq6py/~zelda/classes
    -Djava.security.policy=
    java.policy RMIClient1 kq6py.eng.sun.com
```

Win32:

```
cd \home\zelda\classes
java -Djava.rmi.server.codebase=
    file:c:\home\zelda\classes
    -Djava.security.policy=
    java.policy RMIClient1 kq6py.eng.sun.com
```

The commands to run the RMIclient1 program use the following options:

- The `java.rmi.server.codebase` property specifies where the publicly accessible classes for downloading are located.

- The `java.security.policy` property specifies the policy file with the permissions needed to run the client program and access the remote server classes.

- The `RMIClient1` is the client program class being executed, and `kq6py` is the host name of the machine where the remote server classes are.

Run the RMIClient2 Program

In this example, `RMIClient2` is started from the `/home/zelda/classes` directory. The lines beginning at `java` should all be on one line with spaces where the lines break. The properties specified with the `-D` option to the `java` interpreter command are program attributes that manage the behavior of the program for this invocation.

NOTE In this example, the host machine is kq6py. To make this example work, substitute the host name with the name of your own machine.

Unix:

```
cd /home/zelda/classes
java -Djava.rmi.server.codebase=http://kq6py/~zelda/classes
    -Djava.security.policy=
    java.policy RMIClient2 kq6py.eng.sun.com
```

Win32:

```
cd \home\zelda\classes
java -Djava.rmi.server.codebase=
    file:c:\home\zelda\public_html\classes
    -Djava.security.policy=
    java.policy RMIClient2 kq6py.eng.sun.com
```

The commands to run the `RMIClient2` program use the following options:

- The `java.rmi.server.codebase` property specifies where the publicly accessible classes are located.

- The `java.rmi.server.hostname` property is the complete host name of the server where the publicly accessible classes reside.

- The java.rmi.security.policy property specifies the policy file with the permissions needed to run the remote server object and access the remote server classes for download.

- The RMIClient2 is the client program being exectured and kq6py is the host name of the machine where the remote server classes are.

RemoteServer Class

The RemoteServer class (page 105) extends UnicastRemoteObject and implements the remotely accessible sendData and getData methods declared in the Send interface (page 106). UnicastRemoteObject implements a number of java.lang.Object methods for remote objects and includes constructors and static methods to make a remote object available to receive method calls from client programs.

```
class RemoteServer extends UnicastRemoteObject implements
Send {
    private String text;
    public RemoteServer() throws RemoteException {
      super();
    }
    public void sendData(String gotText) {
      text = gotText;
    }
    public String getData(){
     return text;
    }
}
```

The main method installs the RMISecurityManager and opens a connection with a port on the machine where the server program runs. The RMI security manager determines whether there is a policy file that lets downloaded code perform tasks that require permissions.

The main method creates a name for the RemoteServer object, which includes the server name (kq6py) where the RMI Registry and remote object run, and the name Send. By default the server name uses port 1099. If you want to use a different port, you can add it with a colon where 4321 is the port number: kq6py.eng.sun.com:4321. If you change the port here, you must start the RMI Registry (page 93) with the same port number. The try block creates a RemoteServer instance and binds the name to the remote object to the RMI Registry with the Naming.rebind(name,remoteServer) statement. The string passed to the rebind and lookup methods is the name of the host on which the name server is running.

```
    public static void main(String[] args) {
        if (System.getSecurityManager() == null) {
          System.setSecurityManager(new RMISecurityManager());
        }
        String name = "//kq6py.eng.sun.com/Send";
        try {
          Send remoteServer = new RemoteServer();
          Naming.rebind(name, remoteServer());
          System.out.println("RemoteServer bound");
        } catch (java.rmi.RemoteException e) {
          System.out.println("Cannot crate remote server object");
        } catch(java.net.malformedURLException e) {
          System.out.println("Cannot look up server object");
        }
      }
    }
```

NOTE The remoteServer object is type Send (see the instance declaration at top of class) because the interface available to clients is the Send interface and its methods, not the RemoteServer class and its methods.

Send Interface

The Send interface (page 106) declares the methods implemented in the Remote-Server class. These are the remotely accessible methods:

```
public interface Send extends Remote {
  public void sendData(String text) throws RemoteException;
  public String getData() throws RemoteException;
}
```

RMIClient1 Class

The RMIClient1 (page 102) class establishes a connection to the remote server program in its main method and sends data to the remote server object in its actionPerformed method.

actionPerformed Method

The actionPerformed method calls the RemoteServer.sendData method to send text to the remote server object.

```
public void actionPerformed(ActionEvent event){
  Object source = event.getSource();
  if (source == button) {
//Send data over socket
    String text = textField.getText();
    try {
      send.sendData(text);
    } catch (Exception e) {
      System.out.println("Cannot send data to server);
    }
    textField.setText(new String(""));
  }
}
```

main Method

The main method installs the RMISecurityManager and creates a name to use to look up the RemoteServer server object. The client uses the Naming.lookup method to look up the RemoteServer object in the RMI Registry running on the server. The security manager determines whether there is a policy file that lets downloaded code perform tasks that require permissions.

```
RMIClient1 frame = new RMIClient1();
...
if (System.getSecurityManager() == null) {
  System.setSecurityManager(new RMISecurityManager());
}
try {
  //args[0] contains name of server where Send runs
  String name = "//" + args[0] + "/Send";
  send = ((Send) Naming.lookup(name));
} catch (java.rmi.NotBoundException e) {
  System.out.println("Cannot look up remote server object");
} catch (java.rmi.RemoteException e) {
  System.out.println("Cannot look up remote server object");
} catch (java.net.MalformedURLException e) {
  System.out.println("Cannot look up remote server object");
}
...
```

RMIClient2 Class

The RMIClient2 class (page 104) establishes a connection with the remote server program and gets the data from the remote server object and displays it. The code to do this is in the actionPerformed and main methods.

actionPerformed Method

The actionPerformed method calls the RemoteServer.getData method to retrieve the data sent by the client program. This data is appended to the TextArea object for display to the user on the server side.

```
public void actionPerformed(ActionEvent event) {
    Object source = event.getSource();
    if (source == button) {
        try {
            String text = send.getData();
            textArea.append(text);
        } catch (java.rmi.RemoteException e) {
            System.out.println("Cannot access data in server");
        }
    }
}
```

main Method

The main method installs the RMISecurityManager and creates a name to use to look up the RemoteServer server object. The args[0] parameter provides the name of the server host. The client uses the Naming.lookup method to look up the RemoteServer object in the RMI Registry running on the server.

The security manager determines whether there is a policy file that lets downloaded code perform tasks that require permissions.

```
RMIClient2 frame = new RMIClient2();
...
if (System.getSecurityManager() == null) {
    System.setSecurityManager(new RMISecurityManager());
}
try {
    ring name = "//" + args[0] + "/Send";
        send = ((Send) Naming.lookup(name));
} catch (java.rmi.NotBoundException e) {
    System.out.println("Cannot look up remote server object");
} catch (java.rmi.RemoteException e) {
    System.out.println("Cannot look up remote server object");
} catch (java.net.MalformedURLException e) {
    System.out.println("Cannot look up remote server object");
}
...
```

Exercises

1. What is the RMI Registry?

2. What do you have to start first, the server program or the RMI Registry?

3. What does the RMISecurityManager do?

4. Is the `Send` or `RemoteServer` object available to clients?

More Information

You can find more information on the RMI API in "RMI" in *The Java™ Tutorial, Second Edition* [Cam98].

Code for This Lesson

- RMIClient1

- RMIClient2

- RemoteServer

- Send Interface

RMIClient1 Program

```java
import java.awt.Color;
import java.awt.BorderLayout;
import java.awt.event.*;
import javax.swing.*;
import java.io.*;
import java.net.*;
import java.rmi.*;
import java.rmi.server.*;

class RMIClient1 extends JFrame implements ActionListener {
  JLabel text, clicked;
  JButton button;
  JPanel panel;
  JTextField textField;
  static Send send;
  RMIClient1() { //Begin Constructor
    text = new JLabel("Text to send:");
    textField = new JTextField(20);
    button = new JButton("Click Me");
    button.addActionListener(this);
    panel = new JPanel();
```

```
      panel.setLayout(new BorderLayout());
      panel.setBackground(Color.white);
      getContentPane().add(panel);
      panel.add(BorderLayout.NORTH, text);
      panel.add(BorderLayout.CENTER, textField);
      panel.add(BorderLayout.SOUTH, button);
   } //End Constructor

  public void actionPerformed(ActionEvent event){
    Object source = event.getSource();
    if (source == button) {
//Send data over net
      String text = textField.getText();
      try {
        send.sendData(text);
      } catch (java.rmi.RemoteException e) {
        System.out.println("Cannot send data to server");
      }
      textField.setText(new String(""));
    }
  }

  public static void main(String[] args) {
    RMIClient1 frame = new RMIClient1();
    frame.setTitle("Client One");
    WindowListener l = new WindowAdapter() {
      public void windowClosing(WindowEvent e) {
        System.exit(0);
      }
    };
    frame.addWindowListener(l);
    frame.pack();
    frame.setVisible(true);
    if (System.getSecurityManager() == null) {
      System.setSecurityManager(new RMISecurityManager());
    }

    try {
      String name = "//" + args[0] + "/Send";
      send = ((Send) Naming.lookup(name));
    } catch (java.rmi.NotBoundException e) {
      System.out.println(
        "Cannot look up remote server object");
    } catch(java.rmi.RemoteException e) {
      System.out.println(
        "Cannot look up remote server object");
    } catch(java.net.MalformedURLException e) {
```

```
        System.out.println(
          "Cannot look up remote server object");
    }
  }
}
```

RMIClient2 Program

```java
import java.awt.Color;
import java.awt.BorderLayout;
import java.awt.event.*;
import javax.swing.*;
import java.io.*;
import java.net.*;
import java.rmi.*;
import java.rmi.server.*;

class RMIClient2 extends JFrame implements ActionListener {
  JLabel text, clicked;
  JButton button;
  JPanel panel;
  JTextArea textArea;
  static Send send;
  RMIClient2(){ //Begin Constructor
    text = new JLabel("Text received:");
    textArea = new JTextArea();
    button = new JButton("Click Me");
    button.addActionListener(this);
    panel = new JPanel();
    panel.setLayout(new BorderLayout());
    panel.setBackground(Color.white);
    getContentPane().add(panel);
    panel.add(BorderLayout.NORTH, text);
    panel.add(BorderLayout.CENTER, textArea);
    panel.add(BorderLayout.SOUTH, button);
  } //End Constructor

  public void actionPerformed(ActionEvent event) {
    Object source = event.getSource();
    if (source == button) {
      try {
        String text = send.getData();
        textArea.append(text);
      } catch (java.rmi.RemoteException e) {
        System.out.println("Cannot access data in server");
      }
    }
  }
```

```
    public static void main(String[] args) {
      RMIClient2 frame = new RMIClient2();
      frame.setTitle("Client Two");
      WindowListener l = new WindowAdapter() {
        public void windowClosing(WindowEvent e) {
          System.exit(0);
        }
      };
      frame.addWindowListener(l);
      frame.pack();
      frame.setVisible(true);
      if (System.getSecurityManager() == null) {
        System.setSecurityManager(new RMISecurityManager());
      }
      try {
        String name = "//" + args[0] + "/Send";
        send = ((Send) Naming.lookup(name));
      } catch (java.rmi.NotBoundException e) {
        System.out.println("Cannot access data in server");
      } catch(java.rmi.RemoteException e) {
        System.out.println("Cannot access data in server");
      } catch(java.net.MalformedURLException e) {
        System.out.println("Cannot access data in server");
      }
    }
  }
}
```

RemoteServer Program

```
import java.io.*;
import java.net.*;
import java.rmi.*;
import java.rmi.server.*;

class RemoteServer extends UnicastRemoteObject implements
Send {
  private String text;
  public RemoteServer() throws RemoteException {
    super();
  }
  public void sendData(String gotText) {
    text = gotText;
  }
  public String getData(){
    return text;
  }

  public static void main(String[] args) {
    if (System.getSecurityManager() == null) {
```

```
      System.setSecurityManager(new RMISecurityManager());
    }
    String name = "//kq6py.eng.sun.com/Send";
    try {
      Send remoteServer = new RemoteServer();
      Naming.rebind(name, remoteServer);
      System.out.println("RemoteServer bound");
    } catch (java.rmi.RemoteException e) {
      System.out.println(
        "Cannot create remote server object");
    } catch (java.net.MalformedURLException e) {
      System.out.println(
        "Cannot look up server object");
    }
  }
}
```

Send Interface

```
import java.rmi.Remote;
import java.rmi.RemoteException;

public interface Send extends Remote {
  public void sendData(String text) throws RemoteException;
  public String getData() throws RemoteException;
}
```

Socket Communications

In Lesson 8, Remote Method Invocation (page 89), multiple client programs communicate with one server program without your writing any explicit code to establish the communication or field the client requests. This is because the RMI API is built on sockets, which enable network communications, and threads, which allow the server program to handle simultaneous requests from multiple clients. To help you understand what you get for free with the RMI API and to introduce the APIs for sockets and multithreaded programming, this lesson presents a simple sockets-based program with a multithreaded server.

Threads let a program perform multiple tasks at one time. Using threads in a server program to field simultaneous requests from multiple client programs is one common use, but threads can be used in programs in many other ways, too. For example, you can start a thread to play sound during an animation sequence or start a thread to load a large text file while the window to display the text in the file appears. These uses for threads are not covered in this lesson.

Covered in This Lesson

- What Are Sockets and Threads?
- About the Examples
- Example 1: Single-Threaded Server Example
- Example 2: Multithreaded Server Example
- Exercises

- More Information
- Code for This Lesson

What Are Sockets and Threads?

A socket is a software endpoint that establishes bidirectional communication between a server program and one or more client programs. Figure 9-1 shows how a socket associates the server program with a specific hardware port on the machine where it runs so any client program anywhere in the network with a socket associated with that same port can communicate with the server program.

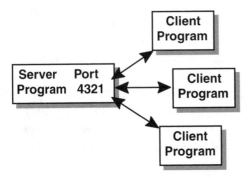

Figure 9-1   Sockets Connecting a Server Program to One or More Client Programs

A server program typically provides resources to a network of client programs. Client programs send requests to the server program, and the server program responds to the request. One way to handle requests from more than one client is to make the server program multithreaded. A thread is a sequence of instructions that run independently of the program and any other threads.

A multithreaded server creates a thread for each communication it accepts from a client. Using threads, a multithreaded server program can accept a connection from a client, start a thread for that communication, and continue listening for requests from other clients.

About the Examples

There are two examples for this lesson. Both are adapted from the FileIO Program (page 61). Example 1 sets up a client and server communication between one server program and one client program. The server program is not multithreaded and cannot handle requests from more than one client. Example 2 converts the server program to a multithreaded version so it can handle requests from more than one client.

Client-Side Behavior

The SocketClient client program (page 116) shown in Figure 9-2 presents a simple user interface and prompts for text input. When you click the Click Me button, the text is sent to the server program. The client program expects an echo from the server and prints the echo on its standard output.

Figure 9-2   Client Program

Server-Side Behavior

The SocketServer program (page 118) shown in Figure 9-3 presents a simple user interface. When you click the Click Me button, the text received from the client is displayed. The server echoes the text it receives whether or not you click the Click Me button.

Figure 9-3   Server Program

Compile and Run

Following are the compiler and interpreter commands to compile and run the example. To run the example, start the server program first; if you do not, the client program cannot establish the socket connection.

```
javac SocketServer.java
javac SocketClient.java
java SocketServer
java SocketClient
```

Example 1: Single-Threaded Server Example

Server-Side Program

The SocketServer program (page 118) establishes a socket connection on Port 4321 in its listenSocket method. It reads data sent to it and sends that same data back to the server in its actionPerformed method.

listenSocket Method

The listenSocket method creates a ServerSocket object with the port number on which the server program is going to listen for client communications. The port number must be an available port, which means the number cannot be reserved or already in use. For example, Unix systems reserve ports 1 through 1023 for administrative functions, leaving port numbers greater than 1023 available for use.

```
public void listenSocket(){
  try {
    server = new ServerSocket(4321);
  } catch (IOException e) {
    System.out.println("Could not listen on port 4321");
    System.exit(-1);
  }
```

Next, the listenSocket method creates a Socket connection for the requesting client. This code executes when a client starts up and requests the connection on the host and port where this server program is running. When the connection is successfully established, the server.accept method returns a new Socket object.

```
try{
  client = server.accept();
} catch (IOException e) {
  System.out.println("Accept failed: 4321");
  System.exit(-1);
}
```

Then, the `listenSocket` method creates a `BufferedReader` object to read the data sent over the socket connection from the client program. It also creates a `PrintWriter` object to send the data received from the client back to the server.

```
try{
  in = new BufferedReader(
            new  InputStreamReader(client.getInputStream()));
  out = new PrintWriter(client.getOutputStream(), true);
} catch (IOException e) {
  System.out.println("Read failed");
  System.exit(-1);
}
```

Last, the `listenSocket` method loops on the input stream to read data as it comes in from the client and writes to the output stream to send the data back.

```
while (true) {
  try {
    line = in.readLine();
//Send data back to client
    out.println(line);
  } catch (IOException e) {
    System.out.println("Read failed");
    System.exit(-1);
  }
}
```

actionPerformed Method

The `actionPerformed` method is called by the Java platform for action events such as button clicks. This `actionPerformed` method uses the text stored in the `line` object to initialize the `textArea` object so the retrieved text can be displayed to the user.

```
public void actionPerformed(ActionEvent event) {
  Object source = event.getSource();
  if (source == button) {
    textArea.setText(line);
  }
}
```

Client-Side Program

The `SocketClient` program (page 116) establishes a connection to the server program on a particular host and port number in its `listenSocket` method, and sends the data entered by the user to the server program in its actionPerformed method. The `actionPerformed` method also receives the data back from the server and prints it to the command line.

listenSocket Method

The `listenSocket` method first creates a `Socket` object with the computer name (kq6py) and port number (4321) where the server program is listening for client connection requests. Next, it creates a `PrintWriter` object to send data over the socket connection to the server program. It also creates a `BufferedReader` object to read the text sent by the server back to the client.

NOTE To make this example work, substitute the host name kq6py with the name of your own machine.

```java
public void listenSocket() {
 //Create socket connection
   try {
      socket = new Socket("kq6py", 4321);
      out = new PrintWriter(socket.getOutputStream(), true);
      in = new BufferedReader(new InputStreamReader(
                         socket.getInputStream()));
   } catch (UnknownHostException e) {
      System.out.println("Unknown host: kq6py");
      System.exit(1);
   } catch (IOException e) {
      System.out.println("No I/O");
      System.exit(1);
   }
}
```

actionPerformed Method

The `actionPerformed` method is called by the Java platform for action events such as button clicks. This `actionPerformed` method code gets the text in the `textField` object and passes it to the `PrintWriter` object (`out`), which sends it over the socket connection to the server program. The `actionPerformed` method then makes the `Textfield` object blank so it is ready for more user input. Last, it receives the text sent back to it by the server and prints the text.

```java
public void actionPerformed(ActionEvent event) {
   Object source = event.getSource();
   if (source == button) {
 //Send data over socket
```

```
        String text = textField.getText();
        out.println(text);
        textField.setText(new String(""));
        out.println(text);
      }
  //Receive text from server
      try {
        String line = in.readLine();
        System.out.println("Text received: " + line);
      } catch (IOException e){
        System.out.println("Read failed");
        System.exit(1);
      }
    }
}
```

Example 2: Multithreaded Server Example

The example in its current form works between the server program and only one client program. To allow multiple client connections as shown in Figure 9-4, the server program has to be converted to a multithreaded server program.

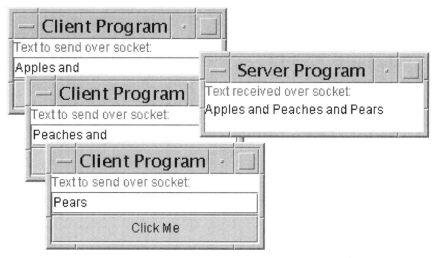

Figure 9-4   Three Clients Sending Data to One Server Program

The multithreaded server program, SocketThrdServer (page 120), creates a new thread for every client request. This way each client has its own connection to the server for passing data back and forth. When running multiple threads, you have to be sure that one thread cannot interfere with the data in another thread.

In this example, the listenSocket method loops on the server.accept call waiting for client connections and creates an instance of the ClientWorker class for each client connection it accepts. The textArea component that displays the text received from the client connection is passed to the Client-Worker instance with the accepted client connection.

```
public void listenSocket() {
  try {
    server = new ServerSocket(4321);
  } catch (IOException e) {
    System.out.println("Could not listen on port 4321");
    System.exit(-1);
  }
  while (true) {
    ClientWorker w;
    try{
//server.accept returns a client connection
        w = new ClientWorker(server.accept(), textArea);
      Thread t = new  Thread(w);
      t.start();
    } catch (IOException e) {
      System.out.println("Accept failed: 4321");
      System.exit(-1);
    }
  }
}
```

The important changes in this version of the server program over the non-threaded server program are that the line and client variables are no longer instance variables of the server class but instead are handled inside the ClientWorker class.

The ClientWorker class implements the Runnable interface, which has one method—run. The run method executes independently in each thread. If three clients request connections, three ClientWorker instances are created, a thread is started for each ClientWorker instance, and the run method executes for each thread.

In the following example, the run method creates the input buffer and output writer, loops on the input stream waiting for input from the client, sends the data it receives back to the client, and sets the text in the text area:

```
class ClientWorker implements Runnable {
  private Socket client;
  private JTextArea textArea;

//Constructor
  ClientWorker(Socket client, JTextArea textArea) {
```

```
      this.client = client;
      this.textArea = textArea;
  }

  public void run() {
    String line;
    BufferedReader in = null;
    PrintWriter out = null;
    try{
      in = new BufferedReader(new InputStreamReader(
        client.getInputStream()));
      out = new  PrintWriter(client.getOutputStream(), true);
    } catch (IOException e) {
      System.out.println("in or out failed");
      System.exit(-1);
    }

    while (true) {
      try {
        line = in.readLine();
//Send data back to client
        out.println(line);
        textArea.append(line);
      } catch (IOException e) {
        System.out.println("Read failed");
        System.exit(-1);
      }
    }
  }
}
```

The API documentation for the JTextArea.append method states this method is thread safe, which means its implementation includes code that allows one thread to finish its append operation before another thread can start an append operation. This prevents one thread from overwriting all or part of a string of appended text and corrupting the output.

If the JTextArea.append method were not thread safe, you would need to wrap the call to textArea.append(line) in a synchronized method and replace the call in the run method to textArea.append(line) with a call to the appendText(line) method instead.

The synchronized keyword gives this thread a lock on the textArea when the appendText method is called, so no other thread can change the textArea until this method completes. Lesson 11, Developing the Example (page 153), uses synchronized methods for writing data out to a series of files.

The `finalize` method is called by the Java VM before the program exits to give the program a chance to clean up and release resources. Multithreaded programs should close all `Files` and `Sockets` they use before exiting so they do not face resource starvation. The call to `server.close` in the `finalize` method closes the `Socket` connection used by each thread in this program.

```
protected void finalize() {
//Objects created in run method are finalized when
//program terminates and thread exits
  try {
     server.close();
   } catch (IOException e) {
     System.out.println("Could not close socket");
     System.exit(-1);
   }
 }
```

Exercises

1. How do you handle server requests from more than one client?
2. What does it mean when the API documentation states that a method is thread safe?
3. What is the `synchronize` keyword for?
4. What does the `finalize` method do?

More Information

Learn more about sockets in "All about Sockets" in *The Java™ Tutorial, Second Edition* [Cam98].

Code for This Lesson

- SocketClient
- SocketServer
- SocketThrdServer

SocketClient Program

```
import java.awt.Color;
import java.awt.BorderLayout;
```

```
import java.awt.event.*;
import javax.swing.*;
import java.io.*;
import java.net.*;

class SocketClient extends JFrame implements ActionListener
{
   JLabel text, clicked;
   JButton button;
   JPanel panel;
   JTextField textField;
   Socket socket = null;
   PrintWriter out = null;
   BufferedReader in = null;
   SocketClient(){ //Begin Constructor
     text = new JLabel("Text to send over socket:");
     textField = new JTextField(20);
     button = new JButton("Click Me");
     button.addActionListener(this);
     panel = new JPanel();
     panel.setLayout(new BorderLayout());
     panel.setBackground(Color.white);
     getContentPane().add(panel);
     panel.add("North", text);
     panel.add("Center", textField);
     panel.add("South", button);
   } //End Constructor

  public void actionPerformed(ActionEvent event) {
     Object source = event.getSource();
     if (source == button) {
//Send data over socket
        String text = textField.getText();
        out.println(text);
        textField.setText(new String(""));
//Receive text from server
       try{
         String line = in.readLine();
         System.out.println("Text received :" + line);
       } catch (IOException e) {
         System.out.println("Read failed");
         System.exit(1);
       }
     }
  }

  public void listenSocket() {
//Create socket connection
```

```
      try{
        socket = new Socket("kq6py", 4321);
        out = new PrintWriter(socket.getOutputStream(), true);
        in = new BufferedReader(
            new InputStreamReader(socket.getInputStream()));
      } catch (UnknownHostException e) {
        System.out.println("Unknown host: kq6py");
        System.exit(1);
      } catch  (IOException e) {
        System.out.println("No I/O");
        System.exit(1);
      }
    }
    public static void main(String[] args) {
      SocketClient frame = new SocketClient();
      frame.setTitle("Client Program");
      WindowListener l = new WindowAdapter() {
        public void windowClosing(WindowEvent e) {
          System.exit(0);
        }
      };
      frame.addWindowListener(l);
      frame.pack();
      frame.setVisible(true);
      frame.listenSocket();
    }
  }
```

SocketServer Program

```
import java.awt.Color;
import java.awt.BorderLayout;
import java.awt.event.*;
import javax.swing.*;
import java.io.*;
import java.net.*;

class SocketServer extends JFrame implements ActionListener
{
    JButton button;
    JLabel label = new JLabel("Text received over socket:");
    JPanel panel;
    JTextArea textArea = new JTextArea();
    ServerSocket server = null;
    Socket client = null;
    BufferedReader in = null;
    PrintWriter out = null;
    String line;
```

```java
    SocketServer(){ //Begin Constructor
      button = new JButton("Click Me");
      button.addActionListener(this);
      panel = new JPanel();
      panel.setLayout(new BorderLayout());
      panel.setBackground(Color.white);
      getContentPane().add(panel);
      panel.add("North", label);
      panel.add("Center", textArea);
      panel.add("South", button);
    } //End Constructor

  public void actionPerformed(ActionEvent event) {
     Object source = event.getSource();
     if(source == button) {
         textArea.setText(line);
     }
  }
  public void listenSocket() {
    try{
      server = new ServerSocket(4321);
    } catch (IOException e) {
      System.out.println("Could not listen on port 4321");
      System.exit(-1);
    }

    try {
      client = server.accept();
    } catch (IOException e) {
      System.out.println("Accept failed: 4321");
      System.exit(-1);
    }

    try {
      in = new BufferedReader(
          new InputStreamReader(client.getInputStream()));
      out = new PrintWriter(client.getOutputStream(), true);
    } catch (IOException e) {
      System.out.println("Accept failed: 4321");
      System.exit(-1);
    }

    while (true) {
      try{
        line = in.readLine();
//Send data back to client
        out.println(line);
      } catch (IOException e) {
```

```
                System.out.println("Read failed");
                System.exit(-1);
            }
        }
    }

    protected void finalize() {
//Clean up
        try {
            in.close();
            out.close();
            server.close();
        } catch (IOException e) {
            System.out.println("Could not close.");
            System.exit(-1);
        }
    }
    public static void main(String[] args) {
        SocketServer frame = new SocketServer();
        frame.setTitle("Server Program");
        WindowListener l = new WindowAdapter() {
            public void windowClosing(WindowEvent e) {
                System.exit(0);
            }
        };
        frame.addWindowListener(l);
        frame.pack();
        frame.setVisible(true);
        frame.listenSocket();
    }
}
```

SocketThrdServer Program

```
import java.awt.Color;
import java.awt.BorderLayout;
import java.awt.event.*;
import javax.swing.*;

import java.io.*;
import java.net.*;

class ClientWorker implements Runnable {
    private Socket client;
    private JTextArea textArea;

    ClientWorker(Socket client, JTextArea textArea) {
        this.client = client;
```

```
    this.textArea = textArea;
  }

  public void run() {
    String line;
    BufferedReader in = null;
    PrintWriter out = null;
    try {
      in = new BufferedReader(new InputStreamReader(
        client.getInputStream()));
      out = new PrintWriter(client.getOutputStream(), true);
    } catch (IOException e) {
      System.out.println("in or out failed");
      System.exit(-1);
    }

    while (true) {
      try {
        line = in.readLine();
//Send data back to client
        out.println(line);
        textArea.append(line);
      } catch (IOException e) {
        System.out.println("Read failed");
        System.exit(-1);
      }
    }
  }
}

class SocketThrdServer extends JFrame{

  JLabel label = new JLabel("Text received over socket:");
  JPanel panel;
  JTextArea textArea = new JTextArea();
  ServerSocket server = null;

  SocketThrdServer(){ //Begin Constructor
    panel = new JPanel();
    panel.setLayout(new BorderLayout());
    panel.setBackground(Color.white);
    getContentPane().add(panel);
    panel.add("North", label);
    panel.add("Center", textArea);
  } //End Constructor

  public void listenSocket() {
    try {
```

```
      server = new ServerSocket(4321);
    } catch (IOException e) {
      System.out.println("Could not listen on port 4321");
      System.exit(-1);
    }
    while (true) {
      ClientWorker w;
      try{
        w = new ClientWorker(server.accept(), textArea);
        Thread t = new Thread(w);
        t.start();
      } catch (IOException e) {
        System.out.println("Accept failed: 4321");
        System.exit(-1);
      }
    }
  }

  protected void finalize(){
//Objects created in run method are finalized when
//program terminates and thread exits
    try {
        server.close();
    } catch (IOException e) {
        System.out.println("Could not close socket");
        System.exit(-1);
    }
  }

  public static void main(String[] args) {
        SocketThrdServer frame = new SocketThrdServer();
        frame.setTitle("Server Program");
        WindowListener l = new WindowAdapter() {
                public void windowClosing(WindowEvent e) {
                        System.exit(0);
                }
        };
        frame.addWindowListener(l);
        frame.pack();
        frame.setVisible(true);
        frame.listenSocket();
  }
}
```

User Interfaces Revisited

I<small>N</small> Lesson 4, Building a User Interface (page 25), you learned how to use Java Foundation Classes (JFC) Project Swing components to build a simple user interface with very basic backend functionality. Lesson 8, Remote Method Invocation (page 89), also showed you how to use the RMI API to send data from a client program to a server program on the Net where the data can be accessed by other client programs.

This lesson takes the RMI application from the Lesson 8 (page 89), creates a more involved user interface and data model, and uses a different layout manager. These changes give you the beginnings of a very simple electronic-commerce application that consists of two types of client programs: One lets users place purchase orders, and the other lets order processors view the orders.

Covered in This Lesson

- About the Example
- Fruit Order (RMIClient1) Code
- Server Program Code
- View Order (RMIClient2) Code
- Exercises
- More Information
- Code for This Lesson

About the Example

This is a very simple electronic commerce example for instructional purposes only. It has three programs: two client programs—one for ordering fruit and another for viewing the fruit order—and one server program that is a repository for the order information.

The fruit order data is wrapped in a single data object defined by the DataOrder class. The fruit order client retrieves the data from the user interface components where the user enters it, stores the data in a DataOrder instance, and sends the DataOrder instance to the server program. The view order client retrieves the DataOrder instance from the server, gets the data out of the DataOrder instance, and displays the retrieved data in its user interface.

Fruit Order Client (RMIClient1)

The RMIClient1 program (page 139) shown in Figure 10-1 presents a user interface and prompts the user to order apples, peaches, and pears at $1.25 each.

Figure 10-1   Fruit Order Client Program

After the user enters the number of each item to order, he or she presses the Return key to commit the order and update the running total. The Tab key or mouse moves the cursor to the next field. At the bottom, the user provides a credit card number and customer ID. When the user clicks Purchase, all values entered into the form are stored in a DataOrder instance, which is then sent to the server program.

The user must press the Return key for the total to update. If the Return key is not pressed, an incorrect total is sent across the net with the order. The Exercises section (page 138) for this lesson asks you to change the code so that incorrect totals are not sent across the net because the user did not press the Return key.

Server Program

The Send interface and RemoteServer class have one getOrder method to return an instance of DataOrder, and one setOrder method to accept an instance of DataOrder. Fruit order clients call the send method to send data to the server, and view order clients call the get method to retrieve the data. In this example, the server program has no user interface.

View Order Client (RMIClient2)

The RMIClient2 program (page 143) shown in Figure 10-2 presents a user interface. When the user clicks View Order, the program gets a DataOrder instance from the server program, retrieves its data, and displays the data on the screen.

Figure 10-2 View Order Client Program

Compile and Run the Example

The code for this lesson is compiled and run the same way as the code in the section <u>Program Behavior</u> (page 90) in Lesson 8, Remote Method Invocation. This summarized version includes steps to handle the DataOrder class introduced in this lesson.

Compile

Unix:

```
cd /home/zelda/classes
javac Send.java
javac RemoteServer.java
javac RMIClient2.java
javac RMIClient1.java
rmic -d . RemoteServer
cp RemoteServer*.class /home/zelda/public_html/classes
cp Send.class /home/zelda/public_html/classes
cp DataOrder.class /home/zelda/public_html/classes
```

Win32:

```
cd \home\zelda\classes
javac Send.java
javac RemoteServer.java
javac RMIClient2.java
javac RMIClient1.java
rmic -d . RemoteServer
copy RemoteServer*.class \home\zelda\public_html\classes
copy Send.class \home\zelda\public_html\classes
copy DataOrder.class \home\zelda\public_html\classes
```

Start the RMI Registry

Unix:

```
cd /home/zelda/public_html/classes
unsetenv CLASSPATH
rmiregistry  &
```

Win32:

```
cd \home\zelda\public_html\classes
set CLASSPATH=
start rmiregistry
```

Start the Server

Unix:

```
cd /home/zelda/public_html/classes
java -Djava.rmi.server.codebase=http://kq6py/~zelda/classes
    -Djava.rmi.server.hostname=kq6py.eng.sun.com
    -Djava.security.policy=java.policy RemoteServer
```

Win32:

```
cd \home\zelda\public_html\classes
java -Djava.rmi.server.codebase=
    file:c:\home\zelda\public_html\classes
    -Djava.rmi.server.hostname=kq6py.eng.sun.com
    -Djava.security.policy=java.policy RemoteServer
```

Start the RMIClient1 Program

Unix:

```
cd /home/zelda/classes
java -Djava.rmi.server.codebase=http://kq6py/~zelda/classes
    -Djava.security.policy=
    java.policy RMIClient1 kq6py.eng.sun.com
```

Win32:

```
cd \home\zelda\classes
java -Djava.rmi.server.codebase=
    file:c:\home\zelda\public_html\classes
    -Djava.security.policy=
    java.policy RMIClient1 kq6py.eng.sun.com
```

Start the RMIClient2 Program

Unix:

```
cd /home/zelda/classes
java -Djava.rmi.server.codebase=http://kq6py/~zelda/classes
    -Djava.security.policy=
    java.policy RMIClient2 kq6py.eng.sun.com
```

Win32:

```
cd \home\zelda\classes
java -Djava.rmi.server.codebase=
    file:c:\home\zelda\public_html\classes
    -Djava.security.policy=
    java.policy RMIClient2 kq6py.eng.sun.com
```

Fruit Order (RMIClient1) Code

The RMIClient1 code uses the label, text field, text area, and button components shown in Figure 10-3 to create the user interface for ordering fruit.

— Fruit $1.25 Each	· □

Select Items	Specify Quantity
Apples	2
Peaches	1
Pears	4
Total Items:	7
Total Cost:	8.75
Credit Card:	1234-4321-1234-31
Customer ID:	munchkin
Reset	Purchase

Figure 10-3   User Interface Components

On the display, the user interface components are arranged in a two-column grid with labels in the left column and the input and output data fields (text fields and text areas) aligned in the right column.

The user enters his or her apples, peaches, and pears order into the text fields and presses the Return key after each fruit entry. When the Return key is pressed, the text field behavior updates the item and cost totals displayed in the text areas.

The Reset button clears the display and the underlying variables for the total cost and total items. The Purchase button sends the order data to the server program. If the Reset button is clicked before the Purchase button, null values are sent to the server.

Instance Variables

The following lines declare the Project Swing component classes that the RMIClient1 class uses. These instance variables can be accessed by any method in the instantiated class. In the following example, they are built in the constructor and accessed in the `actionPerformed` method implementation:

```
JLabel col1, col2;
JLabel totalItems, totalCost;
JLabel cardNum, custID;
JLabel applechk, pearchk, peachchk;
JButton purchase, reset;
JPanel panel;
JTextField appleqnt, pearqnt, peachqnt;
JTextField creditCard, customer;
JTextArea items, cost;
static Send send;
int itotal=0;
double icost=0;
```

Constructor

The constructor is fairly long because it creates all the components, sets the layout to a two-column grid, and places the components in the grid on a panel.

The `Reset` and `Purchase` buttons and the `appleQnt`, `pearQnt`, and `peachQnt` text fields are added to the `RMIClient1` object so the `RMIClient1` object will listen for action events from these components. When the user clicks one of the buttons or presses Return in a text field, an action event causes the platform to call the `RMIClient1.actionPerformed` method where the behaviors for these components are defined.

As explained in Lesson 4, Building a User Interface (page 25), a class declares the `ActionListener` interface and implements the `actionPerformed` method if it needs to handle action events such as button clicks and text field Returns. Other user interface components generate different action events and, as a result, require you to declare different interfaces and implement different methods.

```
//Create left and right column labels
  col1 = new JLabel("Select Items");
  col2 = new JLabel("Specify Quantity");

//Create labels and text field components
  applechk = new JLabel("  Apples");
  appleqnt = new JTextField();
  appleqnt.addActionListener(this);

  pearchk = new JLabel("  Pears");
  pearqnt = new JTextField();
  pearqnt.addActionListener(this);
```

```
peachchk = new JLabel("   Peaches");
peachqnt = new JTextField();
peachqnt.addActionListener(this);

cardNum = new JLabel("   Credit Card:");
creditCard = new JTextField();
customer = new JTextField();
custID = new JLabel("   Customer ID:");

//Create labels and text area components
totalItems = new JLabel("Total Items:");
totalCost = new JLabel("Total Cost:");
items = new JTextArea();
cost = new JTextArea();

//Create buttons and make action listeners
purchase = new JButton("Purchase");
purchase.addActionListener(this);
reset = new JButton("Reset");
reset.addActionListener(this);
```

In the following lines, a JPanel component is created and added to the top-level frame, and the layout manager and background color for the panel are specified. The layout manager determines how user interface components are arranged on the panel.

The example in Lesson 4 (page 25) used the BorderLayout layout manager. This example uses the GridLayout layout manager, which arranges components in a grid using the number of rows and columns you specify. The example uses a two-column grid with an unlimited number of rows, as indicated by the zero (unlimited rows) and two (two columns) in the statement panel.set-Layout(new GridLayout(0,2)). Components are added to a panel using GridLayout going across and down.

The layout manager and color are set on the panel, and the panel is added to the content pane with a call to the getContentPane method of the JFrame class. A content pane lets different types of components work together in Project Swing.

```
//Create a panel for the components
panel = new JPanel();

//Set panel layout to 2-column grid
//on a white background
panel.setLayout(new GridLayout(0,2));
panel.setBackground(Color.white);
```

```
//Add components to panel columns
//going left to right and top to bottom
  getContentPane().add(panel);
  panel.add(col1);
  panel.add(col2);
  panel.add(applechk);
  panel.add(appleqnt);
  panel.add(peachchk);
  panel.add(peachqnt);
  panel.add(pearchk);
  panel.add(pearqnt);
  panel.add(totalItems);
  panel.add(items);
  panel.add(totalCost);
  panel.add(cost);
  panel.add(cardNum);
  panel.add(creditCard);
  panel.add(custID);
  panel.add(customer);
  panel.add(reset);
  panel.add(purchase);
```

Event Handling

The `actionPerformed` method provides behavior in the event the `Purchase` or Reset button is clicked or a Return is pressed in the `appleQnt`, `peachQnt`, or `pearQnt` text fields. The Reset button is similar to the `purchase` button, and the other text fields are similar to `appleQnt`, so this section will focus on the Purchase button, the `appleQnt` text field, and the `DataOrder` class.

The `actionPerformed` method in the `RMIClient1` class retrieves the event, declares its variables, and creates an instance of the `DataOrder` class.

```
public void actionPerformed(ActionEvent event) {
    Object source = event.getSource();
    Integer applesNo, peachesNo, pearsNo, num;
    Double cost;
    String number, text, text2;
    DataOrder order = new DataOrder();
```

The `DataOrder` class defines fields that wrap and store the fruit order data. As you can see by the class definition that follows, the `DataOrder` class has no methods. It does, however, implement the `Serializable` interface.

An object created from a class that implements the `Serializable` interface can be serialized. Object serialization transforms an object's data to a byte stream that represents the state of the data. The serialized form of the data contains enough information so that the receiving program can create an object with its data in the same state as it was when first serialized.

The RMI API uses object serialization to send data over the network, and many Java API classes are serializable. So if you use RMI to send, for example, a JTextArea over the network, everything should work just fine. But in this example, a special DataOrder object class was created to wrap the data, so this DataObject class has to be serializable so the RMI services can serialize the data and send it between the client and server programs. You can see an example of sending individual Java API objects over the network in Appendix A, Cryptography (page 217).

```
import java.io.*;
class DataOrder implements Serializable{
  String apples, peaches, pears, cardnum, custID;
  double icost;
  int itotal;
}
```

Purchase Button

The Purchase button behavior involves retrieving data from the user interface components, initializing the DataOrder instance, and sending the DataOrder instance to the server program.

```
if (source == purchase) {
  order.cardnum = creditCard.getText();
  order.custID = customer.getText();
  order.apples = appleqnt.getText();
  order.peaches = peachqnt.getText();
  order.pears = pearqnt.getText();
  order.itotal = itotal;
  order.icost = icost;
//Send data over net
  try {
    send.sendOrder(order);
  } catch (java.rmi.RemoteException e) {
    System.out.println("Cannot send data to server");
  }
}
```

appleQnt Text Field

The appleQnt text field behavior involves retrieving the number of pears the user wants to order, adding the number to the items total, using the number to calculate the cost, and adding the cost of pears to the total cost.

```
//If Return in apple quantity text field
//Calculate totals
    if (source == appleqnt) {
        number = appleqnt.getText();
        if (number.length() > 0) {
          applesNo = Integer.valueOf(number);
          itotal += applesNo.intValue();
        } else {
         /* else no need to change the total */
        }
    }
```

The total number of items is retrieved from the itotal variable and displayed in the user interface.

```
num = new Integer(itotal);
text = num.toString();
this.items.setText(text);
```

Similarly, the total cost is calculated and displayed in the user interface using the icost variable.

```
icost = (itotal * 1.25);
cost = new Double(icost);
text2 = cost.toString();
this.cost.setText(text2);
```

NOTE   The cost text area component is referenced as this.cost because the actionPerformed method also has a cost variable of type Double. To reference the instance text area and not the local Double by the same name, you have to reference it as this.cost.

Cursor Focus

Users can use the Tab key to move the cursor from one component to another within the user interface. The default Tab key movement steps through all user interface components including the text areas in the order they were added to the panel.

Because the user does not interact with the text areas, there is no reason for the cursor to go there. The example program includes a call in its constructor to pearqnt.setNextFocusableComponent to make the cursor move from the pearqnt text field, to the creditcard text field bypassing the total cost and total items text areas when the Tab key is pressed.

```
    cardNum = new JLabel("   Credit Card:");
    creditCard = new JTextField();
//Make cursor go to creditCard component
    pearqnt.setNextFocusableComponent(creditCard);
```

Converting Strings to Numbers and Back

To calculate the items ordered and their cost, the string values retrieved from the appleQnt, peachQnt, and pearQnt text fields have to be converted to their number equivalents.

The string value is returned in the number variable. To be sure the user actually entered a value, the string length is checked. If the length is not greater than zero, the user pressed Return without entering a value. In this case, the else statement does nothing. If the length is greater than zero, an instance of the java.lang.Integer class is created from the string. The Integer.intValue method is called next to produce the integer (int) equivalent of the string value so it can be added to the items total kept in the itotal integer variable.

```
if (number.length() > 0) {
  pearsNo = Integer.valueOf(number);
  itotal += pearsNo.intValue();
} else {
  /* else no need to change the total */
}
```

To display the running item and cost totals in their respective text areas, the totals have to be converted back to strings. The code at the end of the action-Performed method and shown next does this.

To display the total items, a java.lang.Integer object is created from the itotal integer variable. The Integer.toString method is called to produce the String equivalent of the integer (int). This string is passed to the call to this.cost.setText(text2) to update the Total Cost field in the display.

```
num = new Integer(itotal);
text = num.toString();
this.items.setText(text);
icost = (itotal * 1.25);
cost = new Double(icost);
text2 = cost.toString();
this.cost.setText(text2);
```

Until now, all data types used in the examples have been classes. However, the int and double data types are not classes; they are primitive data types.

The `int` primitive type contains a single whole 32-bit integer value that can be positive or negative. You can use the standard arithmetic operators (+, -, *, and /) to perform arithmetic operations on the integer. The `Integer` class not only contains a whole 32-bit integer value that can be positive or negative but provides methods for working on the value. For example, the `Integer.intValue` method lets you convert an `Integer` to an `int` to perform arithmetic operations.

The `double` primitive type contains a 64-bit double-precision floating point value. The `Double` class not only contains a 64-bit double-precision floating point value but provides methods for working on the value. For example, the `Double.doubleValue` method lets you convert a `Double` to a `double` to perform arithmetic operations.

Server Program Code

The server program consists of the `RemoteServer` class that implements the `get` and `set` methods declared in the `Send` interface. The important thing to note about this interface and class is data of any type and size can be easily passed from one client through the server to another client using the RMI API. No special handling is needed for large amounts of data or for special considerations for different data types, which can sometimes be issues when using socket communications.

Send Interface

The server program is available to the `RMIClient1` program through its `Send` interface, which declares the remote server send and get methods.

```
import java.rmi.Remote;
import java.rmi.RemoteException;

public interface Send extends Remote {
   public void sendOrder(DataOrder order)
     throws RemoteException;
   public DataOrder getOrder() throws RemoteException;
}
```

RemoteServer Class

The `RemoteServer` class implements the methods declared by the `Send` interface.

```
import java.awt.event.*;
import java.io.*;
```

```java
import java.net.*;
import java.rmi.*;
import java.rmi.server.*;

class RemoteServer extends UnicastRemoteObject implements
Send {
  private DataOrder order;
  public RemoteServer() throws RemoteException {
    super();
  }
  public void sendOrder(DataOrder order) {
    this.order = order;
  }
  public DataOrder getOrder() {
    return this.order;
  }

  public static void main(String[] args) {
    if(System.getSecurityManager() == null) {
      System.setSecurityManager(new RMISecurityManager());
    }
    String name = "//kq6py.eng.sun.com/Send";
    try {
      Send remoteServer = new RemoteServer();
      Naming.rebind(name, remoteServer);
      System.out.println("RemoteServer bound");
    } catch (java.rmi.RemoteException e) {
      System.out.println(
        "Cannot create remote server object");
    } catch (java.net.MalformedURLException e) {
      System.out.println(
        "Cannot look up server object");
    }
  }
}
```

View Order Client (RMIClient2) Code

The RMIClient2 program (page 143) uses text areas and buttons to display order information (see Figure 10-4).

The code is very similar to the RMIClient1 class, so rather than repeat a lot of what you have already read, this section highlights how the order data is retrieved.

The first lines in the code that follows retrieve the credit card number and the number of apples, peaches, and pears ordered from the server program. The retrieved values are then set in the corresponding text areas.

Figure 10-4 Fruit Order Retrieval Program

The last lines retrieve the cost and item totals, which are `double` and `integer`, respectively. The total cost value is converted to a `java.lang.Double` object, and the total items value is converted to a `java.lang.Integer` object and then calls the `toString` method on each to get the string equivalents. Finally, the strings can be used to set the values for the corresponding text areas.

```
DataOrder order = new DataOrder();
if (source == view) {
  try {
    order = send.getOrder();
    creditNo.setText(order.cardnum);
    customerNo.setText(order.custID);
    applesNo.setText(order.apples);
    peachesNo.setText(order.peaches);
    pearsNo.setText(order.pears);
    cost = order.icost;
    price = new Double(cost);
    unit = price.toString();
    icost.setText(unit);
    items = order.itotal;
    itms = new Integer(items);
    i = itms.toString();
    itotal.setText(i);
```

Exercises

The example program has been kept simple for instructional purposes and would need a number of improvements to be an enterprise-worthy application. The following exercises ask you to improve the program in several ways.

Calculations and Pressing Return

If the user enters a value for apples, peaches, or pears and moves to the next field without pressing the Return key, no calculation is made. When the user clicks the Purchase key, the order is sent, but the item and cost totals are incorrect. So in this application, relying on the Return key action event is not a good design; modify the `actionPerformed` method so this does not happen. You will find one way to modify the `RMIClient1` code on page 147.

Non-Number Errors

If the user enters a non-number value for apples, peaches, or pears, the program presents a stack trace indicating an illegal number format. A good program will catch and handle the error, rather than produce a stack trace. One possible way to modify the `RMIClient1` code is on page 147.

HINT   Find where the code throws the error and enclose it in a `try` and `catch` block, which was introduced in the section <u>Exception Handling</u> (page 52). The error to catch is `java.lang.NumberFormatException`.

Extra Credit

The RMIClient2 Program (page 143) produces a stack trace if it gets null data from the `DataOrder` object and tries to use it to set the text on the text area component. Add code to test for null fields in the `DataOrder` object, and supply an alternative value in the event a null field is found. No solution for this exercise is provided.

If someone enters 2 apples and 2 pears, and then decides he wants 3 apples, the calculation produces a total of 7 items at $8.75 when it should be 5 items at $6.25. See if you can fix this problem. No solution for this exercise is provided.

The `DataOrder` class should really handle apples, peaches, pears, cardnum, and custID as integers instead of strings. This not only makes more sense but dramatically reduces the packet size when the data is sent over the Net. Change the DataOrder class to handle this information as integers. You will also need to change some code in the RMIClient1 and RMIClient2 classes because the user interface components handle this data as text. No solution for this exercise is provided.

More Information

You can find more information on event listening in "Writing Event Listeners" in *The Java™ Tutorial, Second Edition* [Cam98].

"Variables and Data Types" in *The Java™ Tutorial, Second Edition* [Cam98] provides more information on primitive data types.

See *The JFC Swing Tutorial: A Guide to Constructing GUIs* [Wal99] for more information on Project Swing.

Code for This Lesson

- RMIClient1
- RMIClient2
- RMIClient1 Improved

RMIClient1 Program

```
import java.awt.Color;
import java.awt.GridLayout;
import java.awt.event.*;
import javax.swing.*;
import java.io.*;
import java.net.*;
import java.rmi.*;
import java.rmi.server.*;

class RMIClient1 extends JFrame  implements ActionListener {
    JLabel col1, col2;
    JLabel totalItems, totalCost;
    JLabel cardNum, custID;
```

```java
        JLabel applechk, pearchk, peachchk;
        JButton purchase, reset;
        JPanel panel;
        JTextField appleqnt, pearqnt, peachqnt;
        JTextField creditCard, customer;
        JTextArea items, cost;
        static Send send;
        int itotal=0;
        double icost=0;
        RMIClient1(){ //Begin Constructor

//Create left and right column labels
        col1 = new JLabel("Select Items");
        col2 = new JLabel("Specify Quantity");

//Create labels and text field components
        applechk = new JLabel("   Apples");
        appleqnt = new JTextField();
        appleqnt.addActionListener(this);
        pearchk = new JLabel("   Pears");
        pearqnt = new JTextField();
        pearqnt.addActionListener(this);
        peachchk = new JLabel("   Peaches");
        peachqnt = new JTextField();
        peachqnt.addActionListener(this);
        cardNum = new JLabel("   Credit Card:");
        creditCard = new JTextField();
        pearqnt.setNextFocusableComponent(creditCard);
        customer = new JTextField();
        custID = new JLabel("   Customer ID:");

//Create labels and text area components
        totalItems = new JLabel("Total Items:");
        totalCost = new JLabel("Total Cost:");
        items = new JTextArea();
        cost = new JTextArea();

//Create buttons and make action listeners
       purchase = new JButton("Purchase");
       purchase.addActionListener(this);
       reset = new JButton("Reset");
       reset.addActionListener(this);

//Create a panel for the components
        panel = new JPanel();

//Set panel layout to 2-column grid
//on a white background
        panel.setLayout(new GridLayout(0,2));
        panel.setBackground(Color.white);
```

```
//Add components to panel columns
//going left to right and top to bottom
    getContentPane().add(panel);
    panel.add(col1);
    panel.add(col2);
    panel.add(applechk);
    panel.add(appleqnt);
    panel.add(peachchk);
    panel.add(peachqnt);
    panel.add(pearchk);
    panel.add(pearqnt);
    panel.add(totalItems);
    panel.add(items);
    panel.add(totalCost);
    panel.add(cost);
    panel.add(cardNum);
    panel.add(creditCard);
    panel.add(custID);
    panel.add(customer);
    panel.add(reset);
    panel.add(purchase);
  } //End Constructor

  public void actionPerformed(ActionEvent event) {
    Object source = event.getSource();
    Integer applesNo, peachesNo, pearsNo, num;
    Double cost;
    String number, text, text2;
    DataOrder order = new DataOrder();

//If Purchase button pressed . . .
    if (source == purchase) {
//Get data from text fields
      order.cardnum = creditCard.getText();
      order.custID = customer.getText();
      order.apples = appleqnt.getText();
      order.peaches = peachqnt.getText();
      order.pears = pearqnt.getText();
      order.itotal = itotal;
      order.icost = icost;
      try{
//Send data over net
        send.sendOrder(order);
      } catch (java.rmi.RemoteException e) {
        System.out.println("Cannot send data to server");
      }
    }
```

```
//If Reset button pressed
//Clear all fields
    if (source == reset) {
       creditCard.setText("");
       appleqnt.setText("");
       peachqnt.setText("");
       pearqnt.setText("");
       creditCard.setText("");
       customer.setText("");
       icost = 0;
       itotal = 0;
    }

//If Return in apple quantity text field
//Calculate totals
    if (source == appleqnt) {
      number = appleqnt.getText();
      if (number.length() > 0) {
         applesNo = Integer.valueOf(number);
         itotal += applesNo.intValue();
      } else {
        /* else no need to change the total */
      }
    }

//If Return in peach quantity text field
//Calculate totals
    if (source == peachqnt) {
       number = peachqnt.getText();
       if (number.length() > 0) {
          peachesNo = Integer.valueOf(number);
          itotal += peachesNo.intValue();
       } else {
         /* else no need to change the total */
       }
    }

//If Return in pear quantity text field
//Calculate totals
    if (source == pearqnt){
       number = pearqnt.getText();
       if (number.length() > 0){
          pearsNo = Integer.valueOf(number);
          itotal += pearsNo.intValue();
       } else {
         /* else no need to change the total */
       }
    }
```

```
        num = new Integer(itotal);
        text = num.toString();
        this.items.setText(text);
        icost = (itotal * 1.25);
        cost = new Double(icost);
        text2 = cost.toString();
        this.cost.setText(text2);
    }

    public static void main(String[] args){
      RMIClient1 frame = new RMIClient1();
      frame.setTitle("Fruit $1.25 Each");
      WindowListener l = new WindowAdapter() {
        public void windowClosing(WindowEvent e) {
          System.exit(0);
        }
      };
      frame.addWindowListener(l);
      frame.pack();
      frame.setVisible(true);
      if(System.getSecurityManager() == null) {
        System.setSecurityManager(new RMISecurityManager());
      }
      try {
        String name = "//" + args[0] + "/Send";
        send = ((Send) Naming.lookup(name));
      } catch (java.rmi.NotBoundException e) {
        System.out.println(
          "Cannot look up remote server object");
      } catch (java.rmi.RemoteException e) {
        System.out.println(
          "Cannot look up remote server object");
      } catch (java.net.MalformedURLException e) {
        System.out.println(
          "Cannot look up remote server object");
      }
    }
}
```

RMIClient2 Program

```
import java.awt.Color;
import java.awt.GridLayout;
import java.awt.event.*;
import javax.swing.*;
import java.io.*;
import java.net.*;
import java.rmi.*;
```

```
import java.rmi.server.*;
import java.util.*;

class RMIClient2 extends JFrame implements ActionListener {
    JLabel creditCard, custID;
    JLabel apples, peaches, pears, total, cost, clicked;
    JButton view, reset;
    JPanel panel;
    JTextArea creditNo, customerNo;
    JTextArea applesNo, peachesNo, pearsNo, itotal, icost;
    static Send send;
    String customer;

  RMIClient2(){ //Begin Constructor
//Create labels
    creditCard = new JLabel("Credit Card:");
    custID = new JLabel("Customer ID:");
    apples = new JLabel("Apples:");
    peaches = new JLabel("Peaches:");
    pears = new JLabel("Pears:");
    total = new JLabel("Total Items:");
    cost = new JLabel("Total Cost:");

//Create text area components
    creditNo = new JTextArea();
    customerNo = new JTextArea();
    applesNo = new JTextArea();
    peachesNo = new JTextArea();
    pearsNo = new JTextArea();
    itotal = new JTextArea();
    icost = new JTextArea();

//Create buttons
    view = new JButton("View Order");
    view.addActionListener(this);
    reset = new JButton("Reset");
    reset.addActionListener(this);

//Create panel for 2-column layout
//Set white background color
    panel = new JPanel();
    panel.setLayout(new GridLayout(0,2));
    panel.setBackground(Color.white);

//Add components to panel columns
//going left to right and top to bottom
    getContentPane().add(panel);
    panel.add(creditCard);
```

```
            panel.add(creditNo);
            panel.add(custID);
            panel.add(customerNo);
            panel.add(apples);
            panel.add(applesNo);
            panel.add(peaches);
            panel.add(peachesNo);
            panel.add(pears);
            panel.add(pearsNo);
            panel.add(total);
            panel.add(itotal);
            panel.add(cost);
            panel.add(icost);
            panel.add(view);
            panel.add(reset);
        } //End Constructor

    public void actionPerformed(ActionEvent event) {
        Object source = event.getSource();
        String text=null, unit, i;
        double cost;
        Double price;
        int items;
        Integer itms;
        DataOrder order = new DataOrder();

//If View button pressed
//Get data from server and display it
//Extra Credit: If a DataOrder field is empty, the program
//produces a stack trace when it tries to setText on a user
//interface
//component with empty data. Add code to find empty fields
//and assign alternate data in the event null fields are
//found
        if (source == view) {
            try {
                order = send.getOrder();
                creditNo.setText(order.cardnum);
                customerNo.setText(order.custID);
                applesNo.setText(order.apples);
                peachesNo.setText(order.peaches);
                pearsNo.setText(order.pears);
                cost = order.icost;
                price = new Double(cost);
                unit = price.toString();
                icost.setText(unit);
                items = order.itotal;
                itms = new Integer(items);
```

```java
            i = itms.toString();
            itotal.setText(i);
        } catch (java.rmi.RemoteException e) {
            System.out.println("Cannot get data from server");
        }
    }


//If Reset button pressed
//Clear all fields
    if( source == reset) {
        creditNo.setText("");
        customerNo.setText("");
        applesNo.setText("");
        peachesNo.setText("");
        pearsNo.setText("");
        itotal.setText("");
        icost.setText("");
    }
}

    public static void main(String[] args) {
        RMIClient2 frame = new RMIClient2();
        frame.setTitle("Fruit Order");
        WindowListener l = new WindowAdapter() {
            public void windowClosing(WindowEvent e) {
                System.exit(0);
            }
        };
        frame.addWindowListener(l);
        frame.pack();
        frame.setVisible(true);
        if(System.getSecurityManager() == null) {
            System.setSecurityManager(new RMISecurityManager());
        }

    try {
        String name = "//" + args[0] + "/Send";
        send = ((Send) Naming.lookup(name));
    } catch (java.rmi.NotBoundException e) {
        System.out.println("Cannot access data in server");
    } catch(java.rmi.RemoteException e) {
        System.out.println("Cannot access data in server");
    } catch(java.net.MalformedURLException e) {
        System.out.println("Cannot access data in server");
    }
  }
}
```

RMIClient1 Improved Program

```java
import java.awt.Color;
import java.awt.GridLayout;
import java.awt.event.*;
import javax.swing.*;
import java.io.*;
import java.net.*;
import java.rmi.*;
import java.rmi.server.*;

class RMIClient1Improved extends JFrame  implements Action-
Listener {
    JLabel col1, col2;
    JLabel totalItems, totalCost;
    JLabel cardNum, custID;
    JLabel applechk, pearchk, peachchk;
    JButton purchase, reset;
    JPanel panel;
    JTextField appleqnt, pearqnt, peachqnt;
    JTextField creditCard, customer;
    JTextArea items, cost;
    static Send send;

    RMIClient1Improved(){ //Begin Constructor
//Create left and right column labels
    col1 = new JLabel("Select Items");
    col2 = new JLabel("Specify Quantity");

//Create labels and text field components
    applechk = new JLabel("    Apples");
    appleqnt = new JTextField();
    appleqnt.addActionListener(this);
    pearchk = new JLabel("    Pears");
    pearqnt = new JTextField();
    pearqnt.addActionListener(this);
    peachchk = new JLabel("    Peaches");
    peachqnt = new JTextField();
    peachqnt.addActionListener(this);
    cardNum = new JLabel("    Credit Card:");
    creditCard = new JTextField();
    pearqnt.setNextFocusableComponent(creditCard);
    customer = new JTextField();
    custID = new JLabel("    Customer ID:");

//Create labels and text area components
    totalItems = new JLabel("Total Items:");
    totalCost = new JLabel("Total Cost:");
```

```
        items = new JTextArea();
        cost = new JTextArea();

//Create buttons and make action listeners
        purchase = new JButton("Purchase");
        purchase.addActionListener(this);
        reset = new JButton("Reset");
        reset.addActionListener(this);

//Create a panel for the components
        panel = new JPanel();

//Set panel layout to 2-column grid
//on a white background
        panel.setLayout(new GridLayout(0,2));
        panel.setBackground(Color.white);

//Add components to panel columns
//going left to right and top to bottom
        getContentPane().add(panel);
        panel.add(col1);
        panel.add(col2);
        panel.add(applechk);
        panel.add(appleqnt);
        panel.add(peachchk);
        panel.add(peachqnt);
        panel.add(pearchk);
        panel.add(pearqnt);
        panel.add(totalItems);
        panel.add(items);
        panel.add(totalCost);
        panel.add(cost);
        panel.add(cardNum);
        panel.add(creditCard);
        panel.add(custID);
        panel.add(customer);
        panel.add(reset);
        panel.add(purchase);
    } //End Constructor

  public void actionPerformed(ActionEvent event){
    Object source = event.getSource();
    Integer applesNo, peachesNo, pearsNo, num;
    Double cost;
    String text, text2;
    DataOrder order = new DataOrder();

//If Purchase button pressed  . . .
    if (source == purchase) {
```

```
//Get data from text fields
    order.cardnum = creditCard.getText();
    order.custID = customer.getText();
    order.apples = appleqnt.getText();
    order.peaches = peachqnt.getText();
    order.pears = pearqnt.getText();
//Calculate total items
    if (order.apples.length() > 0) {

//Catch invalid number error
        try {
          applesNo = Integer.valueOf(order.apples);
          order.itotal += applesNo.intValue();
        } catch(java.lang.NumberFormatException e) {
          appleqnt.setText("Invalid Value");
        }
    } else {
      /* else no need to change the total */
    }

    if (order.peaches.length() > 0){
//Catch invalid number error
        try{
          peachesNo = Integer.valueOf(order.peaches);
          order.itotal += peachesNo.intValue();
        } catch(java.lang.NumberFormatException e) {
          peachqnt.setText("Invalid Value");
        }
    } else {
      /* else no need to change the total */
    }

    if (order.pears.length() > 0) {
//Catch invalid number error
        try {
          pearsNo = Integer.valueOf(order.pears);
          order.itotal += pearsNo.intValue();
        } catch(java.lang.NumberFormatException e) {
          pearqnt.setText("Invalid Value");
        }
    } else {
      /* else no need to change the total */
    }

//Display running total
    num = new Integer(order.itotal);
    text = num.toString();
    this.items.setText(text);
```

```java
//Calculate and display running cost
    order.icost = (order.itotal * 1.25);
    cost = new Double(order.icost);
    text2 = cost.toString();
    this.cost.setText(text2);
    try {
       send.sendOrder(order);
     } catch (java.rmi.RemoteException e) {
       System.out.println("Cannot send data to server");
     }
  }

//If Reset button pressed
//Clear all fields
    if (source == reset) {
     creditCard.setText("");
     appleqnt.setText("");
     peachqnt.setText("");
     pearqnt.setText("");
     creditCard.setText("");
     customer.setText("");
     order.icost = 0;
     cost = new Double(order.icost);
     text2 = cost.toString();
     this.cost.setText(text2);
     order.itotal = 0;
     num = new Integer(order.itotal);
     text = num.toString();
     this.items.setText(text);
   }
  }

  public static void main(String[] args) {
      RMIClient1Improved frame = new RMIClient1Improved();
      frame.setTitle("Fruit $1.25 Each");
      WindowListener l = new WindowAdapter() {
         public void windowClosing(WindowEvent e) {
            System.exit(0);
          }
      };
      frame.addWindowListener(l);
      frame.pack();
      frame.setVisible(true);

    if(System.getSecurityManager() == null) {
      System.setSecurityManager(new RMISecurityManager());
    }
```

```
    try {
        String name = "//" + args[0] + "/Send";
        send = ((Send) Naming.lookup(name));
    } catch (java.rmi.NotBoundException e) {
        System.out.println("Cannot look up remote server
object");
    } catch(java.rmi.RemoteException e) {
        System.out.println("Cannot look up remote server
object");
    } catch(java.net.MalformedURLException e) {
        System.out.println("Cannot look up remote server
object");
    }
  }
}
```

Developing the Example

THE program in its current form lets sending clients overwrite each other's data before receiving clients have a chance to get and process it. This lesson adapts the server code so all orders are processed (nothing is overwritten) in the order received by the server.

This lesson shows you how to use object serialization in the server program to save the orders to files where they can be retrieved in the order they were saved. This lesson also shows you how to use the Collections API to maintain and display a list of unique customer IDs.

Covered in This Lesson

- Tracking Orders
- Maintaining and Displaying a Customer List
- Exercises
- More Information
- Code for This Lesson

Tracking Orders

The changes to the example program, so that it uses serialization to keep track of the orders received and processed, are primarily in the RemoteServer class. The full code is on page 162.

sendOrder Method

The sendOrder method in the RemoteServer class accepts a DataOrder instance as input and stores each order in a separate file where the file name is a number. The first order received is stored in a file named *1*, the second order is stored in a file named *2*, and so on. To keep track of the file names, the value variable is incremented by 1 each time the sendOrder method is called, is converted to a String, and is used for the file name in the serialization process.

Objects are serialized by creating a serialized output stream and writing the object to it. In the code, the first line in the try block creates a FileOutput-Stream with the file name to which the serialized object is to be written. The next line creates an ObjectOutputFileStream from the file output stream. Following is the serialized output stream to which the order object is written in the last line of the try block:

```
public synchronized void sendOrder(DataOrder order)
   throws java.io.IOException {
   value += 1;
   String orders = String.valueOf(value);

   try {
      FileOutputStream fos = new FileOutputStream(orders);
      oos = new ObjectOutputStream(fos);
      oos.writeObject(order);
   } catch (java.io.FileNotFoundException e) {
      System.out.println(e.toString());
   } finally {
      if (oos != null) {
         oos.close();
      }
   }
}
```

getOrder Method

The getOrder method in the RemoteServer class does what the sendOrder method does in reverse using the get variable to keep track of which orders have been viewed. First, this method checks the value variable. If it is equal to zero, there are no orders to get from a file and view; if it is greater than the value in the get variable, there is at least one order to get from a file and view. As each order is viewed, the get variable is incremented by 1.

```
public synchronized DataOrder getOrder()
   throws java.io.IOException {
```

```
    DataOrder order = null;
    ObjectInputStream ois = null;

    if (value == 0) {
       System.out.println("No Orders To Process");
    }

    if (value > get) {
      get += 1;
      String orders = String.valueOf(get);
      try {
         FileInputStream fis = new FileInputStream(orders);
         ois = new ObjectInputStream(fis);
         order = (DataOrder)ois.readObject();
      } catch (java.io.FileNotFoundException e) {
        System.out.println(e.toString());
      } catch (java.io.IOException e) {
        System.out.println(e.toString());
      } catch (java.lang.ClassNotFoundException e) {
        System.out.println("No data available");
      } finally {
        if (oos != null) {
          oos.close();
        }
      }
    } else {
      System.out.println("No Orders To Process");
    }
  return order;
}
```

Other Changes to Server Code

You might have noticed the sendOrder and getOrder methods are synchronized, declared to throw java.io.IOException, and have a finally clause in their try and catch blocks.

The synchronized keyword lets the RemoteServer instance handle the get and send requests one at a time. For example, there could be many instances of RMIClient1 sending data to the server. The sendOrder method needs to write the data in order to file one request at a time. In this way, data sent by one RMIClient1 client does not overwrite or collide with the data sent by another RMIClient1. The getOrder method is also synchronized so the server can retrieve data for one RMIClient2 instance before retrieving data for another RMIClient2 instance.

The finally clause is added to the try and catch blocks of the sendOrder and getOrder methods in order to close the object output and input streams and free up any system resources associated with them. The close method for the ObjectInputStream and ObjectOutputStream classes throws java.io.IOException checked exception, which, as you might remember from the section <u>Exception Handling</u> (page 52), has to be either caught or declared in the throws clause of the method signatures. Because a finally clause cannot specify an exception, the best thing to do in this example is to declare java.io.IOException in the method signatures for the sendOrder and getOrder methods.

Adding the java.io.IOException checked exception to the method signatures means the Send interface has to be changed so that the sendOrder and getOrder methods throw java.io.IOException in addition to RemoteException:

```
public interface Send extends Remote {
  public void sendOrder(DataOrder order)
      throws RemoteException, java.io.IOException;
  public DataOrder getOrder()
      throws RemoteException, java.io.IOException;
}
```

This change to the Send interface means you have to add the catch clause shown below to the RMIClient1 and RMIClient2 programs to handle the java.io.IOException thrown by the sendOrder and getOrder methods.

RMIClient1

```
      try{
         send.sendOrder(order);
      } catch (java.rmi.RemoteException e) {
         System.out.println("Cannot send data to server");
//Need to catch this exception
      } catch (java.io.IOException e) {
         System.out.println("Unable to write to file");
      }
```

RMIClient2

```
      if (source == view) {
        try {
          order = send.getOrder();
          creditNo.setText(order.cardnum);
          customerNo.setText(order.custID);
          applesNo.setText(order.apples);
          peachesNo.setText(order.peaches);
```

```
      pearsNo.setText(order.pears);
      cost = order.icost;
      price = new Double(cost);
      unit = price.toString();
      icost.setText(unit);
      items = order.itotal;
      itms = new Integer(items);
      i = itms.toString();
      itotal.setText(i);
   } catch (java.rmi.RemoteException e) {
     System.out.println("Cannot access data in server");
  //Need to catch this exception
   } catch (java.io.IOException e) {
     System.out.println("Unable to write to file");
   }
 }
```

Maintaining and Displaying a Customer List

This section adds methods to the RMIClient2 program to manage a list of unique customer IDs. The addCustomer method uses the Collections API to create the list, and the getData method uses the Collections API to retrieve the list. The getData method also uses Project Swing APIs to display the customer list in a dialog box.

About Collections

A collection is an object that contains other objects and provides methods for working on the objects it contains. A collection can consist of the same types of objects, but it can contain objects of different types, too. The customer IDs are all objects of type String and represent the same type of information—a customer ID. You could also have a collection object that contains objects of type String, Integer, and Double, if it makes sense in your program.

The Collection classes available to use in programs implement Collection interfaces. The Collection interface implementations for each Collection class let collection objects be manipulated independently of their representation details. There are three primary types of collection interfaces: List, Set, and Map. This section focuses on the List and Set collections.

Set implementations do not permit duplicate elements, but List implementations do. Duplicate elements have the same data type and value. For example, two customer IDs of type String containing the value Zelda are duplicate.

However, an element of type String containing the value *1* and an element of type Integer containing the value *1* are not duplicate.

The API provides two general-purpose Set implementations: HashSet, which stores its elements in a hash table, and TreeSet, which stores its elements in a balanced binary tree called a red-black tree. The example for this lesson uses the HashSet implementation because it currently has the best performance. Figure 11-1 shows the Collection interfaces on the right and the class hierarchy for the java.util.HashSet on the left. You can see that the HashSet class implements the Set interface.

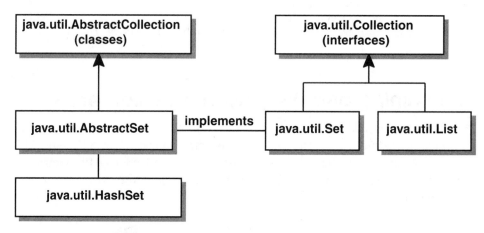

Figure 11-1   Collections API Interfaces and Class Hierarchy

Creating a Set

This example adapts the RMIClient2 class from Lesson 10, User Interfaces Revisited (page 123), to collect customer IDs in a Set and send the list of customer IDs to the command line whenever the View button is clicked.

The collection object is a Set, so if the same customer enters multiple orders, there is only one element for that customer in the list of customer IDs. If the program tries to add an element that is the same as an element already in the set, the second element is simply not added. No error is thrown, and there is nothing you have to do in your code.

The actionPerformed method in the RMIClient2 class calls the addCustomer method to add a customer ID to the set when the order processor clicks the View button. The addCustomer method implementation that follows adds the customer ID to the set and prints a notice that the customer ID has been added:

```
...
Set s = new HashSet();
...
public void addCustomer(String custID) {
  s.add(custID);
  System.out.println("Customer ID added");
}
```

Accessing Data in a Set

The getData method is called from the actionPerformed method in the RMIClient2 class when the order processor clicks the View button. The get-Data method sends the elements currently in the set to the command line. The next section shows you how to display the output in a dialog box.

To traverse the set, an object of type Iterator is returned from the set. The Iterator object has a hasNext method that lets you test if there is another element in the set, a next method that lets you move over the elements in the set, and a remove method that lets you remove an element.

The example getData method shows two ways to access data in the set. The first way uses an iterator, and the second way simply calls System. out.println on the set. In the iterator approach, the element returned by the next method is sent to the command line until there are no more elements in the set.

NOTE   A HashSet does not guarantee the order of the elements in the set. Elements are sent to the command line in the order they occur in the set, but that order is not necessarily the same as the order in which the elements were placed in the set.

```
public void getData() {
  //Iterator approach
  if (s.size()!=0) {
    Iterator it = s.iterator();
    while (it.hasNext()) {
      System.out.println(it.next());
    }
  //Call System.out.println on the set
    System.out.println(s);
  } else {
    System.out.println("No customer IDs available");
  }
}
```

Here is the command line output assuming that three customer IDs (noel, munchkin, and samantha) were added to the set. Note how the System. out.println(s) invocation displays the three customer IDs between square brackets ([]) separated by commas:

```
Customer ID added
noel
munchkin
samantha
[noel, munchkin, samantha]
```

Displaying Data in a Dialog Box

The getData method modified to display the set data in the dialog box is shown in Figure 11-2.

Figure 11-2   Display Customer Data in Dialog Box

```
public void getData() {
  if (s.size()!=0) {
    Iterator it = s.iterator();
    while (it.hasNext()) {
        System.out.println(it.next());
    }
    System.out.println(s);
    JOptionPane.showMessageDialog(frame, s.toString(),
      "Customer List", JOptionPane.PLAIN_MESSAGE);
  } else {
    System.out.println("No customer IDs available");
  }
}
```

Following is a description of the `JOptionPane` line that displays the dialog box:

Parameter	Description
`JOptionPane.showMessageDialog(frame,`	Shows a simple message dialog box attached to this application's `frame`. This is the `frame` that is instantiated in the main method as `frame = new RMIClient2()`.
`s.toString()`	Displays the contents of the set in the dialog box.
`"Customer List"`	Is the text for the title.
`JOptionPane.PLAIN_MESSAGE)`	Creates a plain message dialog box. No icon, such as a question or warning symbol, is included with the message.

Exercises

Modify the `try` and `catch` blocks in the `RMIClient1` and `RMIClient2` classes so they display error text in a dialog box instead of sending it to the command line. See RMIClient2 (page 164) for the solution.

To test the program, run the `RMIClient2` program without starting the server. You should see the error dialog box shown in Figure 11-3.

Figure 11-3   Error Dialog

More Information

You can find more information on serialization in "Reading and Writing (But No 'Rithmetic)" in *The Java™ Tutorial, Second Edition* [Cam98].

You can find more information on Collections in "Collections" in *The Java™ Tutorial, Second Edition* [Cam98].

You can find more information on dialog boxes in "How to Make Dialogs" in *The JFC Swing Tutorial* [Wal99].

Code for This Lesson

- RemoteServer
- RMIClient2

RemoteServer Program

```java
import java.awt.event.*;
import java.io.*;
import java.net.*;
import java.rmi.*;
import java.rmi.server.*;

class RemoteServer extends UnicastRemoteObject
  implements Send {
  Integer num = null;
  int value = 0, get = 0;
  ObjectOutputStream oos = null;

  public RemoteServer() throws RemoteException {
    super();
  }

  public synchronized void sendOrder(DataOrder order)
    throws java.io.IOException {
    value += 1;
    String orders = String.valueOf(value);
    try {
```

```
      FileOutputStream fos = new FileOutputStream(orders);
      oos = new ObjectOutputStream(fos);
      oos.writeObject(order);
  } catch (java.io.FileNotFoundException e) {
    System.out.println("File not found");
  } finally {
    if (oos != null) {
      oos.close();
    }
  }
}

public synchronized DataOrder getOrder()
  throws java.io.IOException {
  DataOrder order = null;
  ObjectInputStream ois = null;
  if (value == 0) {
    System.out.println("No Orders To Process");
  }
  if (value > get) {
    get += 1;
    String orders = String.valueOf(get);
    try {
      FileInputStream fis = new FileInputStream(orders);
      ois = new ObjectInputStream(fis);
      order = (DataOrder)ois.readObject();
    } catch (java.io.FileNotFoundException e) {
      System.out.println("File not found");
    } catch (java.io.IOException e) {
      System.out.println("Unable to read file");
    } catch (java.lang.ClassNotFoundException e){
      System.out.println("No data available");
    } finally {
      if (oos != null) {
        oos.close();
      }
    }
  } else {
    System.out.println("No Orders To Process");
  }
 return order;
}

public static void main(String[] args) {
  if(System.getSecurityManager() == null) {
    System.setSecurityManager(new RMISecurityManager());
  }
  String name = "//kq6py.eng.sun.com/Send";
```

```
      try {
        Send remoteServer = new RemoteServer();
        Naming.rebind(name, remoteServer);
        System.out.println("RemoteServer bound");
      } catch (java.rmi.RemoteException e) {
        System.out.println(
          "Cannot create remote server object");
      } catch (java.net.MalformedURLException e) {
        System.out.println("Cannot look up server object");
      }
    }
  }
```

RMIClient2

```
    import java.awt.Color;
    import java.awt.GridLayout;
    import java.awt.event.*;
    import javax.swing.*;
    import java.io.*;
    import java.net.*;
    import java.rmi.*;
    import java.rmi.server.*;
    import java.io.FileInputStream.*;
    import java.io.RandomAccessFile.*;
    import java.io.File;
    import java.util.*;

    class RMIClient2 extends JFrame implements ActionListener {
      JLabel creditCard, custID, apples, peaches, pears, total,
    cost, clicked;
      JButton view, reset;
      JPanel panel;
       JTextArea creditNo, customerNo, applesNo, peachesNo,
    pearsNo, itotal, icost;
      static Send send;
      String customer;
      Set s = new HashSet();
      static RMIClient2 frame;

      RMIClient2(){ //Begin Constructor
    //Create labels
        creditCard = new JLabel("Credit Card:");
        custID = new JLabel("Customer ID:");
        apples = new JLabel("Apples:");
        peaches = new JLabel("Peaches:");
        pears = new JLabel("Pears:");
        total = new JLabel("Total Items:");
```

```
            cost = new JLabel("Total Cost:");
//Create text areas
            creditNo = new JTextArea();
            customerNo = new JTextArea();
            applesNo = new JTextArea();
            peachesNo = new JTextArea();
            pearsNo = new JTextArea();
            itotal = new JTextArea();
            icost = new JTextArea();
//Create buttons
            view = new JButton("View Order");
            view.addActionListener(this);
            reset = new JButton("Reset");
            reset.addActionListener(this);
//Create panel for 2-column layout
//Set white background color
            panel = new JPanel();
            panel.setLayout(new GridLayout(0,2));
            panel.setBackground(Color.white);
//Add components to panel columns
//going left to right and top to bottom
            getContentPane().add(panel);
            panel.add(creditCard);
            panel.add(creditNo);
            panel.add(custID);
            panel.add(customerNo);
            panel.add(apples);
            panel.add(applesNo);
            panel.add(peaches);
            panel.add(peachesNo);
            panel.add(pears);
            panel.add(pearsNo);
            panel.add(total);
            panel.add(itotal);
            panel.add(cost);
            panel.add(icost);
            panel.add(view);
            panel.add(reset);
      } //End Constructor

    public void addCustomer(String custID) {
      System.out.println(custID);
      s.add(custID);
      System.out.println("Customer ID added");
    }

    public void getData() {
      if (s.size()!=0) {
```

```
      Iterator it = s.iterator();
      while (it.hasNext()) {
        System.out.println(it.next());
      }
      System.out.println(s);
      JOptionPane.showMessageDialog(frame, s.toString(),
                  "Customer List", JOptionPane.PLAIN_MESSAGE);
    } else {
      System.out.println("No customer IDs available");
    }
  }

  public void actionPerformed(ActionEvent event) {
    Object source = event.getSource();
    String unit, i;
    double cost;
    Double price;
    int items;
    Integer itms;
    DataOrder order = new DataOrder();

//If View button pressed
//Get data from server and display it
    if (source == view) {
       try {
         order  = send.getOrder();
         creditNo.setText(order.cardnum);
         customerNo.setText(order.custID);
//Call addCustomer method
         addCustomer(order.custID);
         applesNo.setText(order.apples);
         peachesNo.setText(order.peaches);
         pearsNo.setText(order.pears);
         cost = order.icost;
         price = new Double(cost);
         unit = price.toString();
         icost.setText(unit);
         items = order.itotal;
         itms = new Integer(items);
         i = itms.toString();
         itotal.setText(i);
       } catch (java.rmi.RemoteException e) {
           System.out.println(
             "Cannot access data in server");
       } catch (java.io.IOException e) {
         System.out.println("Unable to write to file");
       }
       getData();
```

```
        }

//If Reset button pressed
//Clear all fields
    if (source == reset) {
        creditNo.setText("");
        customerNo.setText("");
        applesNo.setText("");
         peachesNo.setText("");
        pearsNo.setText("");
        itotal.setText("");
        icost.setText("");
    }
  }

  public static void main(String[] args) {
        frame = new RMIClient2();
        frame.setTitle("Fruit Order");
        WindowListener l = new WindowAdapter() {
          public void windowClosing(WindowEvent e) {
            System.exit(0);
          }
        };
        frame.addWindowListener(l);
        frame.pack();
        frame.setVisible(true);
    if (System.getSecurityManager() == null) {
      System.setSecurityManager(new RMISecurityManager());
    }
    try {
      String name = "//" + args[0] + "/Send";
      send = ((Send) Naming.lookup(name));
    } catch (java.rmi.RemoteException e) {
      System.out.println("Cannot create remote server
object");
    } catch (java.net.MalformedURLException e) {
      System.out.println("Cannot look up server object");
    } catch (java.rmi.NotBoundException e) {
      System.out.println("Cannot access data in server");
    }
  }
}
```

Internationalization

MORE and more companies, large and small, are doing business around the world using many different languages. Effective communication is always good business, so it follows that adapting an application to a local language adds to profitability through better communication and increased satisfaction.

The Java 2 platform provides internationalization features that let you separate culturally dependent data from the application (internationalization) and adapt it to as many cultures as needed (localization).

This lesson takes the two client programs from Lesson 11, Developing the Example (page 153), internationalizes them, and localizes the text for France, Germany, and the United States.

Covered in This Lesson

- Identify Culturally Dependent Data
- Create Keyword and Value Pair File
- Internationalize Application Text
- Internationalize Numbers
- Compile and Run the Application
- Exercises
- More Information
- Code for This Lesson

Identify Culturally Dependent Data

To internationalize an application, the first thing you need to do is to identify the culturally dependent data in your application. Culturally dependent data is any data that varies from one culture or country to another. Text is the most obvious and pervasive example of culturally dependent data, but other things like number formats, sounds, times, and dates should be considered, too.

The RMIClient1 and RMIClient2 classes have culturally dependent data visible to the user. This data is included in the bulleted list that follows. Figure 12-1 shows the Fruit Order client, which displays some of the culturally dependent data mentioned in the bulleted list.

Figure 12-1   Culturally Dependent Data

- Titles and labels (window titles, column heads, and left column labels)
- Buttons (Purchase, Reset, View)
- Numbers (values for item and cost totals)
- Error messages

Although the application has a server program, it is not being internationalized and localized. The only visible culturally dependent data in the server program is the error message text. The server program runs in one place, and the assumption is that it is not seen by anyone other than the system administrator who understands the language in which the error message is hard coded. In this example, that language is United States English.

All error messages in the RMIClient1 and RMIClient2 programs are handled in try and catch blocks. This way you have access to the error text for translation into another language.

```
//Access to error text
public void someMethod(){
  try {
    //do something
  } catch (java.util.NoSuchElementException {
    System.out.println("Print some error text");
  }
}
```

Methods can be coded to declare the exception in their throws clause, but this way you cannot access the error message text thrown when the method tries to access unavailable data in the set. In this case, the system-provided text for this error message is sent to the command line regardless of the locale in use for the application. The point here is that it is better to use try and catch blocks wherever possible if there is any chance the application will be internationalized so you can access and localize the error message text.

```
//No access to error text
public void someMethod()
  throws java.util.NoSuchElementException{
  //do something
}
```

Following is a list of the title, label, button, number, and error text visible to the user and, therefore, subject to internationalization and localization. This data was taken from both the RMIClient1 and RMIClient2 classes.

- Labels: Apples, Peaches, Pears, Total Items, Total Cost, Credit Card, Customer ID

- Titles: Fruit $1.25 Each, Select Items, Specify Quantity

- Buttons: Reset, View, Purchase

- Number Values: Value for total items, Value for total cost

- Errors: Invalid Value, Cannot send data to server, Cannot look up remote server object, No data available, No customer IDs available, Cannot access data in server

Create Keyword and Value Pair Files

Because all text visible to the user will be moved out of the application and translated, your application needs a way to access the translated text during execution. This is done with properties files that specify a list of keyword and value pairs for each language to be used. The application code loads the properties file for a given language and references the keywords instead of using hard-coded text.

So, for example, you could map the keyword purchase to Kaufen in the German file, Achetez in the French file, and Purchase in the United States English file. In your application, you load the properties file for the language you want to use and reference the keyword purchase in your code. During execution, when the purchase keyword is encountered, Achetez, Kaufen, or Purchase is loaded, depending on the language file in use.

Keyword and value pairs are stored in properties files because they contain information about a program's properties or characteristics. Property files are plain-text format, and you need one file for each language you intend to use.

In this example, there are three properties files, one each for the English, French, and German translations. Because this application currently uses hard-coded English text, the easiest way to begin the internationalization process is to use the hard-coded text to set up the key and value pairs for the English properties file.

The properties files follow a naming convention so the application can locate and load the correct file at runtime. The naming convention uses language and country codes that you should make part of the file name. Both the language and country are included because the same language can vary between countries. For example, United States English and Australian English are a little different, and Swiss German and Austrian German differ from each other and from the German spoken in Germany.

Following are the names of the properties files for the German (de_DE), French (fr_FR), and American English (en_US) translations where de, fr, and en indicate the German (Deutsche), French, and English languages; DE, FR, and US indicate Germany (Deutschland), France, and the United States:

- MessagesBundle_de_DE.properties
- MessagesBundle_en_US.properties
- MessagesBundle_fr_FR.properties

Following is the English language properties file. Keywords are to the left of the equal (=) sign, and text values are on the right:

```
apples = Apples:
peaches = Peaches:
pears = Pears:
items = Total Items:
cost=Total Cost:
card=Credit Card:
```

```
customer=Customer ID:
title=Fruit 1.25 Each
1col=Select Items
2col=Specify Quantity
reset=Reset
view=View
purchase = Purchase
invalid = Invalid Value
send = Cannot send data to server
nolookup = Cannot look up remote server object
nodata = No data available
noID = No customer IDs available
noserver = Cannot access data in server
```

You can hand this file off to your French and German translators and ask them to provide the French and German equivalents for the text to the right of the equal (=) sign. Keep a copy because you will need the keywords to internationalize your application text.

The properties file with German translations produces the fruit order client user interface shown in Figure 12-2.

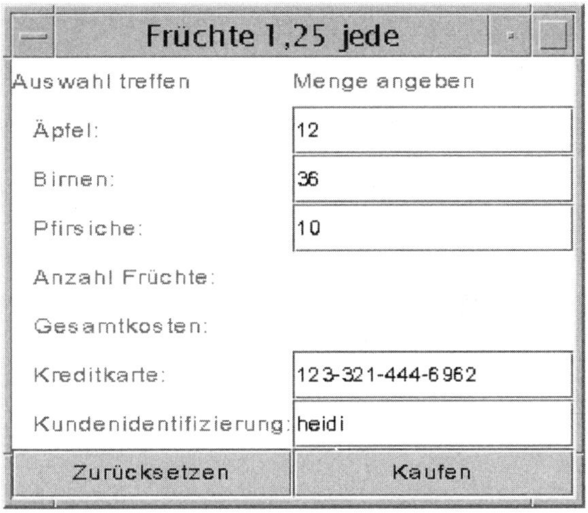

Figure 12-2   German User Interface

German Translations

```
apples=Äpfel:
peaches=Birnen:
pears=Pfirsiche:
items=Anzahl Früchte:
cost=Gesamtkosten:
card=Kreditkarte:
```

```
customer=Kundenidentifizierung:
title=Früchte 1,25 jede
1col=Auswahl treffen
2col=Menge angeben
reset=Zurücksetzen
view=Sehen Sie an
purchase=Kaufen
invalid=Ungültiger Wert
send=Datenübertragung zum Server nicht möglich
nolookup=Das Server läßt sich nicht zu finden
nodata=Keine Daten verfügbar
noID=Keine Kundenidentifizierungen verfügbar
noserver=Kein Zugang zu den Daten beim Server
```

The properties file with French translations produces the fruit order client user interface shown in Figure 12-3.

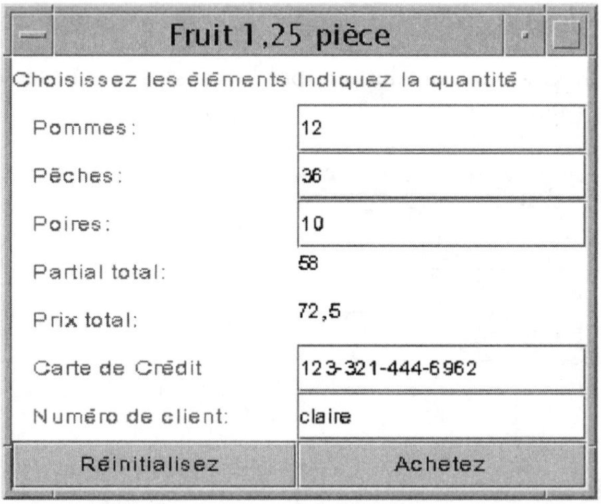

Figure 12-3   French User Interface

French Translations

```
apples=Pommes:
peaches=Pêches:
pears=Poires:
items=Partial total:
cost=Prix total:
card=Carte de Crédit
customer=Numêro de client:
title=Fruit 1,25 pièce
```

```
1col=Choisissez les éléments
2col= Indiquez la quantité
reset=Réinitialisez
view=Visualisez
purchase=Achetez
invalid=Valeur incorrecte
send=Les données n'ont pu être envoyées au serveur
nolookup=Accès impossible à l'objet du serveur distant
nodata=Aucune donnée disponible
noID=dentifiant du client indisponible
noserver=Accès aux données du serveur impossible
```

Internationalize Application Text

This section walks through internationalizing the RMIClient1 code. The RMIClient2 code is almost identical so you can apply the same steps to that program on your own.

Instance Variables

In addition to adding an import statement for the java.util.* package where the internationalization classes are, this program needs the following instance variable declarations for the internationalization process:

```
//Initialized in main method
  static String language, country;
  Locale currentLocale;
  static ResourceBundle messages;
//Initialized in actionPerformed method
  NumberFormat numFormat;
```

main Method

The program is designed so the user specifies the language to use at the command line. Therefore, the first change to the main method is to add the code to check the command line parameters. Specifying the language at the command line means that once the application is internationalized, you can easily change the language without recompiling.

NOTE This style of programming makes it possible for the same user to run the program in different languages. In most cases, the program will use one language and not rely on command line arguments to set the country and language.

The String[] args parameter to the main method contains arguments passed to the program from the command line. This code expects three command line arguments when the user wants a language other than English. The first argument is the name of the machine on which the program is running. This value is passed to the program when it starts and is needed because this is a networked program using the RMI API.

The other two arguments specify the language and country codes. If the program is invoked with one command line argument (the machine name only), the country and language are assumed to be United States English.

As an example, here is how the program is started with command line arguments to specify the machine name and German language (de DE). Everything goes on one line.

```
java -Djava.rmi.server.codebase=http://kq6py/~zelda/classes
    -Djava.security.policy=
    java.policy RMIClient1 kq6py.eng.sun.com de DE
```

The main method code follows. The currentLocale instance variable is initialized from the language and country information passed in at the command line, and the messages instance variable is initialized from the currentLocale.

The messages object provides access to the translated text for the language in use. It takes two parameters: The first parameter, MessagesBundle, is the prefix of the family of translation files this application uses, and the second parameter is the Locale object that tells the ResourceBundle which translation to use. If the application is invoked with de DE command line parameters, this code creates a ResourceBundle variable to access the MessagesBundle _de_DE.properties file:

```
public static void main(String[] args){
//Check for language and country codes
  if (args.length != 3) {
    language = new String("en");
    country = new String ("US");
    System.out.println("English");
  } else {
    language = new String(args[1]);
    country = new String(args[2]);
    System.out.println(language + country);
  }

//Create locale and resource bundle
  currentLocale = new Locale(language, country);
```

```
  messages = ResourceBundle.getBundle(
    "MessagesBundle", currentLocale);
  WindowListener l = new WindowAdapter() {
    public void windowClosing(WindowEvent e) {
      System.exit(0);}
  };

//Create the RMIClient1 object
  RMIClient1 frame = new RMIClient1();
  frame.addWindowListener(l);
  frame.pack();
  frame.setVisible(true);
  if (System.getSecurityManager() == null) {
    System.setSecurityManager(new RMISecurityManager());
  }

  try {
    String name = "//" + args[0] + "/Send";
    send = ((Send) Naming.lookup(name));
  } catch (java.rmi.NotBoundException e) {
    System.out.println(messages.getString("nolookup"));
  } catch(java.rmi.RemoteException e) {
    System.out.println(messages.getString("nolookup"));
  } catch(java.net.MalformedURLException e) {
    System.out.println(messages.getString("nolookup"));
  }
}
```

The applicable error text is accessed by calling the getString method on the ResourceBundle and passing it the keyword that maps to the applicable error text:

```
try {
  String name = "//" + args[0] + "/Send";
  send = ((Send) Naming.lookup(name));
} catch (java.rmi.NotBoundException e) {
  System.out.println(messages.getString("nolookup"));
} catch(java.rmi.RemoteException e) {
  System.out.println(messages.getString("nolookup"));
} catch(java.net.MalformedURLException e) {
  System.out.println(messages.getString("nolookup"));
}
```

Constructor

The window title is set by calling the getString method on the ResourceBundle and passing it the keyword that maps to the title text. You must pass the keyword exactly as it appears in the translation file, or you will get a runtime error indicating the resource is unavailable.

```
RMIClient1(){
//Set window title
  setTitle(messages.getString("title"));
```

The next thing the constructor does is use the `args` parameter to look up the remote server object. If there are any errors in this process, the `catch` statements get the applicable error text from the `ResourceBundle` and print it to the command line. User interface objects that display text, such as `JLabel` and `JButton`, are created the same way:

```
//Create left and right column labels
    col1 = new JLabel(messages.getString("1col"));
    col2 = new JLabel(messages.getString("2col"));
...
//Create buttons and make action listeners
    purchase = new JButton(messages.getString("purchase"));
    purchase.addActionListener(this);
    reset = new JButton(messages.getString("reset"));
    reset.addActionListener(this);
```

actionPerformed Method

In the `actionPerformed` method, the `Invalid Value` error is caught and translated. The `actionPerformed` method also calculates item and cost totals, translates them to the correct format for the language currently in use, and displays them in the user interface:

```
if (order.apples.length() > 0) {
//Catch invalid number error
  try {
    applesNo = Integer.valueOf(order.apples);
    order.itotal += applesNo.intValue();
  } catch(java.lang.NumberFormatException e) {
    appleqnt.setText(messages.getString("invalid"));
  }
} else {
  /* else no need to change the total */
}
```

Internationalize Numbers

A `NumberFormat` object, created from the `currentLocale`, is used to translate numbers to the correct format for the language currently in use. The information in the `currentLocale` tells the `NumberFormat` object what number format to use.

Once you have a `NumberFormat` object, all you do is pass in the value you want translated, and you receive a `String` that contains the number in the correct format. The value can be passed in as any data type used for numbers such as `int`, `Integer`, `double`, or `Double`. No code to convert an `Integer` to an `int` and back again is needed.

```
//Create number formatter
  numFormat = NumberFormat.getNumberInstance(currentLocale);
//Display running total
  text = numFormat.format(order.itotal);
  this.items.setText(text);
//Calculate and display running cost
  order.icost = (order.itotal * 1.25);
  text2 = numFormat.format(order.icost);
  this.cost.setText(text2);
  try {
    send.sendOrder(order);
  } catch (java.rmi.RemoteException e) {
    System.out.println(messages.getString("send"));
  } catch (java.io.IOException e) {
    System.out.println("nodata");
  }
```

Compile and Run the Application

Following are the summarized steps for compiling and running the example program. The complete code listings are on page 183. The important thing when you start the client programs is to include language and country codes if you want a language other than United States English.

Compile

Unix:

```
cd /home/zelda/classes
javac Send.java
javac RemoteServer.java
javac RMIClient2.java
javac RMIClient1.java
rmic -d . RemoteServer
cp RemoteServer*.class /home/zelda/public_html/classes
cp Send.class /home/zelda/public_html/classes
cp DataOrder.class /home/zelda/public_html/classes
```

Win32:

```
cd \home\zelda\classes
javac Send.java
javac RemoteServer.java
javac RMIClient2.java
javac RMIClient1.java
rmic -d . RemoteServer
copy RemoteServer*.class \home\zelda\public_html\classes
copy Send.class \home\zelda\public_html\classes
copy DataOrder.class \home\zelda\public_html\classes
```

Start the RMI Registry

Unix:

```
cd /home/zelda/public_html/classes
unsetenv CLASSPATH
rmiregistry &
```

Win32:

```
cd \home\zelda\public_html\classes
set CLASSPATH=
start rmiregistry
```

Start the Server

Unix:

```
cd /home/zelda/public_html/classes
java -Djava.rmi.server.codebase=http://kq6py/~zelda/classes
    -Djava.rmi.server.hostname=kq6py.eng.sun.com
    -Djava.security.policy=java.policy RemoteServer
```

Win32:

```
cd \home\zelda\public_html\classes
java -Djava.rmi.server.codebase=
    file:c:\home\zelda\public_html\classes
    -Djava.rmi.server.hostname=kq6py.eng.sun.com
    -Djava.security.policy=java.policy RemoteServer
```

Start the RMIClient1 Program in German

Note the addition of de DE for the German language and country at the end of
the command.

Unix:

```
cd /home/zelda/classes
java -Djava.rmi.server.codebase= http://kq6py/~zelda/classes
```

```
    -Djava.security.policy=
    java.policy RMIClient1 kq6py.eng.sun.com de DE
```

Win32:

```
cd \home\zelda\classes
java -Djava.rmi.server.codebase=
    file:c:\home\zelda\public_html\classes
    -Djava.security.policy=
    java.policy RMIClient1 kq6py.eng.sun.com de DE
```

Start the RMIClient2 Program in French

Note the addition of fr FR for the French language and country at the end of the command.

Unix:

```
cd /home/zelda/classes
java -Djava.rmi.server.codebase= http://kq6py/~zelda/classes
    -Djava.security.policy=
    java.policy RMIClient2 kq6py.eng.sun.com fr FR
```

Win32:

```
cd \home\zelda\classes
java -Djava.rmi.server.codebase=
    file:c:\home\zelda\public_html\classes
    -Djava.security.policy=
    java.policy RMIClient2 kq6py.eng.sun.com fr FR
```

Exercises

A real-world scenario for an ordering application like this might be that RMIClient1 is an applet embedded in a Web page. When orders are submitted, order processing staff run RMIClient2 as applications from their local machines.

An interesting exercise would be to convert the RMIClient1 class to its applet equivalent. The translation files would be loaded by the applet from the same directory from which the browser loads the applet class.

One way is to have a separate applet for each language with the language and country codes hard coded. Your Web page can let visitors to your site choose a language by clicking a link that launches a Web page with the appropriate applet. The source code files for the French, German, and English applets start on page 251 in Appendix B, Code Listings.

Following is the HTML code to load the French applet on a Web page:

```
<HTML>
<BODY>
<APPLET CODE=RMIFrenchApp.class WIDTH=300 HEIGHT=300>
  </APPLET>
</BODY> </HTML>
```

NOTE   To run an applet written with Java 2 APIs in a browser, the browser must be enabled for the Java 2 Platform. If your browser is not enabled for the Java 2 Platform, you have to use appletviewer or install Java Plug-in (`http:// java.sun.com/products/plug-in/index.html`). Java Plug-in lets you run applets on Web pages under the 1.2 version of the Java virtual machine (Java VM) instead of the Web browser's default Java VM.

To use appletviewer, type the following where `rmiFrench.html` is the HTML file for the French applet:

```
appletviewer rmiFrench.html
```

Another improvement to the program as it currently stands would be enhancing the error message text. You can locate the errors in the Java API docs (`http://java.sun.com/products/jdk/1.2/docs/api/index.html`) and use the information there to make the error message text user friendly by providing more specific information. You might also want to adapt the client programs to catch and handle the error thrown when an incorrect keyword is used. This is the stack trace provided by the system when this type of error occurs:

```
Exception in thread "main" java.util.MissingResourceException: Can't
find resource   at java.util.ResourceBundle.getObject(Compiled Code)
at java.util.ResourceBundle.getString(Compiled Code)   at
RMIClient1.<init>(Compiled Code)   at RMIClient1.main(Compiled Code)
```

More Information

You can find more information on internationalization in "Internationalization" in *The Java™ Tutorial Continued* [Cam99].

You can find more information on applets in "Writing Applets" in *The Java™ Tutorial Continued* [Cam99].

Code for This Lesson

- RMIClient1
- RMIClient2

RMIClient1

```java
import java.awt.Color;
import java.awt.GridLayout;
import java.awt.event.*;
import javax.swing.*;
import java.io.*;
import java.net.*;
import java.rmi.*;
import java.rmi.server.*;
import java.util.*;
import java.text.*;

class RMIClient1 extends JFrame implements ActionListener {
    JLabel col1, col2;
    JLabel totalItems, totalCost;
    JLabel cardNum, custID;
    JLabel applechk, pearchk, peachchk;
    JButton purchase, reset;
    JPanel panel;
    JTextField appleqnt, pearqnt, peachqnt;
    JTextField creditCard, customer;
    JTextArea items, cost;
    static Send send;

//Internationalization variables
    static Locale currentLocale;
    static ResourceBundle messages;
    static String language, country;
    NumberFormat numFormat;

    RMIClient1() { //Begin Constructor
        setTitle(messages.getString("title"));
//Create left and right column labels
        col1 = new JLabel(messages.getString("1col"));
        col2 = new JLabel(messages.getString("2col"));

//Create labels and text field components
        applechk = new JLabel("   " +
            messages.getString("apples"));
        appleqnt = new JTextField();
        appleqnt.addActionListener(this);
```

```
        pearchk = new JLabel("    " +
          messages.getString("pears"));
        pearqnt = new JTextField();
        pearqnt.addActionListener(this);
        peachchk = new JLabel("    " +
          messages.getString("peaches"));
        peachqnt = new JTextField();
        peachqnt.addActionListener(this);
        cardNum = new JLabel("    " +
          messages.getString("card"));
        creditCard = new JTextField();
        pearqnt.setNextFocusableComponent(creditCard);
        customer = new JTextField();
        custID = new JLabel("    " +
          messages.getString("customer"));

    //Create labels and text area components
        totalItems = new JLabel("    " +
          messages.getString("items"));
        totalCost = new JLabel("    " +
          messages.getString("cost"));
        items = new JTextArea();
        cost = new JTextArea();

    //Create buttons and make action listeners
        purchase = new JButton(messages.getString("purchase"));
        purchase.addActionListener(this);
        reset = new JButton(messages.getString("reset"));
        reset.addActionListener(this);

    //Create a panel for the components
        panel = new JPanel();

    //Set panel layout to 2-column grid
    //on a white background
        panel.setLayout(new GridLayout(0,2));
        panel.setBackground(Color.white);

    //Add components to panel columns
    //going left to right and top to bottom
        getContentPane().add(panel);
        panel.add(col1);
        panel.add(col2);
        panel.add(applechk);
        panel.add(appleqnt);
        panel.add(peachchk);
        panel.add(peachqnt);
        panel.add(pearchk);
```

```
        panel.add(pearqnt);
        panel.add(totalItems);
        panel.add(items);
        panel.add(totalCost);
        panel.add(cost);
        panel.add(cardNum);
        panel.add(creditCard);
        panel.add(custID);
        panel.add(customer);
        panel.add(reset);
        panel.add(purchase);
    } //End Constructor

  public void actionPerformed(ActionEvent event) {
    Object source = event.getSource();
    Integer applesNo, peachesNo, pearsNo, num;
    Double cost;
    String text, text2;
    DataOrder order = new DataOrder();

//If Purchase button pressed
    if (source == purchase) {
//Get data from text fields
      order.cardnum = creditCard.getText();
      order.custID = customer.getText();
      order.apples = appleqnt.getText();
      order.peaches = peachqnt.getText();
      order.pears = pearqnt.getText();
//Calculate total items
      if (order.apples.length() > 0) {
//Catch invalid number error
        try {
          applesNo = Integer.valueOf(order.apples);
          order.itotal += applesNo.intValue();
        } catch (java.lang.NumberFormatException e) {
          appleqnt.setText(messages.getString("invalid"));
        }
      } else {
        /* else no need to change the total */
      }

      if (order.peaches.length() > 0) {
//Catch invalid number error
        try {
          peachesNo = Integer.valueOf(order.peaches);
          order.itotal += peachesNo.intValue();
        } catch(java.lang.NumberFormatException e) {
          peachqnt.setText(messages.getString("invalid"));
```

```
        }
      } else {
        /* else no need to change the total */
      }
      if (order.pears.length() > 0){
//Catch invalid number error
        try {
          pearsNo = Integer.valueOf(order.pears);
          order.itotal += pearsNo.intValue();
        } catch (java.lang.NumberFormatException e) {
          pearqnt.setText(messages.getString("invalid"));
        }
      } else {
        /* else no need to change the total */
      }


//Create number formatter
        numFormat = NumberFormat.getNumberInstance(
          currentLocale);
//Display running total
        text = numFormat.format(order.itotal);
        this.items.setText(text);
//Calculate and display running cost
        order.icost = (order.itotal * 1.25);
        text2 = numFormat.format(order.icost);
        this.cost.setText(text2);
        try{
          send.sendOrder(order);
        } catch (java.rmi.RemoteException e) {
          System.out.println(messages.getString("send"));
        } catch (java.io.IOException e) {
          System.out.println("nodata");
        }
    }


//If Reset button pressed
//Clear all fields
      if (source == reset) {
      creditCard.setText("");
      appleqnt.setText("");
      peachqnt.setText("");
      pearqnt.setText("");
      creditCard.setText("");
      customer.setText("");
      order.icost = 0;
      cost = new Double(order.icost);
      text2 = cost.toString();
      this.cost.setText(text2);
      order.itotal = 0;
```

```
          num = new Integer(order.itotal);
          text = num.toString();
          this.items.setText(text);
        }
      }

    public static void main(String[] args) {
      if (args.length != 3) {
        language = new String("en");
        country = new String ("US");
        System.out.println("English");
      } else {
        language = new String(args[1]);
        country = new String(args[2]);
        System.out.println(language + country);
      }
      currentLocale = new Locale(language, country);
      messages = ResourceBundle.getBundle("MessagesBundle",
  currentLocale);
      WindowListener l = new WindowAdapter() {
        public void windowClosing(WindowEvent e) {
          System.exit(0);
        }
      };
      RMIClient1 frame = new RMIClient1();
      frame.addWindowListener(l);
      frame.pack();
      frame.setVisible(true);
      if(System.getSecurityManager() == null) {
        System.setSecurityManager(new RMISecurityManager());
      }
      try {
        String name = "//" + args[0] + "/Send";
        send = ((Send) Naming.lookup(name));
      } catch (java.rmi.NotBoundException e) {
        System.out.println(messages.getString("nolookup"));
      } catch(java.rmi.RemoteException e){
        System.out.println(messages.getString("nolookup"));
      } catch(java.net.MalformedURLException e) {
        System.out.println(messages.getString("nolookup"));
      }
    }
  }
```

RMIClient2

```
import java.awt.Color;
import java.awt.GridLayout;
import java.awt.event.*;
```

```java
import javax.swing.*;
import java.io.*;
import java.net.*;
import java.rmi.*;
import java.rmi.server.*;
import java.io.FileInputStream.*;
import java.io.RandomAccessFile.*;
import java.io.File;
import java.util.*;
import java.text.*;

class RMIClient2 extends JFrame implements ActionListener {
   JLabel creditCard, custID, apples, peaches, pears, total,
cost, clicked;
   JButton view, reset;
   JPanel panel;
    JTextArea creditNo, customerNo, applesNo, peachesNo,
pearsNo, itotal, icost;
   static Send send;
   String customer;
   Set s = null;
   RMIClient2 frame;

//Internationalization variables
   static Locale currentLocale;
   static ResourceBundle messages;
   static String language, country;
   NumberFormat numFormat;

   RMIClient2(){ //Begin Constructor
     setTitle(messages.getString("title"));
//Create labels
     creditCard = new JLabel(messages.getString("card"));
     custID = new JLabel(messages.getString("customer"));
     apples = new JLabel(messages.getString("apples"));
     peaches = new JLabel(messages.getString("peaches"));
     pears = new JLabel(messages.getString("pears"));
     total = new JLabel(messages.getString("items"));
     cost = new JLabel(messages.getString("cost"));

//Create text areas
     creditNo = new JTextArea();
     customerNo = new JTextArea();
     applesNo = new JTextArea();
     peachesNo = new JTextArea();
     pearsNo = new JTextArea();
     itotal = new JTextArea();
     icost = new JTextArea();
```

```
//Create buttons
    view = new JButton(messages.getString("view"));
    view.addActionListener(this);
    reset = new JButton(messages.getString("reset"));
    reset.addActionListener(this);

//Create panel for 2-column layout
//Set white background color
    panel = new JPanel();
    panel.setLayout(new GridLayout(0,2));
    panel.setBackground(Color.white);

//Add components to panel columns
//going left to right and top to bottom
    getContentPane().add(panel);
    panel.add(creditCard);
    panel.add(creditNo);
    panel.add(custID);
    panel.add(customerNo);
    panel.add(apples);
    panel.add(applesNo);
    panel.add(peaches);
    panel.add(peachesNo);
    panel.add(pears);
    panel.add(pearsNo);
    panel.add(total);
    panel.add(itotal);
    panel.add(cost);
    panel.add(icost);
    panel.add(view);
    panel.add(reset);
  } //End Constructor

 //Create list of customer IDs
  public void addCustomer(String custID){
    s.add(custID);
    System.out.println("Customer ID added");
  }

//Get customer IDs
  public void getData(){
    if (s.size()!=0) {
      Iterator it = s.iterator();
      while (it.hasNext()) {
        System.out.println(it.next());
      }
      System.out.println(s);
```

```
        JOptionPane.showMessageDialog(frame, s.toString(),
                "Customer List", JOptionPane.PLAIN_MESSAGE);
    } else {
      System.out.println("No customer IDs available");
    }
  }

  public void actionPerformed(ActionEvent event) {
     Object source = event.getSource();
     String unit, i;
     double cost;
     Double price;
     int items;
     Integer itms;
     DataOrder order = new DataOrder();

//If View button pressed
//Get data from server and display it
     if (source == view) {
         try {
            order  = send.getOrder();
            creditNo.setText(order.cardnum);
            customerNo.setText(order.custID);
//Get customer ID and add to list
            addCustomer(order.custID);
            applesNo.setText(order.apples);
            peachesNo.setText(order.peaches);
            pearsNo.setText(order.pears);
//Create number formatter
            numFormat = NumberFormat.getNumberInstance(
               currentLocale);
            price = new Double(order.icost);
            unit = numFormat.format(price);
            icost.setText(unit);
            itms = new Integer(order.itotal);
            i = numFormat.format(order.itotal);
            itotal.setText(i);
         } catch (java.rmi.RemoteException e) {
            System.out.println("Cannot access data in
server");
        }catch (java.io.IOException e) {
           System.out.println("nodata");
        }
//Get Customer Information
        getData();
     }
//If Reset button pressed
//Clear all fields
```

```
      if(source == reset){
        creditNo.setText("");
        customerNo.setText("");
        applesNo.setText("");
        peachesNo.setText("");
        pearsNo.setText("");
        itotal.setText("");
        icost.setText("");
      }
  }

  public static void main(String[] args) {
    if(args.length != 3) {
      language = new String("en");
      country = new String ("US");
      System.out.println("English");
    } else {
      language = new String(args[1]);
      country = new String(args[2]);
      System.out.println(language + country);
    }
    currentLocale = new Locale(language, country);
    messages = ResourceBundle.getBundle(
      "MessagesBundle", currentLocale);
    WindowListener l = new WindowAdapter() {
      public void windowClosing(WindowEvent e) {
        System.exit(0);
      }
    };
    RMIClient2 frame = new RMIClient2();
    frame.addWindowListener(l);
    frame.pack();
    frame.setVisible(true);
    if(System.getSecurityManager() == null) {
      System.setSecurityManager(new RMISecurityManager());
    }
    try {
      String name = "//" + args[0] + "/Send";
      send = ((Send) Naming.lookup(name));
    } catch (java.rmi.NotBoundException e) {
      System.out.println(messages.getString("nolookup"));
    } catch(java.rmi.RemoteException e) {
      System.out.println(messages.getString("nolookup"));
    } catch(java.net.MalformedURLException e) {
      System.out.println(messages.getString("nolookup"));
    }
  }
}
```

Packages and JAR File Format

A package is a convenient way to organize groups of related classes so they are easier to locate and use, and in development, you should organize application files into packages, too. Packages also help you control access to class data at runtime.

When your application is fully tested, debugged, and ready for deployment, use the Java Archive™ (JAR) file format to bundle the application. JAR file format lets you bundle executable files with any other related application files so they can be deployed as one unit.

This lesson shows you how to organize the program files from Lesson 12, Internationalization (page 169), into packages and to deploy the executable and other related files to production using JAR file format.

Covered in This Lesson

- Setting Up Class Packages
- Compile and Run the Example
- Using JAR Files to Deploy
- Exercises
- More Information

Setting Up Class Packages

It is easy to organize class files into packages. All you do is put related class files in the same directory, give the directory a name that relates to the purpose of the classes, and add a line to the top of each class file that declares the package name, which is the same as the directory name where they reside. For example, the class and other related files for the program files from Lesson 12, Internationalization (page 169), can be divided into three groups of files: fruit order client, view order client, and server files. Although these three sets of classes are related to each other, they have different functions and will be deployed separately.

Create the Directories

To organize the internationalization program into three packages, you could create the following three directories and move the listed source files into them:

client1 package/directory

- RMIEnglishApp.java

- RMIFrenchApp.java

- RMIGermanApp.java

- MessagesBundle_de_DE.properties

- MessagesBundle_en_US.properties

- MessagesBundle_fr_FR.properties

- index.html

- rmiFapp.html

- rmiGapp.html

- rmiEapp.html

- java.policy

client2 package/directory

- RMIClient2.java

- MessagesBundle_de_DE.properties

- MessagesBundle_en_US.properties

- MessagesBundle_fr_FR.properties

- java.policy

server package/directory

- DataOrder.java

- RemoteServer.java

- Send.java
- java.policy

Declare the Packages

Each *.java file needs a package declaration at the top that reflects the name of the directory. In addition, the fruit order (client1 package) and view order (client2 package) client class files need an import statement for the server package because they have to access the remote server object at runtime. For example, the package declaration and import statements for the RMIClient2 class look like this:

```
//package declaration
  package client2;
//import statements
  import java.awt.Color;
  import java.awt.GridLayout;
  import java.awt.event.*;
  import javax.swing.*;
  import java.io.*;
  import java.net.*;
  import java.rmi.*;
  import java.rmi.server.*;
  import java.util.*;
  import java.text.*;
 //import server package
  import server.*;
```

NOTE If you write an application that will be available for sale, it is important to choose package names that do not conflict with package names from other companies. A good way to avoid this problem is to prefix the package name with com and your company name. For example, the server package could be named com.mycompanyname.server.

Make Classes and Fields Accessible

With class files organized into packages, you have to declare the server classes in the server directory public so they can be instantiated by client programs, which are created from classes in the client1 and client2 directories. If you do not make the server classes public, they can be instantiated only by an object created from a class within the same package.

To make it possible for client programs to access the fruit order data, the fields of the `DataOrder` class have to be `public`, too. The `RemoteServer` class (page 250) and `Send` (page 249) interface need to be `public` classes, but their fields do not need to be public because they do not have public data. Fields and methods without an access specifier such as `public` are package by default and can be accessed only by objects created from classes in the same package. Here is the new DataOrder class:

```
package server;
import java.io.*;

//Make class public
public class DataOrder implements Serializable{

//Make fields public
  public String apples, peaches, pears, cardnum, custID;
  public double icost;
  public int itotal;
  }
```

Change Client Code to Find the Properties Files

In the example, the properties files (Messages_*) are stored in the directories with the client source files. This makes it easier to package and deploy the files later. So the programs can find the properties files, you have to make one small change to the client source code.

The code that creates the `messages` variable needs to include the directory (package) name `client2` as follows:

```
messages = ResourceBundle.getBundle("client2" +
                         File.separatorChar +
                         "MessagesBundle", currentLocale);
```

Compile and Run the Example

Compiling and running the example organized into packages is a little different from compiling and running the example in previous lessons. First, you have to execute the compiler and interpreter commands from one directory above the package directories; second, you have to specify the package directories to the compiler and interpreter commands. You will find this code in the section Application Code (page 240) in Appendix B, Code Listings.

Compile

Unix:

```
cd /home/zelda/classes
javac server/Send.java
javac server/RemoteServer.java
javac client2/RMIClient2.java
javac client1/RMIFrenchApp.java
javac client1/RMIGermanApp.java
javac client1/RMIEnglishApp.java
rmic -d . server.RemoteServer
cp server/RemoteServer*.class
   /home/zelda/public_html/classes
cp server/Send.class /home/zelda/public_html/classes
cp server/DataOrder.class /home/zelda/public_html/classes
```

Win32:

```
cd \home\zelda\classes
javac server\Send.java
javac server\RemoteServer.java
javac client2\RMIClient2.java
javac client1\RMIFrenchApp.java
javac client1\RMIGermanApp.java
javac client1\RMIEnglishApp.java
rmic -d . server.RemoteServer
copy server\RemoteServer*.class
   \home\zelda\public_html\classes
copy server\Send.class \home\zelda\public_html\classes
copy server\DataOrder.class \home\zelda\public_html\classes
```

NOTE The `rmic -d . server.RemoteServer` line uses `server.RemoteServer` instead of `server/RemoteServer`, so the `_stub` and `_skel` classes are generated properly with the package.

Start the RMI Registry

Unix:

```
cd /home/zelda/public_html/classes
unsetenv CLASSPATH
rmiregistry &
```

Win32:

```
cd \home\zelda\public_html\classes
set CLASSPATH=
start rmiregistry
```

Start the Server

Unix:

```
cd /home/zelda/public_html/classes
java -Djava.rmi.server.codebase= http://kq6py/~zelda/classes
    -Djava.rmi.server.hostname=kq6py.eng.sun.com
    -Djava.security.policy=
    server/java.policy server/RemoteServer
```

Win32:

```
cd \home\zelda\public_html\classes
java -Djava.rmi.server.codebase=
    file:c:\home\zelda\public_html\classes
    -Djava.rmi.server.hostname=kq6py.eng.sun.com
    -Djava.security.policy=
    server\java.policy server\RemoteServer
```

Start the RMIGermanApp Program

Following is the HTML code to load the German applet. Note the directory/
package name that is prefixed to the applet class name (client1/RMIFrench-
App.class).

```
<HTML>
<BODY>
<APPLET CODE=client1/RMIGermanApp.class WIDTH=300
HEIGHT=300>
</APPLET>
</BODY>
</HTML>
```

To run the applet with appletviewer, invoke the HTML file from the directory
just above client1 as follows:

```
cd /home/zelda/classes
appletviewer rmiGapp.html
```

Start the RMIClient2 Program in French

Unix:

```
cd /home/zelda/classes
java -Djava.rmi.server.codebase=http://kq6py/~zelda/classes
```

```
    -Djava.security.policy=client2/java.policy
    client2/RMIClient2 kq6py.eng.sun.com fr FR
```

Win32:
```
cd \home\zelda\classes
java -Djava.rmi.server.codebase=
    file:c:\home\zelda\public_html\classes
    -Djava.security.policy=client2\java.policy
    client2\RMIClient2 kq6py.eng.sun.com fr FR
```

Using JAR Files to Deploy

After testing and debugging, the best way to deploy the two client and server files is to bundle the executables and other related application files into three separate JAR files, where you have one JAR file for each client program and one JAR file for the server program.

JAR files use the ZIP file format both to compress and pack files into and to decompress and unpack files from the JAR file. JAR files make it easy to deploy programs that consist of many files. Browsers can easily download applets bundled into JAR files, and the download goes much more quickly than if the applet and its related files were not bundled into a JAR file.

Server Set of Files

Following are the server files:

- RemoteServer.class
- RemoteServer_skel.class
- RemoteServer_stub.class
- Send.class
- DataOrder.class
- java.policy

Compress and Pack Server Files

To compress and pack the server files into one JAR file, type the following command on one line. This command is executed in the same directory with the files. If you execute the command from a directory other than where the files are, you have to specify the full pathname.

```
jar cf server.jar RemoteServer.class RemoteServer_skel.class
   RemoteServer_stub.class  Send.class DataOrder.class
   java.policy
```

jar is the jar command. If you type jar with no options, you get the following help screen. You can see from the help screen that the cf options to the jar command mean to create a new JAR file named server.jar and to put the list of files that follows into it. The new JAR file is placed in the current directory.

```
kq6py% jar Usage: jar {ctxu}[vfm0M] [jar-file] [manifest-
file] [-C dir] files ... Options:
-c create new archive
-t list table of contents for archive
-x extract named (or all) files from archive
-u update existing archive
-v generate verbose output on standard output
-f specify archive file name
-m include manifest information from specified manifest file
-0 store only; use no ZIP compression
-M Do not create a manifest file for the entries
-C change to the specified directory and include the following file
If any file is a directory then it is processed recursively. The
manifest file name and the archive file name needs to be specified
in the same order the 'm' and 'f' flags are specified.
Example 1: to archive two class files into an archive called
classes.jar: jar cvf classes.jar Foo.class Bar.class
Example 2: use an existing manifest file 'mymanifest' and
archive all the files in the foo/ directory into
'classes.jar': jar cvfm classes.jar mymanifest -C foo/ .
To deploy the server files, all you have to do is move the
<CODE>server.jar</CODE> file to a publicly accessible
directory on the server where they are to execute.
```

Decompress and Unpack Server Files

After moving the JAR file to its final location, the compressed and packed files can be decompressed and unpacked so you can start the server. The following command means extract (x) all files from the server.jar file (f):

```
jar xf server.jar
```

NOTE It is also possible to start the server without decompressing and unpacking the JAR file first. You can find out how to do this by referring to the chapter on JAR files in *The Java Tutorial* referenced at the end of this lesson.

Fruit Order Set of Files (RMIClient1)

The fruit order set of files that follow consists of applet classes, Web pages, translation files, and the policy file. Because these files live on the Web, they need to be in a directory accessible to the Web server. The easiest way to deploy the files is to bundle them all into a JAR file and copy them to their location.

- RMIEnglishApp.class
- RMIFrenchApp.class
- RMIGermanApp.class
- index.html (top-level Web page where user chooses language)
- rmiEapp.html (second-level Web page for English)
- rmiFapp.html (second-level Web page for French)
- rmiGapp.html (second-level Web page for German)
- MessagesBundle_de_DE.properties
- MessagesBundle_en_US.properties
- MessagesBundle_fr_FR.properties
- java.policy

Compress and Pack Files

```
jar cf applet.jar RMIEnglishApp.class RMIFrenchApp.class
   RMIGermanApp.class index.html rmiEapp.html rmiFapp.html
     rmiGapp.html
   MessagesBundle_de_DE.properties MessagesBundle_en_US.
     properties
   MessagesBundle_fr_FR.properties java.policy
```

To deploy the fruit order client files, copy the `applet.jar` file to its final location.

Decompress and Unpack Files

An applet in a JAR file can be invoked from an HTML file without being unpacked. All you do is specify the ARCHIVE option to the APPLET tag in your Web page; this tells the `appletviewer` tool the name of the JAR file containing the class file. Be sure to include the package directory when you specify the applet class to the CODE option.

When using appletviewer, you can leave the translation files and policy file in the JAR file. When the applet is invoked from the JAR file, it will find the translation files that are also in the JAR file.

```
<HTML>
<BODY>
<APPLET CODE=client1/RMIFrenchApp.class
  ARCHIVE="applet.jar"
    WIDTH=300 HEIGHT=300>
```

```
</APPLET>
</BODY>
</HTML>
```

However, you do need to unpack the Web pages so you can move them to their final location. The following command does this. Everything goes on one line.

```
jar xv applet.jar index.html rmiEapp.html rmiFapp.html rmiGapp.html
```

NOTE   To run the HTML files from a browser, you need to unpack the JAR file, copy the `java.policy` file to your home directory and make sure it has the right name (`.java.policy` for Unix and `java.policy` for Windows), and install Java Plug-In.

View Order Set of Files

The view order set of files (that follows) consists of the application class file and the policy file:

- RMIClient2.class
- java.policy

Compress and Pack Files

```
jar cf vieworder.jar RMIClient2.class java.policy
```

To deploy the view order client files, copy the `vieworder.jar` file to its final location.

Decompress and Unpack Files

```
jar xf vieworder.jar
```

Exercises

1. When you organize classes into a package, what is the package name the same as?

2. When do you have to make a class public?

3. What do you do different to compile and run classes organized into packages?

4. What are JAR files used for?

5. Can applet and server classes be executed from within a JAR file?

More Information

You can find more information on packages in "Creating and Using Packages" in *The Java™ Tutorial Continued* [Cam99].

You can find more information on these and other JAR file format topics in "JAR File Format" in *The Java™ Tutorial Continued* [Cam99].

Object-Oriented Programming

Y OU have probably heard a lot of talk about object-oriented programming. And, if the Java programming language is your first experience with an object-oriented language, you are probably wondering what all the talk is about.

You already know a little about object-oriented programming because, after working the examples in this tutorial, you are somewhat familiar with the object-oriented concepts of class, object, instance, and inheritance plus the access levels `public` and `private`. Essentially, you have been doing object-oriented programming without really thinking about it.

One of the great things about the Java programming language is that its design supports the object oriented model. To help you gain a better understanding of object oriented programming and its benefits, this lesson presents a very brief overview of object-oriented concepts and terminology as they relate to the example code presented in this tutorial. You will find a list of good books on object-oriented programming at the end of this chapter.

Covered in This Lesson

- Object-Oriented Programming Defined
- Inheritance and Polymorphism
- Data Access Levels
- Your Own Classes
- Exercises
- More Information

Object-Oriented Programming Defined

The Java programming language supports generally accepted object-oriented programming techniques that are based on a hierarchy of classes and well-defined and cooperating objects.

Classes

A class is a structure that defines the data and the methods to work on that data. When you write programs in the Java programming language, all program data is wrapped in a class, whether it is a class you write or a class you use from the Java platform API libraries.

For example, the `ExampleProgram` class from Lesson 1, Compiling and Running a Simple Program (page 1), is a programmer-written class that uses the `java.lang.System` class from the Java platform API libraries to print a string literal (character string) to the command line.

```
class ExampleProgram {
    public static void main(String[] args) {
      System.out.println("I'm a simple Program");
    }
}
```

Classes in the Java platform API libraries define a set of objects that share a common structure and behavior. The `java.lang.System` class used in the example provides access to such things as standard input, output, and error streams and access to system properties. In contrast, the `java.lang.String` class defines string literals.

In the `ExampleProgram` class example, you do not see an explicit use of the `String` class; but in the Java programming language, a string literal can be used anywhere a method expects to receive a `String` object.

During execution, the Java platform creates a `String` object from the character string passed to the `System.out.println` call, but your program cannot call any of the `String` class methods because it did not instantiate the `String` object. If you want access to the `String` methods, rewrite the example program to create a `String` object. The `String.concat` method that follows adds text to the original string:

```
class ExampleProgram {
    public static void main(String[] args){
      String text = new String("I'm a simple Program ");
      System.out.println(text);
      String text2 = text.concat(
        "that uses classes and objects");
```

```
        System.out.println(text2);
    }
}
```

The output looks like this:

```
I'm a simple Program
I'm a simple Program that uses classes and objects
```

Objects

Object is another name for instance. A newly created object has data members and methods as defined by its class. In the last example, various `String` objects are created for the concatenation operation: `text` object, `text2` object, a `String` object created *behind the scenes* to pass to the `text` object constructor, and a `String` object created *behind the scenes* from the "`that uses classes and objects`" character string passed to the `String.concat` method.

Also, because `String` objects cannot be edited, the `java.lang.String.concat` method converts the `String` objects to `StringBuffer` (editable) objects to do the concatenation. Besides the `String` object, there is an instance of the `ExampleProgram` class in memory as well. Figure 14-1 shows these objects in memory.

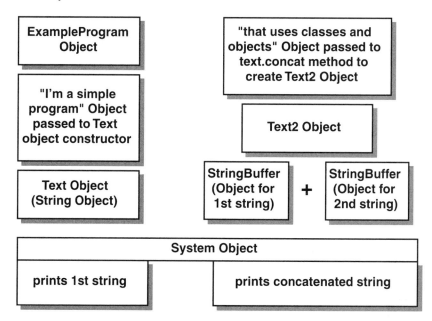

Figure 14-1   Objects in Memory

Well-Defined Boundaries and Cooperation

Class definitions must allow objects to cooperate during execution. In the previous section, you saw how the System, String, and StringBuffer objects cooperated to print a concatenated character string to the command line.

This section changes the example program to display the concatenated character string in a JLabel component in a user interface to illustrate further the concepts of well-defined class boundaries and object cooperation. The program code uses a number of cooperating classes. Each class has its own purpose as summarized below, and, where appropriate, the classes are defined to work with objects of another class.

- ExampleProgram defines the program data and methods to work on that data.
- JFrame defines the top-level window including the window title and frame menu.
- WindowListener defines behavior for (works with) the Close option on the frame menu.
- String defines a character string passed to the label.
- JLabel defines a user interface component to display noneditable text.
- JPanel defines a container and uses the default layout manager (java.awt.FlowLayout) to lay out the objects it contains.

While each class has its own specific purpose, they all work together to create the simple user interface you see in Figure 14-2.

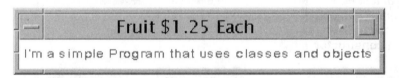

Figure 14-2   Simple User Interface

```
import javax.swing.*;
import java.awt.Color;
import java.awt.event.*;

class ExampleProgram extends JFrame {
  public ExampleProgram() {
    String text = new String("I'm a simple Program ");
```

```
                String text2 = text.concat(
                  "that uses classes and objects");
                JLabel label = new JLabel(text2);
                JPanel panel = new JPanel();
                panel.setBackground(Color.white);
                getContentPane().add(panel);
                panel.add(label);    }

            public static void main(String[] args){
                ExampleProgram frame = new ExampleProgram();
                frame.setTitle("Fruit $1.25 Each");
                WindowListener l = new WindowAdapter() {
                    public void windowClosing(WindowEvent e) {
                      System.exit(0);
                    }
                };
                frame.addWindowListener(l);
                frame.pack();
                frame.setVisible(true);
            }
        }
```

Inheritance and Polymorphism

One object-oriented concept that helps objects work together is inheritance. Inheritance defines relationships among classes in an object-oriented language. The relationship is one of parent to child where the child or extending class inherits all the attributes (methods and data) of the parent class. In the Java programming language, all classes descend from java.lang.Object and inherit its methods .

Figure 14-3 shows the class hierarchy as it descends from java.lang.Object for the classes in the user interface example just given. The java.lang. Object methods are also shown because they are inherited and implemented by all of its subclasses, which includes every class in the Java API libraries. java.lang.Object defines the core set of behaviors that all classes have in common.

As you move down the hierarchy, each class adds its own set of class-specific fields and methods to what it inherits from its superclass. The java. awt.swing.JFrame class inherits fields and methods from java.awt.Frame, which in turn inherits fields and methods from java.awt.Container, which inherits fields and methods from java.awt.Component, which in turn finally

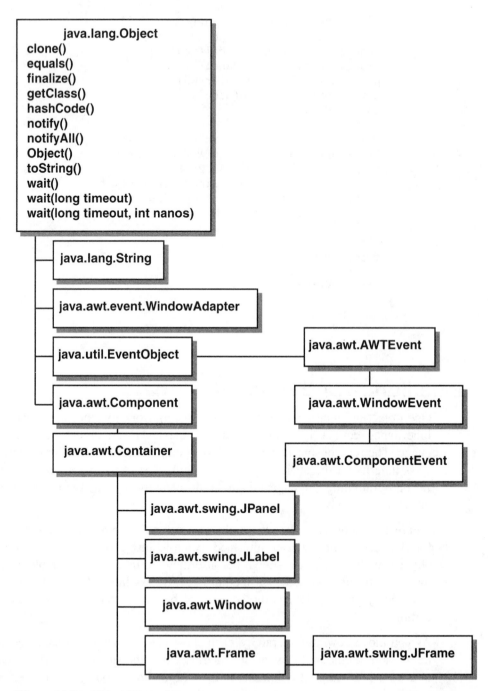

Figure 14-3   Object Hierarchy

inherits from `java.lang.Object`. Each subclass adds its own fields and methods as needed.

Each class in the hierarchy adds its own class-specific behavior to inherited methods. In this way different classes with a common parent can have like-named methods that exhibit behavior appropriate to each class. For example, the `Object` class has a `toString` method inherited by all its subclasses. You can call the `toString` method on any class to get its string representation, but the actual behavior of the `toString` method in each class depends on the class of the object on which it is invoked.

Another way objects work together is to define methods that take other objects as parameters. For example, if you define a method that takes a `java.lang.Object` as a parameter, it can accept any object in the entire Java platform. If you define a method that takes a `java.awt.Component` as a parameter, it can accept any class that derives from `Component`. This form of cooperation is called **polymorphism**.

You saw an example of polymorphism in the section <u>Maintaining and Displaying a Customer List</u> (page 157). A `Collection` object can contain any type of object as long as it descends from `java.lang.Object`. It is repeated here to show you that a `Set` collection can add a `String` object and an `Integer` object to the `Set` because the `Set.add` method is defined to accept any class instance that traces back to the `java.lang.Object` class.

```
String custID = "munchkin";
Integer creditCard =  new Integer(25);
Set s = new HashSet();
s.add(custID);
s.add(creditCard);
```

Data Access Levels

Another way classes work together is through access-level controls. Classes and their fields and methods have access levels to specify how they can be used by other objects during execution. While cooperation among objects is desirable, there are times when you will want to control access explicitly; and specifying access levels is the way to gain that control. When you do not specify an access level, the default access level is in effect.

Classes

Classes can be declared `package`, `public`, `private`, or `protected`. If there is no access level specified, the class is `package` by default.

- `package`: The class can be used only by instances of other classes in the same package.

  ```
  class DbaAppl extends Applet implements ActionListener {
  ```

- `public`: A class can be declared `public` to make it accessible to all class instances regardless of what package its class is in. You might recall that in Lesson 3, Building Applets (page 17), the `Applet` class had to be declared `public` so it could be accessed by the `appletviewer` tool because the appletviewer program is created from classes in another package. In Lesson 12, Internationalization (page 169), the server classes are made `public` so client classes can access them.

  ```
  public class DbaAppl extends Applet
                  implements ActionListener {
  ```

- `private`: A class declared `private` cannot be instantiated by any other class. Usually `private` classes have `public` methods called factory methods that can be called by other classes. These `public` factory methods create (manufacture) an instance of the class and return it to the calling method.

  ```
  private class DbaAppl extends Applet implements ActionListener {
  ```

- `protected`: Only subclasses of a `protected` class can create instances of it.

  ```
  protected class DbaAppl extends Applet implements ActionListener {
  ```

Fields and Methods

Fields and methods can be declared `private`, `protected`, `public`, or `package`. If no access level is specified, the field or method access level is `package` by default.

- `private`: A private field or method is accessible only to the class in which it is defined. In Lesson 7, Database Access and Permissions (page 69), the connection, user name, and password for establishing the database access are all private. This is to prevent an outside class from accessing them and jeopardizing the database connection or from compromising the secret user name and password information.

```
private Connection c;
```

- `protected`: A protected field or method is accessible to the class itself, its subclasses, and the classes in the same package.
- `public`: A public field or method is accessible to any class of any parentage in any package. In Lesson 12 (page 169), server data accessed by client programs is made public.
- `package`: A package field or method is accessible to other classes in the same package.

Global Variables and Methods

The Java programming language does not have global variables and methods because all fields are wrapped in a class and all classes are part of a package. To reference a field or method, you use the package, class, and field or method name.

However, fields declared `public static` can be accessed and changed by any instance regardless of parentage or package (similar to global variable data). If the field is declared `final public static`, its value can never be changed, which makes it similar to a global constant.

Your Own Classes

When you use the Java API library classes, they have already been designed with the above concepts in mind. They all descend from `java.lang.Object`, giving them an inheritance relationship; they have well-defined boundaries, and they are designed to cooperate with each other where appropriate.

For example, you will not find a `String` class that takes an `Integer` object as input because that goes beyond the well-defined boundary for a `String`. You will, however, find the `Integer` class has a method for converting its integer value to a `String` so its value can be displayed in a user interface component, which accepts only `String` objects.

But what about when you write your own classes? How can you be sure your classes have well-defined boundaries, cooperate, and make use of inheritance? One way is to look at what a program needs to do and separate those operations into distinct modules where each operational module is defined by its own class or group of classes.

Well-Defined Boundaries and Cooperation

Looking at the RMIClient2 class from Lesson 11, Developing the Example (page 153), you can see that it performs the following operations: get data, display data, store customer IDs, print customer IDs, and reset the display.

Getting data, displaying the data, and resetting the display are closely related and easily form an operational module. But in a larger program with more data processing, the storing and printing of customer IDs could be expanded to store and print a wider range of data. In such a case, it would make sense to have a separate class for storing data and another class for printing it in various forms.

You could, for example, have a class that defines how to store customer IDs and tracks the number of apples, peaches, and pears sold during the year. You could also have another class that defines report printing. It could access the stored data to print reports on apples, peaches, and pears sold by the month, per customer, or throughout a given season.

Making application code modular by separating out operational units makes it easier to update and maintain the source code. When you change a class, as long as you do not change any part of its public interface, you have to recompile only that one class.

Inheritance

Deciding what classes your program needs means separating operations into modules, but making your code more efficient and easier to maintain means looking for common operations where you can use inheritance. If you need to write a class that does similar things to a class in the Java API libraries, it makes sense to extend that API library class and use its methods rather than write everything from scratch.

The RMIClient2 class from Lesson 11 (page 153) extends JFrame to leverage the ready-made behavior it provides for a program's top-level window, including frame menu closing behavior, background color setting, and a customized title.

Likewise, to add customized behavior to an existing class, extend that class and add the behavior you want. For example, you might want to create a custom `Exception` to use in your program. To do this, write an exception class that extends `java.lang.Exception` and implement it to do what you want.

Access Levels

You should always keep access levels in mind when you declare classes, fields, and methods. Consider which objects really need access to the data, and use packages and access levels to protect your application data from all other objects executing in the system.

Most object-oriented applications declare their data fields `private`. Other objects cannot access their fields directly and make the methods that access the `private` data protected, `public`, or `package` as needed; other objects can manipulate their private data by calling the methods only.

Keeping data private gives an object the control to maintain its data in a valid state. For example, a class can include behavior for verifying that certain conditions are true before and after the data changes. If other objects can access the data directly, it is not possible for an object to maintain its data in a valid state like this.

Another reason to keep data fields private and accessible only through the class methods is to make it easier to maintain source code. You can update your class by changing a field definition and the corresponding method implementation, but other objects that access that data do not need to be changed because their interface to the data (the method signature) has not changed.

Exercises

So that an object has the control it needs to maintain its data in a valid state, it is always best to restrict access as much as possible. In Lesson 13, Packages and JAR File Format (page 193), the server classes and the `DataOrder` class fields had to be made `public` so the client programs could access them. At that time, no access level was specified for the other classes and fields so they are all `package` by default, and all methods have an access level of `public`.

A good exercise is to go back to the client classes from Lesson 12, Internationalization (page 169), and give the classes, fields, and methods an access level so they are not accessed inappropriately by other objects. You will find solutions for the `RMIClient1` and `RMIClient2` client programs in the section <u>Application Code</u> (page 240) in Appendix B, Code Listings.

More Information

You can find more information on object-oriented programming concepts in "Object-Oriented Programming Concepts" in *The Java™ Tutorial, Second Edition* [Cam98].

You might also find the following books useful:

Object-Oriented Analysis and Design with Applications [Boo94] by Grady Booch.

Analysis Patterns: Reusable Object Models [Fow97] by Martin Fowler.

Object Models: Strategies, Patterns, and Applications [Coa96] by Peter Coad, Mark Mayfield, and David North.

Design Patterns: Elements of Reusable Object-Oriented Software [Gam95] by Erich Gamma, Richard Helm, Ralph Johnson, and John Vlissides.

Cryptography

Many people are protective of their credit card numbers—and for good reason. A stolen credit card number with other personal information can give a thief all he or she needs to create mayhem in someone's life. One way to keep credit card and other proprietary information secure when sending it over the net is to encrypt it.

Encryption is the process of applying to plain text a key that transforms that text into unintelligible (cipher) text. Only programs with the key to turn the cipher text back to the original text can decrypt the protected information.

This lesson adapts the example from Lesson 10, User Interfaces Revisited (page 123), to encrypt the credit card number before sending it over the net and to decrypt it on the other side. The order data is not wrapped in a `DataOrder` object as it was in Lesson 10, but is sent over the network as data units of type `String`, `double`, and `int` to illustrate the flexibility of the RMI API.

NOTE   This lesson is an appendix because only residents of the United States and Canada have access to the Cryptographic software, and the descriptions for using this software are somewhat more complex than the material presented in the other lessons.

Covered in This Lesson

- About the Example
- Compiling and Running the Example

- Source Code
- Exercises
- More Information

About the Example

To safely send the credit card number shown in Figure A-1 over the net, the example program gets the plain text credit card number entered by the user and passes the credit card number to its encrypt method.

Figure A-1   Fruit Order Client Program

The encrypt method creates a cipher and session key and uses the session key with the cipher to encrypt the credit card number.

A session key is a secret key generated new each time the Purchase button is clicked. Changing the session key protects against an unauthorized program getting the key and decrypting hundreds and thousands of credit card numbers with it.

The credit card number is encrypted and decrypted with the same session key. This type of cryptography is called **symmetric key encryption** and, in the example, requires that the session key and encrypted credit card number be sent over the Net to the receiving program. Because the session key is sent over the Net, it, too, should be protected against unauthorized access.

To protect the session key, it is encrypted with or wrapped under the public key of the intended recipient. Even if an unauthorized program gets the encrypted session key and credit card number, it would have to recover the session key with the private key corresponding to the public key that encrypted the session key before it could decrypt the credit card number with the session key.

Anything encrypted with a public key can be decrypted only with the private key corresponding to the public key that originally encrypted it. This type of cryptography is called **asymmetric key encryption**. In the example, the public key is made readily available to any client program that requests it, and the private key is kept secret and made available to specific, trusted clients only.

As shown in Figure A-2, this example uses a separate program to generate the public and private key pair. The public key is stored in one file, and the private key is stored in another. The file with the private key must be kept in a very secure place. Many companies keep the private key file on an external storage medium such as tape or disk to prevent an unauthorized person or program from breaking into the system and getting the private key.

The server program loads the public key from the public key file and makes it available to order clients for encrypting the session key. Order processing

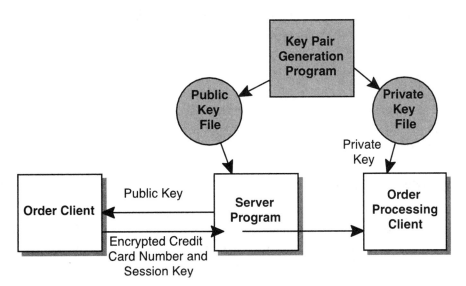

Figure A-2   Public and Private Keys

clients receive the encrypted session key and credit card number, load the private key, use the private key to decrypt the session key, and use the session key to decrypt the credit card number.

Compiling and Running the Example

If you are within the United States or Canada, you can download the javax.crypto package from the java.sun.com Products & APIs (http://java.sun.com/products/jce) page. It contains documentation and a Java Archive (JAR) file with the cryptographic APIs and a cryptographic service provider. A cryptographic service provider (or provider, for short) is a package or set of packages that supplies a concrete implementation of a cryptographic algorithm.

To install the package, copy the JAR file to the jdk1.2/jre/lib/ext directory of your Java 2 SDK, Standard Edition, installation or the jre1.2/lib/ext directory of your Java Runtime Environment (JRE) 1.2 installation. Make sure you have the following entries in the jdk1.2/jre/lib/security/java.security or jre1.2/lib/security/java.security files:

```
security.provider.1=sun.security.provider.Sun
security.provider.2=com.sun.crypto.provider.SunJCE
```

You also need to install a package with an asymmetric algorithm such as the Rivest, Shamir, and Adleman (RSA) Asymmetric-Cipher algorithm. The asymmetric algorithm is needed to create the asymmetric cipher for the public and private key encryption. Add the asymmetric algorithm package to jdk1.2/jre/lib/security/java.security or jre1.2/lib/security java.security as security.provider.3=, and put it in the /jre/lib/ext directory with the other JAR files.

To compile and run the example, refer to a summary of the steps in the section Compile and Run the Example (page 126) in Lesson 10, User Interfaces Revisited.

Source Code

A cipher object is used in the encryption and decryption process. It is created with a specific cryptographic algorithm, depending on the type of encryption in use. In this example, two types of encryption are used: symmetric to encrypt the credit card number and asymmetric to encrypt the session key.

Symmetric key encryption uses a symmetric algorithm such as Data Encryption Standard (DES). The asymmetric key encryption uses an asymmetric algorithm such as Rivest, Shamir, and Adleman (RSA) Asymmetric-Cipher algorithm.

The `javax.crypto` package defines the framework for both symmetric and asymmetric encryption into which concrete cipher implementations can be plugged. The SunJCE provider that comes standard with JCE 1.2 supplies only implementations of symmetric encryption algorithms such as DES. For an implementation of an asymmetric encryption algorithm such as RSA, you need to install a different provider.

The source code shows two ways to do the asymmetric encryption of the session key. One way uses an RSA key to encrypt the symmetric key; the other way uses another asymmetric algorithm to seal (encrypt) the symmetric key. Sealing is the preferred way, but it presents a problem when you use the RSA key because the RSA algorithm imposes a size restriction (discussed later) on the object being encrypted, and the sealing process makes the session key too large to be encrypted with an RSA key.

After the cipher is created with the correct symmetric or asymmetric algorithm, it is initialized for encryption or decryption with a key. In symmetric encryption, the key is a secret key; and in asymmetric encryption, the key is either the public or private key.

Sealing the Symmetric Key

Sealing the symmetric key involves creating a sealed object that uses an asymmetric cipher to seal (encrypt) the session key. The RSA asymmetric algorithm cannot be used because it has the size restrictions described in the next section, and the sealing process makes the session key too large to use with the RSA algorithm.

Sealing the Symmetric Key: Generating the Public and Private Key Pair

You need a program to generate a public and private key pair with an asymmetric algorithm and store them to separate files. The public key is read from its file when a client calls the server method to get the public key. The private key is read from its file when `RMIClient2` needs it to decrypt the session key.

```
import java.security.*;
import java.security.interfaces.*;
import javax.crypto.*;
import java.util.*;
import java.text.NumberFormat;
import java.io.*;
```

```
public class GenerateKey implements Serializable {
  private static PublicKey pubKey;
  private static PrivateKey privKey;
  public static void main(String[] args){

//Generate Key Pair
    try {
      KeyPairGenerator kpg =
        KeyPairGenerator.getInstance("asym algorithm");
      kpg.initialize(1024);
      KeyPair kp = kpg.generateKeyPair();
      pubKey = (PublicKey)kp.getPublic();
      privKey = (PrivateKey)kp.getPrivate();
    } catch (java.security.NoSuchAlgorithmException e) {
      System.out.println(e.toString());
    }
//Store in really safe place on disk
    try {
      String outputFileName =
        System.getProperty("user.home",
      File.separatorChar + "home" +
      File.separatorChar + "zelda") +
      File.separatorChar + "privkey.txt";
      FileOutputStream fstream = new
        FileOutputStream(outputFileName);
      ObjectOutputStream out = new ObjectOutput-
Stream(fstream);
      out.writeObject(privKey);
      out.flush();
      out.close();
      outputFileName = System.getProperty("user.home",
      File.separatorChar + "home" +
      File.separatorChar + "zelda") +
      File.separatorChar + "pubkey.txt";
      fstream = new FileOutputStream(outputFileName);
      out = new ObjectOutputStream(fstream);
      out.writeObject(pubKey);
      out.flush();
      out.close();
    } catch(java.io.IOException e) {
      System.out.println(e.toString());
    }
  }
}
```

Sealing the Symmetric Key:
Send Interface

The Send interface declares and the RemoteServer class implements methods
to handle the encrypted credit card number and the encrypted session key. The

Send interface also defines a method to return the public key when a client requests it. The following is the Send interface:

```
import java.rmi.Remote;
import java.rmi.RemoteException;
import javax.crypto.*;
import java.security.*;

public interface Send extends Remote {
  public PublicKey getPublicKey() throws RemoteException;
  public void sendEncrypted(byte[] encrypted)
    throws RemoteException;
  public byte[] getEncrypted() throws RemoteException;
  public void sendKey(SealedObject cardnum)
    throws RemoteException;
  public SealedObject getKey() throws RemoteException;
  public void sendCustID(String cust) throws RemoteException;
  public String getCustID() throws RemoteException;
  public void sendAppleQnt(String apples)
    throws RemoteException;
  public String getAppleQnt() throws RemoteException;
  public void sendPeachQnt(String peaches)
    throws RemoteException;
  public String getPeachQnt() throws RemoteException;
  public void sendPearQnt(String pears)
    throws RemoteException;
  public String getPearQnt() throws RemoteException;
  public void sendTotalCost(double cost)
    throws RemoteException;
  public double getTotalCost() throws RemoteException;
  public void sendTotalItems(int items)
    throws RemoteException;
  public int getTotalItems() throws RemoteException;
}
```

Sealing the Symmetric Key: RemoteServer Class

The RemoteServer class implements the Send interface and its methods.

```
import java.awt.Color;
import java.awt.BorderLayout;
import java.awt.event.*;
import java.io.*;
import java.net.*;
import java.rmi.*;
import java.rmi.server.*;
import java.security.*;
import javax.crypto.*;
```

```java
class RemoteServer extends UnicastRemoteObject implements
Send, Serializable {
  private SealedObject cardnum;
  private byte[] encrypt;
  private String custID;
  private String apples;
  private String peaches;
  private String pears;
  private int items;
  private double cost;

  public RemoteServer() throws RemoteException {
    super();
  }

  public PublicKey getPublicKey(){
//Load from really safe place on disk
    PublicKey pubKey=null;
    try {
      String inputFileName = System.getProperty("user.home",
            File.separatorChar + "home" +
            File.separatorChar + "zelda") +
            File.separatorChar + "pubkey.txt";
      FileInputStream fstream = new
        FileInputStream(inputFileName);
      ObjectInputStream in = new ObjectInputStream(fstream);
      pubKey = (PublicKey)in.readObject();
      in.close();
    } catch(java.io.IOException e) {
      System.out.println("File not found");
    } catch(java.lang.ClassNotFoundException e) {
      System.out.println("PublicKey class not found");
    }
    return pubKey;
  }
  public void sendKey(SealedObject creditcard) {
    cardnum = creditcard;
  }
  public SealedObject getKey() {
    return cardnum;
  }
  public byte[] getEncrypted() {
    return encrypt;
  }
  public void sendEncrypted(byte[] encrypted) {
    encrypt = encrypted;
  }
  public void sendCustID(String cust) {
```

```
        custID = cust;
    }
    public String getCustID() {
      return custID;
    }
    public void sendAppleQnt(String apps) {
      apples = apps;
    }
    public String getAppleQnt() {
      return apples;
    }
    public void sendPeachQnt(String pchs) {
      peaches = pchs;
    }
    public String getPeachQnt() {
      return peaches;
    }
    public void sendPearQnt(String prs) {
      pears = prs;
    }
    public String getPearQnt() {
      return pears;
    }
    public void sendTotalCost(double cst) {
      cost = cst;
    }
    public double getTotalCost() {
      return cost;
    }
    public void sendTotalItems(int itm) {
      items = itm;
    }
    public int getTotalItems() {
      return items;
    }
}
```

Sealing the Symmetric Key:
RMIClient1 Code

The RMIClient1 program (page 265) has an encrypt method to encrypt the credit card number, seal the symmetric key, and send the encrypted credit card number and sealed key to the server.

```
    private void encrypt(String cardnum {
      Cipher c=null, c2=null;
      KeyGenerator keyGen;
      SecretKey secretKey=null;
```

```
    PublicKey pubKey=null;
    SealedObject sealed=null;
    byte[] encrypted=null;
    String s="text";

//Create Cipher for symmetric key encryption (DES)
//Create a key generator
//Create a secret (session) key with key generator
    try {
       c = Cipher.getInstance("DES/ECB/PKCS5Padding");
       keyGen = KeyGenerator.getInstance("DES");
       keyGen.init(new SecureRandom());
       secretKey=keyGen.generateKey();
    } catch (java.security.NoSuchAlgorithmException e) {
       System.out.println("No such algorithm");
    } catch(javax.crypto.NoSuchPaddingException e) {
       System.out.println("No such padding");
    }

//Initialize Cipher for encryption with session key
//Encrypt credit card number with Cipher
    try {
       c.init(Cipher.ENCRYPT_MODE, secretKey);
       encrypted=c.doFinal(s.getBytes());
       System.out.println("Cipher Text:");
       System.out.println(new String(encrypted));
       System.out.println();
    } catch (java.security.InvalidKeyException e) {
       System.out.println("Invalid Key");
    } catch( javax.crypto.IllegalBlockSizeException e) {
       System.out.println("Illegal block size");
    } catch (javax.crypto.BadPaddingException e) {
       System.out.println("Bad Padding");
    }

//Get public key from server
    try {
       pubKey = (PublicKey)send.getPublicKey();
    } catch (java.rmi.RemoteException e){
       System.out.println("Key not availalbe");
    }

//Create Cipher for asymmetric encryption
//Initialize Cipher for encryption with session key
    try {
       c2 = Cipher.getInstance("an asymmetric algorithm");
       c2.init(Cipher.ENCRYPT_MODE, pubKey);
    } catch (java.security.NoSuchAlgorithmException e) {
```

```
        System.out.println("No such algorithm");
    } catch (javax.crypto.NoSuchPaddingException e) {
        System.out.println("No such padding");
    } catch (java.security.InvalidKeyException e) {
        System.out.println("Invalid key");
    }

//Seal session key in SealedObject using asymmetric Cipher
    try{
        sealed = new SealedObject(secretKey, c2);
    } catch (javax.crypto.IllegalBlockSizeException  e) {
        System.out.println("Illegal block size");
    } catch (java.io.IOException e) {
        System.out.println("Unable to seal session key");
    }
//Send encrypted message and
//sealed session key to server
    try {
        send.sendKey(sealed);
        send.sendEncrypted(encrypted);
    } catch(java.rmi.RemoteException e){
        System.out.println("Unable to send key");
    }
}
```

Sealing the Symmetric Key:
RMIClient2 Code

The RMIClient2 program (page 271) has a decrypt method to unseal the symmetric key and decrypt the credit card number.

```
public String decrypt(SealedObject sealed, byte[] encrypted)
{
//Get private key from file
    PrivateKey privkey=null;
    SecretKey seckey=null;
    Cipher c=null;
    String s=null;
    try {
        String inputFileName = System.getProperty("user.home",
            File.separatorChar + "home" +
            File.separatorChar + "zelda") +
            File.separatorChar + "privkey.txt";
        FileInputStream fstream = new FileInputStream(input-
FileName);
        ObjectInput in = new ObjectInputStream(fstream);
        privkey = (PrivateKey)in.readObject();
        in.close();
```

```java
        } catch(java.io.FileNotFoundException e) {
          System.out.println("File not found");
        } catch(java.io.StreamCorruptedException e) {
          System.out.println("Bad data");
        } catch(java.io.IOException e) {
          System.out.println("Unable to read file");
        } catch(java.lang.ClassNotFoundException e) {
          System.out.println("Unable to read private key");
        }

//Create asymmetric Cipher
//Initialize Cipher for decryption with private key
//Unseal wrapped session key using asymmetric cipher
        try {
          c = Cipher.getInstance("An asymmetric algorithm");
          c.init(Cipher.DECRYPT_MODE, privkey);
          seckey = (SecretKey)sealed.getObject(c);
        } catch( javax.crypto.NoSuchPaddingException e) {
          System.out.println("No such padding");
        } catc h(javax.crypto.IllegalBlockSizeException e) {
          System.out.println("Illegal block size");
        } catch (javax.crypto.BadPaddingException e) {
          System.out.println("Bad padding");
        } catch (java.security.NoSuchAlgorithmException e) {
          System.out.println("No such algorithm");
        } catch (java.security.InvalidKeyException e) {
          System.out.println("Invalid key");
        } catch (java.io.IOException e) {
          System.out.println("Unable to get private key");
        } catch (java.lang.ClassNotFoundException e) {
          System.out.println("Secret key not available");
        }

//Create symmetric Cipher
        try {
          c = Cipher.getInstance("DES/ECB/PKCS5Padding");
        } catch (java.security.NoSuchAlgorithmException e) {
          System.out.println("No such algorithm");
        } catch (javax.crypto.NoSuchPaddingException e) {
          System.out.println("No such padding");
        }

//Initialize Cipher for decryption with session key
//Decrypt credit card number with symmetric Cipher
        try
          c.init(Cipher.DECRYPT_MODE, seckey);
          encrypted=c.doFinal(s.getBytes());
          System.out.println("Cipher Text:");
```

```
        System.out.println(new String(encrypted));
        System.out.println();
      } catch (java.security.InvalidKeyException e) {
        System.out.println("Invalid key");
      } catch (javax.crypto.IllegalBlockSizeException e) {
        System.out.println("Illegal block size");
      } catch (javax.crypto.BadPaddingException e) {
        System.out.println("Bad padding");
      }
      return s;
  }
```

Encrypting the Symmetric Key with the RSA Algorithm

The RSA algorithm imposes size restrictions on the object being encrypted. RSA encryption uses the PKCS#1 standard with PKCS#1 block type 2 padding. The PKCS RSA encryption padding scheme needs 11 spare bytes to work. So, if you generate an RSA key pair with a key size of 512 bits, you cannot use the keys to encrypt more than 53 bytes (53 = 64 – 11).

If you have an 8-byte session key, sealing expands it to 3644 bytes, which is over the size restriction imposed by the RSA algorithm. This is because the process of sealing serializes the object to be sealed (the session key, in this case), and then encrypts the serialized contents. Serialization adds more information to the session key, such as the class of the session key, the class signature, and any objects referenced by the session key. The additional information makes the session key too large to be encrypted with an RSA key, and the result is a javax.crypto.IllegalBlockSizeException runtime error. This example uses the RSA algorithm to encrypt the symmetric key without sealing it.

Encrypting the Symmetric Key: Generating the Public and Private Key Pair

You need a program to generate a public and private key pair with the RSA algorithm and store them to separate files. The public key is read from its file when a client calls the method to get the public key. The private key is read from its file when RMIClient2 needs it to decrypt the session key.

```
import java.security.*;
import java.security.interfaces.*;
import javax.crypto.*;
import java.util.*;
import java.text.NumberFormat;
import java.io.*;
```

```
public class GenerateKey implements Serializable {
  private static RSAPublicKey pubKey;
  private static RSAPrivateKey privKey;
  public static void main(String[] args){

//Generate Key Pair
    try {
      KeyPairGenerator kpg = KeyPairGenerator.getIn-
stance("RSA");
      kpg.initialize(1024);
      KeyPair kp = kpg.generateKeyPair();
      pubKey = (RSAPublicKey)kp.getPublic();
      privKey = (RSAPrivateKey)kp.getPrivate();
    } catch (java.security.NoSuchAlgorithmException e){
      System.out.println(e.toString());
    }

//Store in really safe place on disk
    try {
      String outputFileName =
        System.getProperty("user.home",
      File.separatorChar + "home" +
      File.separatorChar + "zelda") +
      File.separatorChar + "privkey.txt";
      FileOutputStream fstream = new
        FileOutputStream(outputFileName);
      ObjectOutputStream out = new
        ObjectOutputStream(fstream);
      out.writeObject(privKey);
      out.flush();
      out.close();
      outputFileName = System.getProperty("user.home",
      File.separatorChar + "home" +
      File.separatorChar + "zelda") +
      File.separatorChar + "pubkey.txt";
      fstream = new FileOutputStream(outputFileName);
      out = new ObjectOutputStream(fstream);
      out.writeObject(pubKey);
      out.flush();
      out.close();
    } catch (java.io.IOException e) {
      System.out.println(e.toString());
    }
  }
}
```

Encrypting the Symmetric Key:
Send Interface

The Send interface declares and the RemoteServer class implements methods
to handle the encrypted credit card number and the encrypted session key. The

Send interface also defines a method to return the public key when a client requests it. Following is the Send interface:

```java
import java.rmi.Remote;
import java.rmi.RemoteException;
import javax.crypto.*;
import java.security.*;

public interface Send extends Remote {
  public PublicKey getPublicKey() throws RemoteException;
  public void sendEncrypted(byte[] encrypted)
    throws RemoteException;
  public byte[] getEncrypted() throws RemoteException;
  public void sendKey(byte[] key) throws RemoteException;
  public byte[] getKey() throws RemoteException;
  public void sendCustID(String cust) throws RemoteException;
  public String getCustID() throws RemoteException;
  public void sendAppleQnt(String apples)
    throws RemoteException;
  public String getAppleQnt() throws RemoteException;
  public void sendPeachQnt(String peaches)
    throws RemoteException;
  public String getPeachQnt() throws RemoteException;
  public void sendPearQnt(String pears)
    throws RemoteException;
  public String getPearQnt() throws RemoteException;
  public void sendTotalCost(double cost)
    throws RemoteException;
  public double getTotalCost() throws RemoteException;
  public void sendTotalItems(int items)
    throws RemoteException;
  public int getTotalItems() throws RemoteException;
}
```

Encrypting the Symmetric Key: RemoteServer Class

The RemoteServer class implements the Send interface and its methods.

```java
import java.awt.Color;
import java.awt.BorderLayout;
import java.awt.event.*;
import java.io.*;
import java.net.*;
import java.rmi.*;
import java.rmi.server.*;
import java.security.*;
import javax.crypto.*;

class RemoteServer extends UnicastRemoteObject
  implements Send, Serializable {
```

```java
    private byte[] encrypt, cardnum;
    private String custID;
    private String apples;
    private String peaches;
    private String pears;
    private int items;
    private double cost;

    public RemoteServer() throws RemoteException {
      super();
    }

    public PublicKey getPublicKey() {
//Load from really safe place on disk
      PublicKey pubKey=null;
      try{
        String inputFileName = System.getProperty("user.home",
        File.separatorChar + "home" +
        File.separatorChar + "zelda") +
        File.separatorChar + "pubkey.txt";
        FileInputStream fstream = new
          FileInputStream(inputFileName);
        ObjectInputStream in = new ObjectInputStream(fstream);
        pubKey = (PublicKey)in.readObject();
        in.close();
      } catch(java.io.IOException e) {
        System.out.println("File not found");
      } catch(java.lang.ClassNotFoundException e){
        System.out.println("PublicKey class not found");
      }
      return pubKey;
    }

    public void sendKey(byte[] creditcard) {
      cardnum = creditcard;
    }
    public byte[] getKey() {
      return cardnum;
    }
    public byte[] getEncrypted() {
      return encrypt;
    }
    public void sendEncrypted(byte[] encrypted) {
      encrypt = encrypted;
    }
    public void sendCustID(String cust) {
      custID = cust;
    }
```

```
      public String getCustID() {
        return custID;
      }
      public void sendAppleQnt(String apps) {
        apples = apps;
      }
      public String getAppleQnt() {
        return apples;
      }
      public void sendPeachQnt(String pchs) {
        peaches = pchs;
      }
      public String getPeachQnt() {
        return peaches;
      }
      public void sendPearQnt(String prs) {
        pears = prs;
      }
      public String getPearQnt() {
        return pears;
      }
      public void sendTotalCost(double cst) {
        cost = cst;
      }
      public double getTotalCost() {
        return cost;
      }
      public void sendTotalItems(int itm) {
        items = itm;
      }
      public int getTotalItems() {
        return items;
      }
    }
```

Encrypting the Symmetric Key: RMIClient1 Code

The RMIClient1 program (page 276) has an encrypt method to encrypt the credit card number and session key, and send the encrypted credit card number and session key to the server.

```
      private void encrypt(String cardnum) {
        Cipher c=null, c2=null;
        KeyGenerator keyGen;
        SecretKey secretKey=null;
        RSAPublicKey pubKey=null;
        byte[] encrypted=null, wrappedKey=null;
```

```
//Create Cipher for symmetric key encryption (DES)
//Create a key generator
//Create a secret (session) key with key generator
    try {
      c = Cipher.getInstance();
      keyGen = KeyGenerator.getInstance("DES");
      keyGen.init(new SecureRandom());
      secretKey=keyGen.generateKey();
    } catch (java.security.NoSuchAlgorithmException e) {
      System.out.println("No such algorithm");
    } catch(javax.crypto.NoSuchPaddingException e) {
      System.out.println("No such padding");
    }

//Initialize Cipher for encryption with session key
//Encrypt credit card number with Cipher
    try {
      c.init(Cipher.ENCRYPT_MODE, secretKey);
      encrypted=c.doFinal(cardnum.getBytes());
      System.out.println("Cipher Text:");
      System.out.println(new String(encrypted));
      System.out.println();
    } catch (java.security.InvalidKeyException e) {
      System.out.println("Invalid Key");
    } catch(javax.crypto.IllegalBlockSizeException e) {
      System.out.println("Illegal block size");
    } catch (javax.crypto.BadPaddingException e) {
      System.out.println("Bad Padding");
    }

//Get public key from server
    try {
      pubKey = (RSAPublicKey)send.getPublicKey();
    } catch (java.rmi.RemoteException e) {
      System.out.println("Key not available");
    }

//Create Cipher for asymmetric encryption (RSA)
//Initialize Cipher for encryption with public key
    try {
      c2 = Cipher.getInstance("RSA");
      c2.init(Cipher.ENCRYPT_MODE, pubKey);
    } catch (java.security.NoSuchAlgorithmException e) {
      System.out.println("No such algorithm");
    } catch (javax.crypto.NoSuchPaddingException e) {
      System.out.println("No such padding");
    } catch (java.security.InvalidKeyException e) {
      System.out.println("Invalid key");
    }
```

```
//Encrypt session key
    try{
     wrappedKey = c2.doFinal(secretKey.getEncoded());
    } catch (javax.crypto.IllegalBlockSizeException  e){
      System.out.println("Illegal block size");
    } catch (javax.crypto.BadPaddingException e) {
      System.out.println("Bad padding");
    }

//Send encrypted message and session key to server
   try {
     send.sendKey(wrappedKey);
     send.sendEncrypted(encrypted);
   } catch (java.rmi.RemoteException e) {
     System.out.println("Unable to send key");
   }
}
```

Encrypting the Symmetric Key:
RMIClient2 Code

The RMIClient2 program (page 283) has a decrypt method to decrypt the symmetric key and credit card number.

```
    public byte[] decrypt(byte[] wrappedKey, byte[] encrypted)
{
    PrivateKey privkey=null;
    SecretKey secretKey=null;
    Cipher c=null, c2=null;
    String s=null;
    SecretKeySpec kspec=null;
    byte[] card=null;

//Get private key from file
   try {
     String inputFileName = System.getProperty("user.home",
         File.separatorChar + "home" +
         File.separatorChar + "zelda") +
         File.separatorChar + "privkey.txt";
     FileInputStream fstream = new FileInputStream(inputFile-
Name);
     ObjectInput in = new ObjectInputStream(fstream);
     privkey = (PrivateKey)in.readObject();
     in.close();
   } catch (java.io.FileNotFoundException e) {
     System.out.println("File not found");
   } catch java.io.StreamCorruptedException e) {
     System.out.println("Bad data");
   } catch (java.io.IOException e) {
     System.out.println("Unable to read file");
```

```
        } catch (java.lang.ClassNotFoundException e) {
          System.out.println("Unable to read private key");
        }

    //Create asymmetric Cipher
    //Initialize Cipher for decryption with private key
    //Decrypt symmetric key
    //Instantiate symmetric key
        try {
          c = Cipher.getInstance("RSA");
          c.init(Cipher.DECRYPT_MODE, privkey);
          byte[] secretKeyBytes = c.doFinal(wrappedKey);
          kspec = new SecretKeySpec(secretKeyBytes, "DES");
        } catch (javax.crypto.IllegalBlockSizeException e) {
          System.out.println("Illegal block size");
        } catch (javax.crypto.BadPaddingException e) {
          System.out.println("Bad padding");
        } catch (javax.crypto.NoSuchPaddingException e) {
           System.out.println("No such padding");
        } catch (java.security.NoSuchAlgorithmException e) {
          System.out.println("No such algorithm");
        } catch (java.security.InvalidKeyException e) {
          System.out.println("Invalid key");
        }

    //Create symmetric Cipher
        try {
          c2 = Cipher.getInstance("DES/ECB/PKCS5Padding");
        } catch (java.security.NoSuchAlgorithmException e) {
           System.out.println("No such algorithm");
         } catch (javax.crypto.NoSuchPaddingException e) {
           System.out.println("No such padding");
         }

    //Initialize Cipher for decryption with session key
    //Decrypt credit card number with symmetric Cipher
        try {
          c2.init(Cipher.DECRYPT_MODE, kspec);
          card=c2.doFinal(encrypted);
          System.out.println("Credit Card Number:");
          System.out.println(new String(card));
          System.out.println();
        } catch (java.security.InvalidKeyException e) {
          System.out.println("Invalid key");
        } catch (javax.crypto.IllegalBlockSizeException e) {
          System.out.println("Illegal block size");
        } catch (javax.crypto.BadPaddingException e) {
          System.out.println("Bad padding");
        }
        return card;
    }
```

Exercises

1. What is the difference between symmetric and asymmetric encryption?

2. What is a `Cipher` object?

3. What happens when an object is sealed?

More Information

You can find more information on RSA key encryption on the Security Dynamics Web site (`http://www.rsa.com/ns.html`) or by using a search engine and searching RSA Cryptography, asymmetric key encryption, or symmetric key encryption.

You might also find this book helpful: *Cryptography: Theory and Practice* [Sti95] by Douglas R. Stinson.

Code Listings

THIS appendix lists application code from Lesson 14, Object-Oriented Programming (page 205), and the cryptography example from Appendix A, Cryptography (page 217).

Covered in This Lesson

- Application Code
- Cryptography Example

Application Code

- RMIClient1
- RMIClient2
- DataOrder
- Send
- RemoteServer
- RMIFrenchApp
- RMIGermanApp
- RMIEnglishApp
- Cryptography Example

Application Code:
RMIClient1

```
//package statement
package client1;

import java.awt.Color;
import java.awt.GridLayout;
import java.awt.event.*;
import javax.swing.*;
import java.io.*;
import java.net.*;
import java.rmi.*;
import java.rmi.server.*;
import java.util.*;
import java.text.*;
import server.*;

class RMIClient1 extends JFrame implements ActionListener {
  private JLabel col1, col2;
  private JLabel totalItems, totalCost;
  private JLabel cardNum, custID;
  private JLabel applechk, pearchk, peachchk;
  private JButton purchase, reset;
  private JPanel panel;
  private JTextField appleqnt, pearqnt, peachqnt;
  private JTextField creditCard, customer;
  private JTextArea items, cost;
  private static Send send;

//Internationalization variables
  private static Locale currentLocale;
  private static ResourceBundle messages;
  private static String language, country;
  private NumberFormat numFormat;

  private RMIClient1(){ //Begin Constructor
    setTitle(messages.getString("title"));

//Create left and right column labels
    col1 = new JLabel(messages.getString("1col"));
    col2 = new JLabel(messages.getString("2col"));

//Create labels and text field components
    applechk = new JLabel("   " +
      messages.getString("apples"));
    appleqnt = new JTextField();
    appleqnt.addActionListener(this);
```

```java
        pearchk = new JLabel("    " +
          messages.getString("pears"));
        pearqnt = new JTextField();
        pearqnt.addActionListener(this);
        peachchk = new JLabel("    " +
          messages.getString("peaches"));
        peachqnt = new JTextField();
        peachqnt.addActionListener(this);
        cardNum = new JLabel("    " + messages.getString("card"));
        creditCard = new JTextField();
        pearqnt.setNextFocusableComponent(creditCard);
        customer = new JTextField();
        custID = new JLabel("    " +
          messages.getString("customer"));

//Create labels and text area components
        totalItems = new JLabel("    " +
          messages.getString("items"));
        totalCost = new JLabel("    " +
          messages.getString("cost"));
        items = new JTextArea();
        cost = new JTextArea();

//Create buttons and make action listeners
        purchase = new JButton(messages.getString("purchase"));
        purchase.addActionListener(this);
        reset = new JButton(messages.getString("reset"));
        reset.addActionListener(this);

//Create a panel for the components
        panel = new JPanel();

//Set panel layout to 2-column grid
//on a white background
        panel.setLayout(new GridLayout(0,2));
        panel.setBackground(Color.white);

//Add components to panel columns
//going left to right and top to bottom
        getContentPane().add(panel);
        panel.add(col1);
        panel.add(col2);
        panel.add(applechk);
        panel.add(appleqnt);
        panel.add(peachchk);
        panel.add(peachqnt);
        panel.add(pearchk);
        panel.add(pearqnt);
```

```
      panel.add(totalItems);
      panel.add(items);
      panel.add(totalCost);
      panel.add(cost);
      panel.add(cardNum);
      panel.add(creditCard);
      panel.add(custID);
      panel.add(customer);
      panel.add(reset);
      panel.add(purchase);
   } //End Constructor

   public void actionPerformed(ActionEvent event) {
    Object source = event.getSource();
    Integer applesNo, peachesNo, pearsNo, num;
    Double cost;
    String text, text2;
    DataOrder order = new DataOrder();

//If Purchase button pressed  . . .
    if (source == purchase) {
//Get data from text fields
      order.cardnum = creditCard.getText();
      order.custID = customer.getText();
      order.apples = appleqnt.getText();
      order.peaches = peachqnt.getText();
      order.pears = pearqnt.getText();

//Calculate total items
      if (order.apples.length() > 0) {
//Catch invalid number error
         try {
           applesNo = Integer.valueOf(order.apples);
           order.itotal += applesNo.intValue();
         } catch (java.lang.NumberFormatException e) {
           appleqnt.setText(messages.getString("invalid"));
         }
      } else {
         /* else no need to change the total */
      }
      if(order.peaches.length() > 0){

//Catch invalid number error
         try {
           peachesNo = Integer.valueOf(order.peaches);
           order.itotal += peachesNo.intValue();
         } catch(java.lang.NumberFormatException e) {
           peachqnt.setText(messages.getString("invalid"));
```

```
            }
          } else {
            /* else no need to change the total */
          }
          if(order.pears.length() > 0){

//Catch invalid number error
            try {
              pearsNo = Integer.valueOf(order.pears);
              order.itotal += pearsNo.intValue();
            } catch (java.lang.NumberFormatException e) {
              pearqnt.setText(messages.getString("invalid"));
            }
          } else {
            /* else no need to change the total */
          }

//Create number formatter
            numFormat = NumberFormat.getNumberInstance(
              currentLocale);
//Display running total
            text = numFormat.format(order.itotal);
            this.items.setText(text);
//Calculate and display running cost
            order.icost = (order.itotal * 1.25);
            text2 = numFormat.format(order.icost);
            this.cost.setText(text2);
            try {
              send.sendOrder(order);
            } catch (java.rmi.RemoteException e) {
              System.out.println(messages.getString("send"));
            } catch (java.io.IOException e) {
              System.out.println("Unable to write to file");
            }
          }
//If Reset button pressed
//Clear all fields
        if (source == reset) {
          creditCard.setText("");
          appleqnt.setText("");
          peachqnt.setText("");
          pearqnt.setText("");
          creditCard.setText("");
          customer.setText("");
          order.icost = 0;
          cost = new Double(order.icost);
          text2 = cost.toString();
          this.cost.setText(text2);
```

```
      order.itotal = 0;
      num = new Integer(order.itotal);
      text = num.toString();
      this.items.setText(text);
    }
  }

  public static void main(String[] args) {
    if (args.length != 3) {
      language = new String("en");
      country = new String ("US");
      System.out.println("English");
    } else {
      language = new String(args[1]);
      country = new String(args[2]);
      System.out.println(language + country);
    }
    currentLocale = new Locale(language, country);
                  messages = ResourceBundle.getBundle(
                  "client1" + File.separatorChar +
                  "MessagesBundle", currentLocale);
    WindowListener l = new WindowAdapter() {
      public void windowClosing(WindowEvent e) {
        System.exit(0);
      }
    };

  RMIClient1 frame = new RMIClient1();
    frame.addWindowListener(l);
    frame.pack();
    frame.setVisible(true);
    if(System.getSecurityManager() == null) {
      System.setSecurityManager(new RMISecurityManager());
    }

    try {
      String name = "//" + args[0] + "/Send";
      send = ((Send) Naming.lookup(name));
    } catch (java.rmi.NotBoundException e) {
      System.out.println(messages.getString("nolookup"));
    } catch (java.rmi.RemoteException e) {
      System.out.println(messages.getString("nolookup"));
    } catch (java.net.MalformedURLException e) {
      System.out.println(messages.getString("nolookup"));
    }
  }
}
```

Application Code:
RMIClient2

```java
//package statement
package client2;

import java.awt.Color;
import java.awt.GridLayout;
import java.awt.event.*;
import javax.swing.*;
import java.io.*;
import java.net.*;
import java.rmi.*;
import java.rmi.server.*;
import java.io.FileInputStream.*;
import java.io.RandomAccessFile.*;
import java.io.File;
import java.util.*;
import java.text.*;
import server.*;

class RMIClient2 extends JFrame implements ActionListener {
   private JLabel creditCard, custID, apples, peaches, pears,
total, cost, clicked;
   private JButton view, reset;
   private JPanel panel;
   private JTextArea creditNo, customerNo, applesNo,
peachesNo, pearsNo, itotal, icost;
   private static Send send;
   private String customer;
   private Set s = new HashSet();
   private static RMIClient2 frame;

//Internationalization variables
   private static Locale currentLocale;
   private static ResourceBundle messages;
   private static String language, country;
   private NumberFormat numFormat;
   private RMIClient2(){ //Begin Constructor
   setTitle(messages.getString("title"));

//Create labels
       creditCard = new JLabel(messages.getString("card"));
       custID = new JLabel(messages.getString("customer"));
       apples = new JLabel(messages.getString("apples"));
       peaches = new JLabel(messages.getString("peaches"));
       pears = new JLabel(messages.getString("pears"));
       total = new JLabel(messages.getString("items"));
```

```java
        cost = new JLabel(messages.getString("cost"));

//Create text areas
    creditNo = new JTextArea();
    customerNo = new JTextArea();
    applesNo = new JTextArea();
    peachesNo = new JTextArea();
    pearsNo = new JTextArea();
    itotal = new JTextArea();
    icost = new JTextArea();

//Create buttons
    view = new JButton(messages.getString("view"));
    view.addActionListener(this);
    reset = new JButton(messages.getString("reset"));
    reset.addActionListener(this);

//Create panel for 2-column layout
//Set white background color
    panel = new JPanel();
    panel.setLayout(new GridLayout(0,2));
    panel.setBackground(Color.white);

//Add components to panel columns
//going left to right and top to bottom
    getContentPane().add(panel);
    panel.add(creditCard);
    panel.add(creditNo);
    panel.add(custID);
    panel.add(customerNo);
    panel.add(apples);
    panel.add(applesNo);
    panel.add(peaches);
    panel.add(peachesNo);
    panel.add(pears);
    panel.add(pearsNo);
    panel.add(total);
    panel.add(itotal);
    panel.add(cost);
    panel.add(icost);
    panel.add(view);
    panel.add(reset);
  } //End Constructor

//Create list of customer IDs
 public void addCustomer(String custID) {
   s.add(custID);
   System.out.println("Customer ID added");
```

```
      }
  //Get customer IDs
    public void getData() {
      if (s.size()!=0) {
        Iterator it = s.iterator();
        while (it.hasNext()) {
          System.out.println(it.next());
        }
        System.out.println(s);
        JOptionPane.showMessageDialog(frame, s.toString(),
                    "Customer List", JOptionPane.PLAIN_MESSAGE);
      } else {
        System.out.println("No customer IDs available");
      }
    }
    public void actionPerformed(ActionEvent event) {
      Object source = event.getSource();
      String unit, i;
      double cost;
      Double price;
      int items;
      Integer itms;
      DataOrder order = new DataOrder();

//If View button pressed
//Get data from server and display it
      if (source == view) {
        try {
          order = send.getOrder();
          creditNo.setText(order.cardnum);
          customerNo.setText(order.custID);

//Add customerID to list
          addCustomer(order.custID);
          applesNo.setText(order.apples);
          peachesNo.setText(order.peaches);
          pearsNo.setText(order.pears);

//Create number formatter
          numFormat = NumberFormat.getNumberInstance(current-
Locale);
          price = new Double(order.icost);
          unit = numFormat.format(price);
          icost.setText(unit);
          itms = new Integer(order.itotal);
          i = numFormat.format(order.itotal);
          itotal.setText(i);
        } catch (java.rmi.RemoteException e) {
```

```
                JOptionPane.showMessageDialog(frame,
                  "Cannot get data from server", "Error",
                    JOptionPane.ERROR_MESSAGE);
              } catch (java.io.IOException e) {
                System.out.println("Unable to write to file");
              }
          //Display Customer IDs
            getData();
      }

//If Reset button pressed
//Clear all fields
        if (source == reset) {
          creditNo.setText("");
          customerNo.setText("");
          applesNo.setText("");
          peachesNo.setText("");
          pearsNo.setText("");
          itotal.setText("");
        icost.setText("");
        }
      }

    public static void main(String[] args) {
      if (args.length != 3) {
        language = new String("en");
        country = new String ("US");
        System.out.println("English");
      } else {
        language = new String(args[1]);
        country = new String(args[2]);
        System.out.println(language + country);
      }

      currentLocale = new Locale(language, country);
      messages = ResourceBundle.getBundle(
                 "client2" + File.separatorChar +
                 "MessagesBundle", currentLocale);
      WindowListener l = new WindowAdapter() {
        public void windowClosing(WindowEvent e) {
          System.exit(0);
        }
      };

      frame = new RMIClient2();
      frame.addWindowListener(l);
      frame.pack();
      frame.setVisible(true);
      if (System.getSecurityManager() == null) {
```

```
        System.setSecurityManager(new RMISecurityManager());
    }

    try {
      String name = "//" + args[0] + "/Send";
      send = ((Send) Naming.lookup(name));
    } catch (java.rmi.NotBoundException e) {
      System.out.println(messages.getString("nolookup"));
    } catch (java.rmi.RemoteException e) {
      System.out.println(messages.getString("nolookup"));
    } catch (java.net.MalformedURLException e) {
      System.out.println(messages.getString("nolookup"));
    }
  }
}
```

Application Code: DataOrder

```
//package statement
package server;

import java.io.*;

public class DataOrder implements Serializable {
  public String apples, peaches, pears, custID, cardnum;
  public double icost;
  public int itotal;
}
```

Application Code: Send

```
//package statement
package server;

import java.rmi.Remote;
import java.rmi.RemoteException;

public interface Send extends Remote {
  public void sendOrder(DataOrder order)
            throws RemoteException, java.io.IOException;
  public DataOrder getOrder()
            throws RemoteException, java.io.IOException;
}
```

Application Code:
RemoteServer

```
//package statement
package server;

import java.awt.event.*;
import java.io.*;
import java.net.*;
import java.rmi.*;
import java.rmi.server.*;

class RemoteServer extends UnicastRemoteObject implements
Send {
  Integer num = null;
  int value = 0, get = 0;
  ObjectOutputStream oos = null;

  public RemoteServer() throws RemoteException {
    super();
  }

  public synchronized void sendOrder(DataOrder order) throws
java.io.IOException{
    value += 1;
    String orders = String.valueOf(value);
    try {
      FileOutputStream fos = new FileOutputStream(orders);
      oos = new ObjectOutputStream(fos);
      oos.writeObject(order);
    } catch (java.io.FileNotFoundException e) {
      System.out.println("File not found");
    } finally {
      if (oos != null) {
        oos.close();
      }
    }
  }

  public synchronized DataOrder getOrder() throws
java.io.IOException{
    DataOrder order = null;
    ObjectInputStream ois = null;

    if (value == 0) {
      System.out.println("No Orders To Process");
    }
    if (value > get) {
```

```
        get += 1;
        String orders = String.valueOf(get);
        try {
          FileInputStream fis = new FileInputStream(orders);
          ois = new ObjectInputStream(fis);
          order = (DataOrder)ois.readObject();
        } catch (java.io.FileNotFoundException e) {
          System.out.println("File not found");
        } catch (java.io.IOException e) {
          System.out.println("Unable to read file");
        } catch (java.lang.ClassNotFoundException e) {
          System.out.println("No data available");
        } finally {
          if (oos != null) {
            oos.close();
          }
        }
      } else {
        System.out.println("No Orders To Process");
      }
    return order;
  }

  public static void main(String[] args) {
    if (System.getSecurityManager() == null) {
      System.setSecurityManager(new RMISecurityManager());
    }
    String name = "G"//kq6py.eng.sun.com/Send";
    try {
      Send remoteServer = new RemoteServer();
      Naming.rebind(name, remoteServer);
      System.out.println("RemoteServer bound");
    } catch (java.rmi.RemoteException e) {
      System.out.println("Cannot create remote server
object");
    } catch (java.net.MalformedURLException e) {
      System.out.println("Cannot look up server object");
    }
  }
}
```

Application Code:
RMIFrenchApp

```
import java.awt.Color;
import java.awt.GridLayout;
import java.awt.event.*;
import javax.swing.*;
```

```
import java.io.*;
import java.net.*;
import java.rmi.*;
import java.rmi.server.*;
import java.util.*;
import java.text.*;
import java.applet.Applet;

//Make public
public class RMIFrenchApp extends Applet implements Action-
Listener {
   JLabel col1, col2;
   JLabel totalItems, totalCost;
   JLabel cardNum, custID;
   JLabel applechk, pearchk, peachchk;
   JButton purchase, reset;
   JTextField appleqnt, pearqnt, peachqnt;
   JTextField creditCard, customer;
   JTextArea items, cost;
   static Send send;

//Internationalization variables
   Locale currentLocale;
   ResourceBundle messages;
   static String language, country;
   NumberFormat numFormat;
   public void init(){
   language = new String("fr");
   country = new String ("FR");
   if (System.getSecurityManager() == null) {
      System.setSecurityManager(new RMISecurityManager());
    }
    currentLocale = new Locale(language, country);
    messages = ResourceBundle.getBundle("MessagesBundle",
currentLocale);
    Locale test = messages.getLocale();
    try {

//Path to host where remote Send object is running
       String name = "//kq6py.eng.sun.com/Send";
       send = ((Send) Naming.lookup(name));
     } catch (java.rmi.NotBoundException e) {
       System.out.println(messages.getString("nolookup"));
     } catch (java.rmi.RemoteException e) {
       System.out.println(messages.getString("nolookup"));
     } catch (java.net.MalformedURLException e) {
       System.out.println(messages.getString("nolookup"));
     }
```

```
//Create left and right column labels
    col1 = new JLabel(messages.getString("1col"));
    col2 = new JLabel(messages.getString("2col"));

//Create labels and text field components
    applechk = new JLabel("   " +
      messages.getString("apples"));
    appleqnt = new JTextField();
    appleqnt.addActionListener(this);
    pearchk = new JLabel("   " +
      messages.getString("pears"));
    pearqnt = new JTextField();
    pearqnt.addActionListener(this);
    peachchk = new JLabel("   " +
      messages.getString("peaches"));
    peachqnt = new JTextField();
    peachqnt.addActionListener(this);
    cardNum = new JLabel("   " +
      messages.getString("card"));
    creditCard = new JTextField();
    pearqnt.setNextFocusableComponent(creditCard);
    customer = new JTextField();
    custID = new JLabel("   " +
      messages.getString("customer"));

//Create labels and text area components
    totalItems = new JLabel("   "
      + messages.getString("items"));
    totalCost = new JLabel("   "
      + messages.getString("cost"));
    items = new JTextArea();
    cost = new JTextArea();

//Create buttons and make action listeners
    purchase = new JButton(messages.getString("purchase"));
    purchase.addActionListener(this);
    reset = new JButton(messages.getString("reset"));
    reset.addActionListener(this);

//Set panel layout to 2-column grid
//on a white background
    setLayout(new GridLayout(0,2));
    setBackground(Color.white);

//Add components to panel columns
//going left to right and top to bottom
    add(col1);
    add(col2);
```

```
            add(applechk);
            add(appleqnt);
            add(peachchk);
            add(peachqnt);
            add(pearchk);
            add(pearqnt);
            add(totalItems);
            add(items);
            add(totalCost);
            add(cost);
            add(cardNum);
            add(creditCard);
            add(custID);
            add(customer);
            add(reset);
            add(purchase);
        } //End Constructor

    public void actionPerformed(ActionEvent event) {
        Object source = event.getSource();
        Integer applesNo, peachesNo, pearsNo, num;
        Double cost;
        String text, text2;
        DataOrder order = new DataOrder();

//If Purchase button pressed  . . .
        if (source == purchase) {
//Get data from text fields
            order.cardnum = creditCard.getText();
            order.custID = customer.getText();
            order.apples = appleqnt.getText();
            order.peaches = peachqnt.getText();
            order.pears = pearqnt.getText();

//Calculate total items
        if (order.apples.length() > 0){
//Catch invalid number error
            try {
                applesNo = Integer.valueOf(order.apples);
                order.itotal += applesNo.intValue();
            } catch (java.lang.NumberFormatException e) {
                appleqnt.setText(messages.getString("invalid"));
            }
        } else {
            /* else no need to change the total */
        }

        if (order.peaches.length() > 0) {
```

```java
//Catch invalid number error
    try
      peachesNo = Integer.valueOf(order.peaches);
      order.itotal += peachesNo.intValue();
    } catch (java.lang.NumberFormatException e) {
      peachqnt.setText(messages.getString("invalid"));
    }
  } else {
    /* else no need to change the total */
  }

  if (order.pears.length() > 0) {
//Catch invalid number error
    try{
      pearsNo = Integer.valueOf(order.pears);
      order.itotal += pearsNo.intValue();
    } catch(java.lang.NumberFormatException e) {
      pearqnt.setText(messages.getString("invalid"));
    }
  } else {
    /* else no need to change the total */
  }

//Create number formatter
    numFormat = NumberFormat.getNumberInstance(
      currentLocale);
//Display running total
    text = numFormat.format(order.itotal);
    this.items.setText(text);
//Calculate and display running cost
    order.icost = (order.itotal * 1.25);
    text2 = numFormat.format(order.icost);
    this.cost.setText(text2);
    try {
      send.sendOrder(order);
    } catch (java.rmi.RemoteException e) {
      System.out.println(messages.getString("send"));
    }catch (java.io.IOException e) {
      System.out.println("Unable to write to file");
    }
  }

//If Reset button pressed
//Clear all fields
  if (source == reset) {
    creditCard.setText("");
    appleqnt.setText("");
    peachqnt.setText("");
```

```
            peargnt.setText("");
            creditCard.setText("");
            customer.setText("");
            order.icost = 0;
            cost = new Double(order.icost);
            text2 = cost.toString();
            this.cost.setText(text2);
            order.itotal = 0;
            num = new Integer(order.itotal);
            text = num.toString();
            this.items.setText(text);
        }
    }
}
```

Application Code: RMIGermanApp

```
    import java.awt.Color;
    import java.awt.GridLayout;
    import java.awt.event.*;
    import javax.swing.*;
    import java.io.*;
    import java.net.*;
    import java.rmi.*;
    import java.rmi.server.*;
    import java.util.*;
    import java.text.*;
    import java.applet.Applet;

    //Make public
    public class RMIGermanApp extends Applet
      implements ActionListener {
        JLabel col1, col2;
        JLabel totalItems, totalCost;
        JLabel cardNum, custID;
        JLabel applechk, pearchk, peachchk;
        JButton purchase, reset;
        JTextField applegnt, peargnt, peachgnt;
        JTextField creditCard, customer;
        JTextArea items, cost;
        static Send send;

    //Internationalization variables
        Locale currentLocale;
        ResourceBundle messages;
        static String language, country;
        NumberFormat numFormat;
        public void init(){
```

```java
        language = new String("de");
        country = new String ("DE");
        if (System.getSecurityManager() == null) {
          System.setSecurityManager(new RMISecurityManager());
        }
        currentLocale = new Locale(language, country);
        messages = ResourceBundle.getBundle("MessagesBundle",
                                            currentLocale);
        Locale test = messages.getLocale();
        try {

//Path to host where remote Send object is running
        String name = "//kq6py.eng.sun.com/Send";
        send = ((Send) Naming.lookup(name));
        } catch (java.rmi.NotBoundException e) {
          System.out.println(messages.getString("nolookup"));
        } catch java.rmi.RemoteException e) {
          System.out.println(messages.getString("nolookup"));
        } catch (java.net.MalformedURLException e) {
          System.out.println(messages.getString("nolookup"));
        }

//Create left and right column labels
        col1 = new JLabel(messages.getString("1col"));
        col2 = new JLabel(messages.getString("2col"));

//Create labels and text field components
        applechk = new JLabel("    " +
          messages.getString("apples"));
        appleqnt = new JTextField();
        appleqnt.addActionListener(this);
        pearchk = new JLabel("    " +
          messages.getString("pears"));
        pearqnt = new JTextField();
        pearqnt.addActionListener(this);
        peachchk = new JLabel("    " +
          messages.getString("peaches"));
        peachqnt = new JTextField();
        peachqnt.addActionListener(this);
        cardNum = new JLabel("    " +
          messages.getString("card"));
        creditCard = new JTextField();
        pearqnt.setNextFocusableComponent(creditCard);
        customer = new JTextField();
        custID = new JLabel("   " + messages.getString("customer"));

//Create labels and text area components
        totalItems = new JLabel("    " +
          messages.getString("items"));
```

```java
        totalCost = new JLabel("    " +
          messages.getString("cost"));
        items = new JTextArea();
        cost = new JTextArea();

//Create buttons and make action listeners
        purchase = new JButton(messages.getString("purchase"));
        purchase.addActionListener(this);
        reset = new JButton(messages.getString("reset"));
        reset.addActionListener(this);

//Set panel layout to 2-column grid
//on a white background
        setLayout(new GridLayout(0,2));
        setBackground(Color.white);

//Add components to panel columns
//going left to right and top to bottom
        add(col1);
        add(col2);
        add(applechk);
        add(appleqnt);
        add(peachchk);
        add(peachqnt);
        add(pearchk);
        add(pearqnt);
        add(totalItems);
        add(items);
        add(totalCost);
        add(cost);
        add(cardNum);
        add(creditCard);
        add(custID);
        add(customer);
        add(reset);
        add(purchase);
    } //End Constructor

  public void actionPerformed(ActionEvent event) {
    Object source = event.getSource();
    Integer applesNo, peachesNo, pearsNo, num;
    Double cost;
    String text, text2;
    DataOrder order = new DataOrder();

//If Purchase button pressed  . . .
    if (source == purchase) {
//Get data from text fields
```

```
      order.cardnum = creditCard.getText();
      order.custID = customer.getText();
      order.apples = appleqnt.getText();
      order.peaches = peachqnt.getText();
      order.pears = pearqnt.getText();

//Calculate total items
    if (order.apples.length() > 0) {
//Catch invalid number error
       try {
         applesNo = Integer.valueOf(order.apples);
         order.itotal += applesNo.intValue();
       } catch (java.lang.NumberFormatException e) {
         appleqnt.setText(messages.getString("invalid"));
       }
    } else {
       /* else no need to change the total */
    }

    if (order.peaches.length() > 0) {
//Catch invalid number error
       try {
         peachesNo = Integer.valueOf(order.peaches);
         order.itotal += peachesNo.intValue();
       } catch (java.lang.NumberFormatException e){
         peachqnt.setText(messages.getString("invalid"));
       }
    } else {
       /* else no need to change the total */
    }

    if (order.pears.length() > 0) {
//Catch invalid number error
       try {
         pearsNo = Integer.valueOf(order.pears);
         order.itotal += pearsNo.intValue();
       } catch (java.lang.NumberFormatException e) {
         pearqnt.setText(messages.getString("invalid"));
       }
    } else {
       /* else no need to change the total */
    }

//Create number formatter
    numFormat = NumberFormat.getNumberInstance(
       currentLocale);
//Display running total
    text = numFormat.format(order.itotal);
```

```
        this.items.setText(text);
//Calculate and display running cost
        order.icost = (order.itotal * 1.25);
        text2 = numFormat.format(order.icost);
        this.cost.setText(text2);
        try{
           send.sendOrder(order);
         }catch (java.rmi.RemoteException e) {
          System.out.println(messages.getString("send"));
         }catch (java.io.IOException e) {
          System.out.println("Unable to write to file");
         }
      }

//If Reset button pressed
//Clear all fields
       if source == reset) {
       creditCard.setText("");
       appleqnt.setText("");
       peachqnt.setText("");
       pearqnt.setText("");
       creditCard.setText("");
       customer.setText("");
       order.icost = 0;
       cost = new Double(order.icost);
       text2 = cost.toString();
       this.cost.setText(text2);
       order.itotal = 0;
       num = new Integer(order.itotal);
       text = num.toString();
       this.items.setText(text);
      }
    }
  }
```

Application Code: RMIEnglishApp

```
import java.awt.Color;
import java.awt.GridLayout;
import java.awt.event.*;
import javax.swing.*;
import java.io.*;
import java.net.*;
import java.rmi.*;
import java.rmi.server.*;
import java.util.*;
import java.text.*;
import java.applet.Applet;
```

```java
      //Make public
      public class RMIEnglishApp extends Applet
        implements ActionListener {
        JLabel col1, col2;
        JLabel totalItems, totalCost;
        JLabel cardNum, custID;
        JLabel applechk, pearchk, peachchk;
        JButton purchase, reset;
        JTextField appleqnt, pearqnt, peachqnt;
        JTextField creditCard, customer;
        JTextArea items, cost;
        static Send send;

    //Internationalization variables
        Locale currentLocale;
        ResourceBundle messages;
        static String language, country;
        NumberFormat numFormat;

        public void init() {
         language = new String("en");
         country = new String ("US");
         if (System.getSecurityManager() == null) {
           System.setSecurityManager(new RMISecurityManager());
         }
         currentLocale = new Locale(language, country);
         messages = ResourceBundle.getBundle(
           "MessagesBundle", currentLocale);
         Locale test = messages.getLocale();
         try {

    //Path to host where remote Send object is running
             String name = "//kq6py.eng.sun.com/Send";
             send = ((Send) Naming.lookup(name));
           } catch (java.rmi.NotBoundException e) {
             System.out.println(messages.getString("nolookup"));
           } catch (java.rmi.RemoteException e) {
             System.out.println(messages.getString("nolookup"));
           } catch(java.net.MalformedURLException e) {
             System.out.println(messages.getString("nolookup"));
           }

    //Create left and right column labels
           col1 = new JLabel(messages.getString("1col"));
           col2 = new JLabel(messages.getString("2col"));

    //Create labels and text field components
           applechk = new JLabel("    " +
             messages.getString("apples"));
           appleqnt = new JTextField();
```

```
        appleqnt.addActionListener(this);
        pearchk = new JLabel("    " +
          messages.getString("pears"));
        pearqnt = new JTextField();
        pearqnt.addActionListener(this);
        peachchk = new JLabel("    " +
          messages.getString("peaches"));
        peachqnt = new JTextField();
        peachqnt.addActionListener(this);
        cardNum = new JLabel("    " +
          messages.getString("card"));
        creditCard = new JTextField();
        pearqnt.setNextFocusableComponent(creditCard);
        customer = new JTextField();
        custID = new JLabel("    " +
          messages.getString("customer"));

//Create labels and text area components
        totalItems = new JLabel("    " +
          messages.getString("items"));
        totalCost = new JLabel("    " +
          messages.getString("cost"));
        items = new JTextArea();
        cost = new JTextArea();

//Create buttons and make action listeners
        purchase = new JButton(messages.getString("purchase"));
        purchase.addActionListener(this);
        reset = new JButton(messages.getString("reset"));
        reset.addActionListener(this);

//Set panel layout to 2-column grid
//on a white background
        setLayout(new GridLayout(0,2));
        setBackground(Color.white);

//Add components to panel columns
//going left to right and top to bottom
        add(col1);
        add(col2);
        add(applechk);
        add(appleqnt);
        add(peachchk);
        add(peachqnt);
        add(pearchk);
        add(pearqnt);
        add(totalItems);
        add(items);
```

```
              add(totalCost);
              add(cost);
              add(cardNum);
              add(creditCard);
              add(custID);
              add(customer);
              add(reset);
              add(purchase);
        } //End Constructor

      public void actionPerformed(ActionEvent event) {
        Object source = event.getSource();
        Integer applesNo, peachesNo, pearsNo, num;
        Double cost;
        String text, text2;
        DataOrder order = new DataOrder();
  //If Purchase button pressed  . . .
        if(source == purchase){
  //Get data from text fields
          order.cardnum = creditCard.getText();
          order.custID = customer.getText();
          order.apples = appleqnt.getText();
          order.peaches = peachqnt.getText();
          order.pears = pearqnt.getText();
  //Calculate total items
          if(order.apples.length() > 0){
  //Catch invalid number error
            try {
              applesNo = Integer.valueOf(order.apples);
              order.itotal += applesNo.intValue();
            } catch (java.lang.NumberFormatException e) {
              appleqnt.setText(messages.getString("invalid"));
            }
          } else {
            /* else no need to change the total */
          }
          if(order.peaches.length() > 0){
  //Catch invalid number error
            try{
              peachesNo = Integer.valueOf(order.peaches);
              order.itotal += peachesNo.intValue();
            } catch(java.lang.NumberFormatException e) {
              peachqnt.setText(messages.getString("invalid"));
            }
          } else {
            /* else no need to change the total */
          }
          if (order.pears.length() > 0) {
```

```
//Catch invalid number error
     try {
        pearsNo = Integer.valueOf(order.pears);
        order.itotal += pearsNo.intValue();
     } catch(java.lang.NumberFormatException e) {
        pearqnt.setText(messages.getString("invalid"));
     }
   } else {
     /* else no need to change the total */
   }
//Create number formatter
     numFormat = NumberFormat.getNumberInstance(
        currentLocale);
//Display running total
     text = numFormat.format(order.itotal);
     this.items.setText(text);
//Calculate and display running cost
     order.icost = (order.itotal * 1.25);
     text2 = numFormat.format(order.icost);
     this.cost.setText(text2);
     try {
        send.sendOrder(order);
     } catch (java.rmi.RemoteException e) {
         System.out.println(messages.getString("send"));
     }catch (java.io.IOException e) {
      System.out.println("Unable to write to file");
     }
 }

//If Reset button pressed
//Clear all fields
   if (source == reset) {
     creditCard.setText("");
     appleqnt.setText("");
     peachqnt.setText("");
     pearqnt.setText("");
     creditCard.setText("");
     customer.setText("");
     order.icost = 0;
     cost = new Double(order.icost);
     text2 = cost.toString();
     this.cost.setText(text2);
     order.itotal = 0;
     num = new Integer(order.itotal);
     text = num.toString();
     this.items.setText(text);
   }
 }
}
```

Cryptography Example

Following are the RMIClient1 and RMIClient2 programs from Appendix A, Cryptography (page 217), in their entirety:

- Sealing the Symmetric Key: RMIClient1 Program
- Sealing the Symmetric Key: RMIClient2 Program
- Encrypting the Symmetric Key with the RSA Algorithm: RMIClient1 Program
- Encrypting the Symmetric Key with the RSA Algorithm: RMIClient2 Program

Sealing the Symmetric Key: RMIClient1 Program

```java
import java.awt.Color;
import java.awt.GridLayout;
import java.awt.event.*;
import javax.swing.*;
import java.io.*;
import java.net.*;
import java.rmi.*;
import java.rmi.server.*;
import javax.crypto.*;
import java.security.*;
import java.security.interfaces.*;

class RMIClient1 extends JFrame implements ActionListener {
    JLabel col1, col2;
    JLabel totalItems, totalCost;
    JLabel cardNum, custID;
    JLabel applechk, pearchk, peachchk;

    JButton purchase, reset;
    JPanel panel;
    JTextField appleqnt, pearqnt, peachqnt;
    JTextField creditCard, customer;
    JTextArea items, cost;
    static Send send;
    int itotal=0;
    double icost=0;

    RMIClient1() { //Begin Constructor
//Create left and right column labels
        col1 = new JLabel("Select Items");
        col2 = new JLabel("Specify Quantity");
```

```
//Create labels and text field components
    applechk = new JLabel("   Apples");
    appleqnt = new JTextField();
    appleqnt.addActionListener(this);
    pearchk = new JLabel("   Pears");
    pearqnt = new JTextField();
    pearqnt.addActionListener(this);
    peachchk = new JLabel("   Peaches");
    peachqnt = new JTextField();
    peachqnt.addActionListener(this);
    cardNum = new JLabel("   Credit Card:");
    creditCard = new JTextField();
    pearqnt.setNextFocusableComponent(creditCard);
    customer = new JTextField();
    custID = new JLabel("   Customer ID:");

//Create labels and text area components
    totalItems = new JLabel("Total Items:");
    totalCost = new JLabel("Total Cost:");
    items = new JTextArea();
    cost = new JTextArea();

//Create buttons and make action listeners
    purchase = new JButton("Purchase");
    purchase.addActionListener(this);
    reset = new JButton("Reset");
    reset.addActionListener(this);
    creditCard.setNextFocusableComponent(reset);

//Create a panel for the components
    panel = new JPanel();

//Set panel layout to 2-column grid
//on a white background
    panel.setLayout(new GridLayout(0,2));
    panel.setBackground(Color.white);

//Add components to panel columns
//going left to right and top to bottom
    getContentPane().add(panel);
    panel.add(col1);
    panel.add(col2);
    panel.add(applechk);
    panel.add(appleqnt);
    panel.add(peachchk);
    panel.add(peachqnt);
    panel.add(pearchk);
```

```
        panel.add(pearqnt);
        panel.add(totalItems);
        panel.add(items);
        panel.add(totalCost);
        panel.add(cost);
        panel.add(cardNum);
        panel.add(creditCard);
        panel.add(custID);
        panel.add(customer);
        panel.add(reset);
        panel.add(purchase);
    } //End Constructor

  private void encrypt(String cardnum) {
    Cipher c=null, c2=null;
    KeyGenerator keyGen;
    SecretKey secretKey=null;
    PublicKey pubKey=null;
    SealedObject sealed=null;
    byte[] encrypted=null;
    String s="text";

//Create Cipher for symmetric key encryption (DES)
//Create a key generator
//Create a secret (session) key with key generator
    try{
      c = Cipher.getInstance("DES/ECB/PKCS5Padding");
      keyGen = KeyGenerator.getInstance("DES");
      keyGen.init(new SecureRandom());
      secretKey=keyGen.generateKey();
    } catch (java.security.NoSuchAlgorithmException e) {
      System.out.println("No such algorithm");
    } catch(javax.crypto.NoSuchPaddingException e){
      System.out.println("No such padding");
    }

//Initialize Cipher for encryption with session key
//Encrypt credit card number with Cipher
    try {
      c.init(Cipher.ENCRYPT_MODE, secretKey);
      encrypted=c.doFinal(s.getBytes());
      System.out.println("Cipher Text:");
      System.out.println(new String(encrypted));
      System.out.println();
    } catch (java.security.InvalidKeyException e) {
      System.out.println("Invalid Key");
    } catch (javax.crypto.IllegalBlockSizeException e) {
      System.out.println("Illegal block size");
```

```java
      } catch (javax.crypto.BadPaddingException e) {
        System.out.println("Bad Padding");
      }

//Get public key from server
    try{
        pubKey = (PublicKey)send.getPublicKey();
      } catch (java.rmi.RemoteException e) {
        System.out.println("Key not available");
      }

//Create Cipher for asymmetric encryption (Not RSA)
//Initialize Cipher for encryption with session key
    try {
        c2 = Cipher.getInstance("some asymmetric cipher");
        c2.init(Cipher.ENCRYPT_MODE, pubKey);
      } catch (java.security.NoSuchAlgorithmException e) {
        System.out.println("No such algorithm");
      } catch (javax.crypto.NoSuchPaddingException e) {
        System.out.println("No such padding");
      } catch (java.security.InvalidKeyException e) {
        System.out.println("Invalid key");
      }

//Seal session key in SealedObject using asymmetric Cipher
    try {
        sealed = new SealedObject(secretKey, c2);
      } catch (javax.crypto.IllegalBlockSizeException  e){
       System.out.println("Illegal block size");
      } catch (java.io.IOException e) {
        System.out.println("Unable to seal session key");
      }


//Send encrypted message and
//sealed session key to server
    try {
      send.sendKey(sealed);
      send.sendEncrypted(encrypted);
      } catch (java.rmi.RemoteException e) {
       System.out.println("Unable to send key");
     }
  }

public void actionPerformed(ActionEvent event) {
    Object source = event.getSource();
    Integer applesNo, peachesNo, pearsNo, num;
    Double cost;
```

```
    String number, cardnum, custID, apples, peaches, pears,
text, text2;

//If Purchase button pressed
   if (source == purchase) {
//Get data from text fields
    cardnum = creditCard.getText();
    custID = customer.getText();
    apples = appleqnt.getText();
    peaches = peachqnt.getText();
    pears = pearqnt.getText();

//Calculate total items
    if (apples.length() > 0) {
//Catch invalid number error
       try {
         applesNo = Integer.valueOf(apples);
         itotal += applesNo.intValue();
       } catch (java.lang.NumberFormatException e) {
         appleqnt.setText("Invalid Value");
       }
    } else {
       /* else no need to change the total */
    }
    if(peaches.length() > 0){

//Catch invalid number error
       try {
         peachesNo = Integer.valueOf(peaches);
         itotal += peachesNo.intValue();
       } catch(java.lang.NumberFormatException e) {
         peachqnt.setText("Invalid Value");
       }
    } else {
       /* else no need to change the total */
    }
    if (pears.length() > 0) {

//Catch invalid number error
       try {
         pearsNo = Integer.valueOf(pears);
         itotal += pearsNo.intValue();
       } catch(java.lang.NumberFormatException e) {
         pearqnt.setText("Invalid Value");
       }
    } else {
       /* else no need to change the total */
    }
```

```
//Display running total
    num = new Integer(itotal);
    text = num.toString();
    this.items.setText(text);

//Calculate and display running cost
    icost = (itotal * 1.25);
    cost = new Double(icost);
    text2 = cost.toString();
    this.cost.setText(text2);

//Encrypt credit card number
    encrypt(cardnum);

//Send data over net
    try {
      send.sendCustID(custID);
      send.sendAppleQnt(apples);
      send.sendPeachQnt(peaches);
      send.sendPearQnt(pears);
      send.sendTotalCost(icost);
      send.sendTotalItems(itotal);
    } catch (java.rmi.RemoteException e) {
      System.out.println("sendData exception:
        " + e.getMessage());
    }
  }

//If Reset button pressed
//Clear all fields
    if (source == reset) {
    creditCard.setText("");
    appleqnt.setText("");
    peachqnt.setText("");
    pearqnt.setText("");
    creditCard.setText("");
    customer.setText("");
    icost = 0;
    cost = new Double(icost);
    text2 = cost.toString();
    this.cost.setText(text2);
    itotal = 0;
    num = new Integer(itotal);
    text = num.toString();
    this.items.setText(text);
  }
  }
```

```
      public static void main(String[] args) {
        try {
          UIManager.setLookAndFeel(
            UIManager.getCrossPlatformLookAndFeelClassName());
        } catch (Exception e) {
          System.out.println("Couldn't use the cross-platform"
            + "look and feel: " + e);
        }

        RMIClient1 frame = new RMIClient1();
        frame.setTitle("Fruit $1.25 Each");
        WindowListener l = new WindowAdapter() {
          public void windowClosing(WindowEvent e) {
            System.exit(0);
          }
        };
        frame.addWindowListener(l);
        frame.pack();
        frame.setVisible(true);
        if(System.getSecurityManager() == null) {
          System.setSecurityManager(new RMISecurityManager());
        }

        try {
          String name = "//" + args[0] + "/Send";
          send = ((Send) Naming.lookup(name));
        } catch (Exception e) {
          System.out.println("RMIClient1 exception: " +
            e.getMessage());
          e.printStackTrace();
        }
      }
    }
```

Sealing the Symmetric Key: RMIClient2 Program

```
import java.awt.Color;
import java.awt.GridLayout;
import java.awt.event.*;
import javax.swing.*;
import java.io.*;
import java.net.*;
import java.rmi.*;
import java.rmi.server.*;
import java.io.FileInputStream.*;
import java.io.File;
import java.util.*;
```

```java
import javax.crypto.*;
import java.security.*;

class RMIClient2 extends JFrame implements ActionListener {
    JLabel creditCard;
    JLabel custID, apples, peaches, pears, total, cost,
clicked;
    JButton view, reset;
    JPanel panel;
    JTextArea creditNo, customerNo;
    JTextArea applesNo, peachesNo, pearsNo, itotal, icost;
    Socket socket = null;
    PrintWriter out = null;
    static Send send;
    String customer;

    RMIClient2(){ //Begin Constructor
//Create labels
        creditCard = new JLabel("Credit Card:");
        custID = new JLabel("Customer ID:");
        apples = new JLabel("Apples:");
        peaches = new JLabel("Peaches:");
        pears = new JLabel("Pears:");
        total = new JLabel("Total Items:");
        cost = new JLabel("Total Cost:");

//Create text area components
        creditNo = new JTextArea();
        customerNo = new JTextArea();
        applesNo = new JTextArea();
        peachesNo = new JTextArea();
        pearsNo = new JTextArea();
        itotal = new JTextArea();
        icost = new JTextArea();

//Create buttons
        view = new JButton("View Order");
        view.addActionListener(this);
        reset = new JButton("Reset");
        reset.addActionListener(this);

//Create panel for 2-column layout
//Set white background color
        panel = new JPanel();
        panel.setLayout(new GridLayout(0,2));
        panel.setBackground(Color.white);

//Add components to panel columns
//going left to right and top to bottom
```

```java
      getContentPane().add(panel);
      panel.add(creditCard);
      panel.add(creditNo);
      panel.add(custID);
      panel.add(customerNo);
      panel.add(apples);
      panel.add(applesNo);
      panel.add(peaches);
      panel.add(peachesNo);
      panel.add(pears);
      panel.add(pearsNo);
      panel.add(total);
      panel.add(itotal);
      panel.add(cost);
      panel.add(icost);
      panel.add(view);
      panel.add(reset);
   } //End Constructor

//Decrypt credit card number
  public String decrypt(SealedObject sealed,
    byte[] encrypted) {
//Get private key from file
    PrivateKey privkey=null;
    SecretKey seckey=null;
    Cipher c=null;
    String s=null;
    try {
      String inputFileName = System.getProperty("user.home",
      File.separatorChar + "home" +
      File.separatorChar + "monicap") +
      File.separatorChar + "privkey.txt";
      FileInputStream fstream = new FileInputStream(
        inputFileName);
      ObjectInput in = new ObjectInputStream(fstream);
      privkey = (PrivateKey)in.readObject();
      in.close();
    } catch (java.io.FileNotFoundException e) {
      System.out.println("File not found");
    } catch (java.io.StreamCorruptedException e) {
      System.out.println("Bad data");
    } catch(java.io.IOException e) {
      System.out.println("Unable to read file");
    } catch (java.lang.ClassNotFoundException e) {
      System.out.println("Unable to read private key");
    }

//Create asymmetric Cipher
//Initialize Cipher for decryption with private key
```

```java
//Unseal wrapped session key using asymmetric cipher
    try {
      c = Cipher.getInstance("an asymmetric algorithm");
      c.init(Cipher.DECRYPT_MODE, privkey);
      seckey = (SecretKey)sealed.getObject(c);
    } catch(javax.crypto.NoSuchPaddingException e){
      System.out.println("No such padding");
      } catch (javax.crypto.IllegalBlockSizeException e) {
      System.out.println("Illegal block size");
      } catch (javax.crypto.BadPaddingException e) {
      System.out.println("Bad padding");
      } catch (java.security.NoSuchAlgorithmException e) {
      System.out.println("No such algorithm");
      } catch (java.security.InvalidKeyException e) {
      System.out.println("Invalid key");
      } catch(java.io.IOException e) {
      System.out.println("Unable to get private key");
      } catch(java.lang.ClassNotFoundException e) {
      System.out.println("Secret key not available");
      }

//Create symmetric Cipher
    try {
      c = Cipher.getInstance("DES/ECB/PKCS5Padding");
      } catch (java.security.NoSuchAlgorithmException e) {
      System.out.println("No such algorithm");
      } catch (javax.crypto.NoSuchPaddingException e) {
      System.out.println("No such padding");
      }

//Initialize Cipher for decryption with session key
//Decrypt credit card number with symmetric Cipher
    try {
      c.init(Cipher.DECRYPT_MODE, seckey);
      encrypted=c.doFinal(s.getBytes());
      System.out.println("Cipher Text:");
      System.out.println(new String(encrypted));
      System.out.println();
      } catch (java.security.InvalidKeyException e) {
      System.out.println("Invalid key");
      } catch(javax.crypto.IllegalBlockSizeException e){
      System.out.println("Illegal block size");
      } catch (javax.crypto.BadPaddingException e) {
      System.out.println("Bad padding");
      }
    return s;
  }
```

```
    public void actionPerformed(ActionEvent event){
        Object source = event.getSource();
        String text=null, unit, i;
        SealedObject sealed;
        byte[] encrypted;
        double cost;
        Double price;
        int items;
        Integer itms;

//If View button pressed
//Get data from server and display it
        if (source == view) {
            try {
                sealed = send.getKey();
                encrypted = send.getEncrypted();

//Decrypt credit card number
                String credit = decrypt(sealed, encrypted);
                creditNo.setText(credit);
                text = send.getCustID();
                customerNo.setText(text);
                text = send.getAppleQnt();
                applesNo.setText(text);
                text = send.getPeachQnt();
                peachesNo.setText(text);
                text = send.getPearQnt();
                pearsNo.setText(text);
                cost = send.getTotalCost();
                price = new Double(cost);
                unit = price.toString();
                icost.setText(unit);
                items = send.getTotalItems();
                itms = new Integer(items);
                i = itms.toString();
                itotal.setText(i);
            } catch (java.rmi.RemoteException e) {
            System.out.println("sendData exception: " +
              e.getMessage());
            }
        }

//If Reset button pressed
//Clear all fields
        if (source == reset) {
          creditNo.setText("");
          customerNo.setText("");
          applesNo.setText("");
```

```
            peachesNo.setText("");
            pearsNo.setText("");
            itotal.setText("");
            icost.setText("");
        }
    }

    public static void main(String[] args) {
        RMIClient2 frame = new RMIClient2();
        frame.setTitle("Fruit Order");
        WindowListener l = new WindowAdapter() {
            public void windowClosing(WindowEvent e) {
                System.exit(0);
            }
        };
        frame.addWindowListener(l);
        frame.pack();
        frame.setVisible(true);
      if (System.getSecurityManager() == null) {
        System.setSecurityManager(new RMISecurityManager());
      }

      try {
        String name = "//" + args[0] + "/Send";
        send = ((Send) Naming.lookup(name));
      } catch (java.rmi.NotBoundException e) {
        System.out.println("Cannot access data in server");
      } catch (java.rmi.RemoteException e) {
        System.out.println("Cannot access data in server");
      } catch (java.net.MalformedURLException e) {
        System.out.println("Cannot access data in server");
      }
    }
}
```

Encrypting the Symmetric Key with the RSA Algorithm: RMIClient1 Program

```
import java.awt.Color;
import java.awt.GridLayout;
import java.awt.event.*;
import javax.swing.*;
import java.io.*;
import java.net.*;
import java.rmi.*;
import java.rmi.server.*;
import javax.crypto.*;
import java.security.*;
import java.security.interfaces.*;
```

```
class RMIClient1 extends JFrame implements ActionListener {
    JLabel col1, col2;
    JLabel totalItems, totalCost;
    JLabel cardNum, custID;
    JLabel applechk, pearchk, peachchk;
    JButton purchase, reset;
    JPanel panel;
    JTextField appleqnt, pearqnt, peachqnt;
    JTextField creditCard, customer;
    JTextArea items, cost;
    static Send send;
    int itotal=0;
    double icost=0;

    RMIClient1(){ //Begin Constructor
//Create left and right column labels
        col1 = new JLabel("Select Items");
        col2 = new JLabel("Specify Quantity");

//Create labels and text field components
        applechk = new JLabel("    Apples");
        appleqnt = new JTextField();
        appleqnt.addActionListener(this);
        pearchk = new JLabel("    Pears");
        pearqnt = new JTextField();
        pearqnt.addActionListener(this);
        peachchk = new JLabel("    Peaches");
        peachqnt = new JTextField();
        peachqnt.addActionListener(this);
        cardNum = new JLabel("    Credit Card:");
        creditCard = new JTextField();
        pearqnt.setNextFocusableComponent(creditCard);
        customer = new JTextField();
        custID = new JLabel("    Customer ID:");

//Create labels and text area components
        totalItems = new JLabel("Total Items:");
        totalCost = new JLabel("Total Cost:");
        items = new JTextArea();
        cost = new JTextArea();

//Create buttons and make action listeners
        purchase = new JButton("Purchase");
        purchase.addActionListener(this);
        reset = new JButton("Reset");
        reset.addActionListener(this);
        creditCard.setNextFocusableComponent(reset);
```

```
//Create a panel for the components
    panel = new JPanel();

//Set panel layout to 2-column grid
//on a white background
    panel.setLayout(new GridLayout(0,2));
    panel.setBackground(Color.white);

//Add components to panel columns
//going left to right and top to bottom
    getContentPane().add(panel);
    panel.add(col1);
    panel.add(col2);
    panel.add(applechk);
    panel.add(appleqnt);
    panel.add(peachchk);
    panel.add(peachqnt);
    panel.add(pearchk);
    panel.add(pearqnt);
    panel.add(totalItems);
    panel.add(items);
    panel.add(totalCost);
    panel.add(cost);
    panel.add(cardNum);
    panel.add(creditCard);
    panel.add(custID);
    panel.add(customer);
    panel.add(reset);
    panel.add(purchase);
  } //End Constructor

  private void encrypt(String cardnum) {
    Cipher c=null, c2=null;
    KeyGenerator keyGen;
    SecretKey secretKey=null;
    RSAPublicKey pubKey=null;
    byte[] encrypted=null, wrappedKey=null;

//Create Cipher for symmetric key encryption (RSA)
//Create a key generator
//Create a secret (session) key with key generator
    try {
      c = Cipher.getInstance("DES/ECB/PKCS5Padding");
      keyGen = KeyGenerator.getInstance("RSA");
      keyGen.init(new SecureRandom());
      secretKey=keyGen.generateKey();
    } catch (java.security.NoSuchAlgorithmException e) {
      System.out.println("No such algorithm");
    } catch(javax.crypto.NoSuchPaddingException e){
```

```
                  System.out.println("No such padding");
              }

//Initialize Cipher for encryption with session key
//Encrypt credit card number with Cipher
        try {
          c.init(Cipher.ENCRYPT_MODE, secretKey);
          encrypted=c.doFinal(cardnum.getBytes());
          System.out.println("Cipher Text:");
          System.out.println(new String(encrypted));
          System.out.println();
        } catch (java.security.InvalidKeyException e) {
          System.out.println("Invalid Key");
        } catch(javax.crypto.IllegalBlockSizeException e){
          System.out.println("Illegal block size");
        } catch (javax.crypto.BadPaddingException e) {
          System.out.println("Bad Padding");
        }

//Get public key from server
        try {
          pubKey = (RSAPublicKey)send.getPublicKey();
        } catch (java.rmi.RemoteException e) {
          System.out.println("Key not available");
        }

//Create Cipher for asymmetric encryption (RSA)
//Initialize Cipher for encryption with public key
        try {
          c2 = Cipher.getInstance("RSA");
          c2.init(Cipher.ENCRYPT_MODE, pubKey);
         } catch (java.security.NoSuchAlgorithmException e) {
           System.out.println("No such algorithm");
         } catch (javax.crypto.NoSuchPaddingException e) {
           System.out.println("No such padding");
         } catch (java.security.InvalidKeyException e) {
           System.out.println("Invalid key");
         }

//Encrypt session key
        try{
          wrappedKey = c2.doFinal(secretKey.getEncoded());
        } catch (javax.crypto.IllegalBlockSizeException  e) {
          System.out.println("Illegal block size");
        } catch (javax.crypto.BadPaddingException e) {
          System.out.println("Bad padding");
        }
```

```
//Send encrypted message and session key to server
   try {
     send.sendKey(wrappedKey);
     send.sendEncrypted(encrypted);
   } catch( java.rmi.RemoteException e) {
     System.out.println("Unable to send key");
   }
}

  public void actionPerformed(ActionEvent event) {
   Object source = event.getSource();
   Integer applesNo, peachesNo, pearsNo, num;
   Double cost;
   String number, cardnum, custID, apples, peaches, pears,
text, text2;

//If Purchase button pressed
   if (source == purchase) {
//Get data from text fields
     cardnum = creditCard.getText();
     custID = customer.getText();
     apples = appleqnt.getText();
     peaches = peachqnt.getText();
     pears = pearqnt.getText();

//Calculate total items
     if( apples.length() > 0) {
//Catch invalid number error
       try {
         applesNo = Integer.valueOf(apples);
         itotal += applesNo.intValue();
       } catch(java.lang.NumberFormatException e) {
         appleqnt.setText("Invalid Value");
       }
     } else {
       /* else no need to change the total */
     }

     if (peaches.length() > 0) {
//Catch invalid number error
       try {
         peachesNo = Integer.valueOf(peaches);
         itotal += peachesNo.intValue();
       } catch(java.lang.NumberFormatException e) {
         peachqnt.setText("Invalid Value");
       }
     } else {
```

```
            /* else no need to change the total */
        }

        if (pears.length() > 0) {
//Catch invalid number error
            try {
                pearsNo = Integer.valueOf(pears);
                itotal += pearsNo.intValue();
            } catch (java.lang.NumberFormatException e) {
                pearqnt.setText("Invalid Value");
            }
        } else {
            /* else no need to change the total */
        }

//Display running total
        num = new Integer(itotal);
        text = num.toString();
        this.items.setText(text);
//Calculate and display running cost
        icost = (itotal * 1.25);
        cost = new Double(icost);
        text2 = cost.toString();
        this.cost.setText(text2);
//Encrypt credit card number
        encrypt(cardnum);

//Send data over net
        try{
            send.sendCustID(custID);
            send.sendAppleQnt(apples);
            send.sendPeachQnt(peaches);
            send.sendPearQnt(pears);
            send.sendTotalCost(icost);
            send.sendTotalItems(itotal);
        } catch (java.rmi.RemoteException e) {
            System.out.println("sendData exception: " +
                e.getMessage());
        }
    }

//If Reset button pressed
//Clear all fields
    if ( source == reset) {
        creditCard.setText("");
        appleqnt.setText("");
        peachqnt.setText("");
        pearqnt.setText("");
        creditCard.setText("");
```

```
      customer.setText("");
      icost = 0;
      cost = new Double(icost);
      text2 = cost.toString();
      this.cost.setText(text2);
      itotal = 0;
      num = new Integer(itotal);
      text = num.toString();
    this.items.setText(text);
    }
  }

  public static void main(String[] args) {
    try {
      UIManager.setLookAndFeel(
        UIManager.getCrossPlatformLookAndFeelClassName());
    } catch (Exception e) {
      System.out.println("Couldn't use the cross-platform"
        + "look and feel: " + e);
    }
    RMIClient1 frame = new RMIClient1();
    frame.setTitle("Fruit $1.25 Each");
    WindowListener l = new WindowAdapter() {
      public void windowClosing(WindowEvent e) {
        System.exit(0);
      }
    };

    frame.addWindowListener(l);
    frame.pack();
    frame.setVisible(true);
    if (System.getSecurityManager() == null) {
      System.setSecurityManager(new RMISecurityManager());

    }
    try {
      String name = "//" + args[0] + "/Send";
      send = ((Send) Naming.lookup(name));
    } catch (Exception e) {
      System.out.println("RMIClient1 exception: " +
        e.getMessage());
      e.printStackTrace();
    }
  }
}
```

Encrypting the Symmetric Key with the RSA Algorithm: RMIClient2 Program

```java
import java.awt.Color;
import java.awt.GridLayout;
import java.awt.event.*;
import javax.swing.*;
import java.io.*;
import java.net.*;
import java.rmi.*;
import java.rmi.server.*;
import java.io.FileInputStream.*;
import java.io.RandomAccessFile.*;
import java.io.File;
import java.util.*;
import javax.crypto.*;
import javax.crypto.spec.*;
import java.security.*;

class RMIClient2 extends JFrame implements ActionListener {
    JLabel creditCard;
    JLabel custID, apples, peaches, pears, total, cost,
clicked;
    JButton view, reset;
    JPanel panel;
    JTextArea creditNo;
    JTextArea customerNo, applesNo, peachesNo, pearsNo,
      itotal, icost;
    Socket socket = null;
    PrintWriter out = null;
    static Send send;
    String customer;

    RMIClient2(){ //Begin Constructor]
//Create labels
        creditCard = new JLabel("Credit Card:");
        custID = new JLabel("Customer ID:");
        apples = new JLabel("Apples:");
        peaches = new JLabel("Peaches:");
        pears = new JLabel("Pears:");
        total = new JLabel("Total Items:");
        cost = new JLabel("Total Cost:");

//Create text area components
        creditNo = new JTextArea();
        customerNo = new JTextArea();
        applesNo = new JTextArea();
        peachesNo = new JTextArea();
```

```
        pearsNo = new JTextArea();
        itotal = new JTextArea();
        icost = new JTextArea();

//Create buttons
        view = new JButton("View Order");
        view.addActionListener(this);
        reset = new JButton("Reset");
        reset.addActionListener(this);

//Create panel for 2-column layout
//Set white background color
        panel = new JPanel();
        panel.setLayout(new GridLayout(0,2));
        panel.setBackground(Color.white);

//Add components to panel columns
//going left to right and top to bottom
        getContentPane().add(panel);
        panel.add(creditCard);
        panel.add(creditNo);
        panel.add(custID);
        panel.add(customerNo);
        panel.add(apples);
        panel.add(applesNo);
        panel.add(peaches);
        panel.add(pears);
        panel.add(pearsNo);
        panel.add(total);
        panel.add(itotal);
        panel.add(cost);
        panel.add(icost);
        panel.add(view);
        panel.add(reset);
    } //End Constructor

//Decrypt credit card number
  public byte[] decrypt(byte[] wrappedKey, byte[] encrypted){
    PrivateKey privkey=null;
    SecretKey secretKey=null;
    Cipher c=null, c2=null;
    String s=null;
    SecretKeySpec kspec=null;
    byte[] card=null;

//Get private key from file
    try {
    String inputFileName = System.getProperty("user.home",
    File.separatorChar + "home" +
```

```
            File.separatorChar + "monicap") +
            File.separatorChar + "privkey.txt";
            FileInputStream fstream = new FileInputStream(
                inputFileName);
            ObjectInput in = new ObjectInputStream(fstream);
            privkey = (PrivateKey)in.readObject();
            in.close();
        } catch (java.io.FileNotFoundException e) {
            System.out.println("File not found");
        } catch(java.io.StreamCorruptedException e) {
            System.out.println("Bad data");
        } catch(java.io.IOException e) {
            System.out.println("Unable to read file");
        } catch (java.lang.ClassNotFoundException e) {
            System.out.println("Unable to read private key");
        }

//Create asymmetric Cipher
//Initialize Cipher for decryption with private key
//Decrypt symmetric key
//Instantiate symmetric key
        try{
            c = Cipher.getInstance("RSA");
            c.init(Cipher.DECRYPT_MODE, privkey);
            byte[] secretKeyBytes = c.doFinal(wrappedKey);
            kspec = new SecretKeySpec(secretKeyBytes, "DES");
        } catch(javax.crypto.IllegalBlockSizeException e){
            System.out.println("Illegal block size");
        } catch(javax.crypto.BadPaddingException e){
            System.out.println("Bad padding");
        } catch(javax.crypto.NoSuchPaddingException e){
            System.out.println("No such padding");
        } catch (java.security.NoSuchAlgorithmException e) {
            System.out.println("No such algorithm");
        } catch (java.security.InvalidKeyException e){
            System.out.println("Invalid key");
        }

//Create symmetric Cipher
        try {
            c2 = Cipher.getInstance("DES/ECB/PKCS5Padding");
        } catch (java.security.NoSuchAlgorithmException e) {
            System.out.println("No such algorithm");
        } catch (javax.crypto.NoSuchPaddingException e) {
            System.out.println("No such padding");
        }

//Initialize Cipher for decryption with session key
```

```java
//Decrypt credit card number with symmetric Cipher
    try {
      c2.init(Cipher.DECRYPT_MODE, kspec);
      card=c2.doFinal(encrypted);
      System.out.println("Credit Card Number:");
      System.out.println(new String(card));
      System.out.println();
    } catch (java.security.InvalidKeyException e) {
      System.out.println("Invalid key");
    } catch( javax.crypto.IllegalBlockSizeException e) {
      System.out.println("Illegal block size");
    } catch (javax.crypto.BadPaddingException e) {
      System.out.println("Bad padding");
    }
    return card;
  }
  public void actionPerformed(ActionEvent event){
      Object source = event.getSource();
      String text=null, unit, i;
      byte[] wrappedKey;
      byte[] encrypted;
      double cost;
      Double price;
      int items;
      Integer itms;

//If View button pressed
//Get data from server and display it
      if (source == view) {
        try {
          wrappedKey = send.getKey();
          encrypted = send.getEncrypted();

//Decrypt credit card number
          byte[] credit = decrypt(wrappedKey, encrypted);
          creditNo.setText(new String(credit));
          text = send.getCustID();
          customerNo.setText(text);
          text = send.getAppleQnt();
          applesNo.setText(text);
          text = send.getPeachQnt();
          peachesNo.setText(text);
          text = send.getPearQnt();
          pearsNo.setText(text);
          cost = send.getTotalCost();
          price = new Double(cost);
          unit = price.toString();
          icost.setText(unit);
          items = send.getTotalItems();
```

```
                   itms = new Integer(items);
                   i = itms.toString();
                   itotal.setText(i);
               } catch (java.rmi.RemoteException e) {
                   System.out.println("sendData exception: " +
                                          e.getMessage());
               }
           }

   //If Reset button pressed
   //Clear all fields
       if (source == reset) {
          creditNo.setText("");
          customerNo.setText("");
          applesNo.setText("");
           peachesNo.setText("");
          pearsNo.setText("");
          itotal.setText("");
          icost.setText("");
       }
     }

     public static void main(String[] args) {
           RMIClient2 frame = new RMIClient2();
           frame.setTitle("Fruit Order");
           WindowListener l = new WindowAdapter() {
             public void windowClosing(WindowEvent e) {
               System.exit(0);
             }
           };
           frame.addWindowListener(l);
           frame.pack();
           frame.setVisible(true);
         if (System.getSecurityManager() == null) {
           System.setSecurityManager(new RMISecurityManager());
         }

       try {
         String name = "//" + args[0] + "/Send";
         send = ((Send) Naming.lookup(name));
       } catch (java.rmi.NotBoundException e) {
         System.out.println("Cannot access data in server");
       } catch (java.rmi.RemoteException e) {
         System.out.println("Cannot access data in server");
       } catch (java.net.MalformedURLException e) {
         System.out.println("Cannot access data in server");
       }
     }
   }
```

Further Reading

[Boo94] Grady Booch. *Object-Oriented Analysis and Design with Applications, Second Edition,* Addison-Wesley, Reading, MA, 1994.

[Cam98] Mary Campione and Kathy Walrath. *The Java™ Tutorial, Second Edition: Object-Oriented Programming for the Internet*, Addison Wesley Longman, Reading, MA, 1998.

[Cam99] Mary Campione, Kathy Walrath, and Alison Huml. *The Java™ Tutorial Continued: The Rest of the JDK™,* Addison Wesley Longman, Reading, MA, 1999.

[Coa96] Peter Coad, Mark Mayfield, and David North. *Object Models: Strategies, Patterns, and Applications,* Yourdon Press/Prentice Hall, Upper Saddle River, NJ, 1996.

[Fow97] Martin Fowler. *Analysis Patterns: Reusable Object Models,* Addison Wesley Longman, Reading, MA, 1997.

[Gam95] Erich Gamma, Richard Helm, Ralph Johnson, and John Vlissides. *Design Patterns: Elements of Reusable Object-Oriented Software,* Addison-Wesley, Reading, MA, 1995.

[Hop96] K. C. Hopson, Stephen E. Ingram, and Patrick Chan. *Developing Professional Java™ Applets,* Sams Publishing, Indianapolis, IN, 1996.

[Hun98] Jason Hunter and William Crawford. *Java™ Servlet Programming*, O'Reilly & Associates, Sebastapol, CA, 1998.

[Sti95] Douglas R. Stinson. *Cryptography: Theory and Practice,* CRC Press, Boca Raton, FL, 1995.

[Wal99] Kathy Walrath and Mary Campione. The *JFC Swing Tutorial: A Guide to Constructing GUIs,* Addison Wesley Longman, Reading, MA, 1999.

Index

/* and */ (C-style comments), 5
/** and */ (documentation comments) 5
// (C++-style comments) 5
= (equal operator), 172–173
+ (addition operator), 73

accessEventQueue permission, 58
accessor methods, 10
ACTION parameter, 39, 43
ActionListener interface, 28–29, 31–32, 129
actionPerformed method, 29, 31–32
   customers lists and, 158, 159
   database access and, 72
   file access and, 48–49, 53–55
   internationalization and, 178
   RMI and, 99–101, 129, 131, 133, 138
   sockets communications and, 111, 112–113
adapter classes, 33
addActionListener method, 31
addCustomer method, 157, 158
Algorithms, 220–221, 229, 276–287
APIs (application program interfaces)
   basic description of, 2
   comments and, 5, 6
   consistency across, 21
   documentation for, 6, 7
   Java Plug-in and, 19, 58, 78, 182
   object-oriented programming and, 206
   packages and, 23
   Project Swing adapter classes, 33
   RMI API and socket communications, 107
AppendIO class, 66–68
appendText method, 115
appleQnt text field, 129, 131–135
Applet(s)

basic description of, 17
behavior of, 21–22
building, 17–24
database access by, 74–78
elements of, 19–23
file access by, 55–57
internationalization and, 182
methods for, 21–22
permissions granted to, 57–58
policy files and, 57–58
running, 19, 57–58
starting, 75, 77
structure of, 19–23
Applet class, 19, 21–23, 33
<APPLET> tag, 19, 201
appletviewer tool, 19, 57–58, 201, 212
Application(s)
   building, 9–16
   database access by, 70–74
   elements of, 9–12
   file access by, 48–49
   restricting, 58
   structure of, 9–12
   text, internationalization of, 175–178
ARCHIVE option, 201
Arithmetic operators, 135
ASCII (American Standard Code for Information Interchange), 57, 76, 77
Asymmetric key encryption, 219, 220–221.
   See also Cryptography
AUTOEXEC.BAT, 6
AWT (Abstract Window Toolkit) package, 23, 29
   basic description of, 28
   import statements and, 26–27
   object-oriented programming and, 209–211

Background color, 30
Banners, 58
<BODY> tag, 44
BorderLayout class, 30
BorderLayout layout manager, 30, 130
Browser(s)
  destroy method and, 22
  doPost method and, 42
  enabled for the Java 2 platform, 19
  JAR files and, 199
  policy files and, 58
  running applets and, 19, 58
  windows, top-level containers as, 26
BufferedReader class, 111, 112
button component, 32
Button(s)
  Click Me button, 39, 57, 71, 75, 77, 90–92,
    109–110
  Purchase button, 125, 128–129, 131–132,
    218
  Remove button, 159
  Reset button, 128, 129, 131
  Start button, 6
  Submit button, 38
  View button, 158, 159
Byte data, 48

C (high-level language), 5, 9
C++ (high-level language), 5, 9, 20
catch block, 53, 55, 72, 155–156, 171
Character (alphanumeric) data, 48
Class(es). *See also* Classes (listed by name)
  abstract, 41
  accessor methods and, 10
  basic description of, 9, 10, 206
  declarations, 28–29, 41–42, 195–196, 212
  extending, 20–21
  inheritance and, 209–211, 214–215
  instances of, 11–12, 14
  object-oriented programming and, 206–209,
    213–215
  private, 212
  protected, 212
  public, 195–196, 212
  throwable, 52–53
  writing your own, 213–215

Classes (listed by name)
  Applet class, 19, 21–23, 33
  BufferedReader class, 111, 112
  BorderLayout class, 30
  ClientWorker class, 114
  Collection class, 157
  Color class, 12, 23
  Component class, 21, 211
  Connection class, 71
  Container class, 20, 209–210
  DataOrder class, 124–125, 131–132, 138–
    139, 154, 196, 249
  Double class, 135, 137
  DriverManager class, 71, 75, 77
  ExampleProgram class, 4–5, 206, 207
  ExampServlet class, 41–44
  File class, 52
  FileInputStream class, 49, 51–52
  FileOutputStream class, 49, 51, 154
  Frame class, 26, 28
  Graphics class, 21, 23
  HttpServlet class, 40–43
  Integer class, 134, 137, 211, 213
  IOException class, 40, 42
  Iterator class, 159
  JApplet class, 33
  JButton class, 29
  JFrame class, 28, 29, 31, 130, 207, 209–210,
    214
  JLabel class, 29, 129, 178, 208
  JPanel class, 29, 30, 208
  JTextArea class, 132
  JTextField class, 49
  LessonTwoA class, 12
  LessonTwoB class, 13–14, 17–19
  LessonTwoC class, 12
  LessonTwoD class, 14–16
  LessonTwoE class, 15–16
  Line class, 111
  Locale class, 176
  Math class, 12
  Message class, 176
  NumberFormat class, 178–179
  Object class, 20
  ObjectInputStream class, 156
  ObjectOutputFileStream class, 154
  ObjectOutputStream class, 156

Panel class, 19
PrintWriter class, 42, 111, 112
Project Swing 26
RemoteServer class, 93–106, 125, 135–136, 153–155, 164–167, 222–225, 230–233, 250–251
ResultSet class, 55, 71, 73
RMICLient1 class, 99–100
RMIClient2 class, 100–101
Send class, 93, 99, 106
ServerSocket class, 110–111
ServletException class, 40, 42
SimpleApplet class, 19–20, 22–23
skel class, 93, 94
Socket class, 112
Statement class, 55, 73
StoreData class, 11
StringBuffer class, 207
String class, 71, 73, 206, 207, 211, 213
stub class, 93
skel class, 93
SwingUI class, 28–31, 33
System class, 11–12, 24, 52, 206, 207
TextArea class, 101, 111
TextField class, 49, 51, 55, 112
UnicastRemoteObject class, 98
WindowAdapter class, 33
CLASSPATH environment variable, 4, 6, 94, 95
-classpath option, 4
Click Me button, 39, 57
  database access and, 71, 75, 77
  RMI and, 90–92
  sockets communications and, 109–110
client variable, 114
ClientWorker class, 114
Close option, 208
CODE option, 201
Collection class, 157
Collection interface, 157
Collections, 153, 157–158
Color, background, 30
Color class, 12, 23
Commands
  jar command, 200
  javac command, 4
  javadoc command, 7

policytool command, 57
rmiregistry command, 94
SET CLASSPATH command, 6
sysedit command, 6
Comments
  basic description of, 5–6
  C-style, 5
  C++-style, 5
  javadoc, 5
  JSP tags and, 45
Compiling
  internationalization examples, 179–181
  introduction to, 1–7
  RMI examples, 92–93
  a simple program, 1–7
  socket communications examples, 110
Component class, 21, 211
Components. *See also* Classes (listed by name)
  adding, 30–31
  basic description of, 26
Components (listed by name). *See also* Components
  JButton component, 29, 31, 178
  JPanel component, 130
  Panel component, 19, 21–22, 31
  JTextArea component, 111, 114, 115
Compression, 199–202
Computer, setting up your, 3
Connection class, 71
Constructors
  basic description of, 14–16, 23–31
  file access and, 48, 49, 55
  internationalization and, 177–178
  object-oriented programming and, 207
  RMI and, 129–131, 133–134
Container class, 20, 209–210
Content panes, 130–131
cost variable, 133
creditcard text field, 133
Cryptography
  basic description of, 217–237
  code for, 265–287
  encrypting symmetric keys, 229–236
  generating public and private key pairs, 221–236
  RSA algorithm and, 220–221, 229, 276–287
  sealing symmetric keys, 221–229

Culturally-dependent data, identifying, 170–171. *See also* Internationalization
currentLocale object, 176, 178–179
Cursor focus, 133–134
Customer IDs, 157–160, 214
Customer lists, 157–160, 211, 214

Database(s)
  access to, 69–87
  code for, 79–87
  connections, establishing, 71–72
  management systems (DBMSs), 75
  permissions and, 69–87
  setup, 70
  tables, creating, 70
DataOrder class, 124–125, 131–132, 138–139, 154, 194, 196, 249
Data types
  Double class, 134, 179, 157
  double primitive type, 135, 179
  int primitive type, 134, 179
  Integer class, 134, 157, 179
  String data type, 154, 157, 158, 179
Dba class, 71, 79–81
DbaAppl class, 74–78, 82–84
DbaApplPol class, 76
DbaOdbAppl class, 77–78, 84–86
DbaOdbPol policy file, 78
DbaServlet class, 78, 86–88
DBMSs (database management systems), 75. *See also* Databases
Debugging, 5, 199. *See also* Errors
Decompression, 200–202
decrypt method, 227–229, 235–236
DES (Data Encryption Standards), 220–221
destroy method, 20, 22
Dialog boxes
  with application-specific error text, 54–55
  displaying data in, 160–161
Directories, for packages, 194–195
doc comments, 5–6
doGet method, 43
doPost method, 41, 42, 43
-D option with java command, 95, 97
DOS (Disk Operating System)
  compiling and, 4

  setting the CLASSPATH environment variable and, 6
Double class, 135, 137
Double primitive type, 134, 179, 157
Double-precision floating point values, 135
Double quotes ("), 73
doubleValue method, 135
Downloading
  the Java platform, 3
  the javax.crypto package, 220
  the JavaServer Web Development Kit (JSWDK), 37
DriverManager class, 71, 75, 77
DriverManager.getConnection method, 72
Drivers, 70–73
  database, 70
  JDBC, 70–71, 74, 75
  locating, 75
  ODBC, 74, 77, 78

else statement, 134
encrypt method, 218, 233–235
Enterprise JavaBeans, 90
Equal sign (=) and properties files, 172–173
Errors, 138, 170–171, 178, 182, 229. *See also* Debugging
Event handling
  basic description of, 32, 131–134
  RMI and, 131–134
ExampleProgram class, 4–5, 10 –12, 206, 207
ExampServlet class, 39–44
Exception handling, 52–55, 138, 229
  database access and, 72
  object-oriented programming and, 215
executeQuery method, 73
Extraction, of files, 200

Fields. *See also* Fields (listed by name)
  access levels for, 195–196, 212–213
  declaration of, 195–196
  nonstatic, 12–14
  static, 12–14
Fields (listed by name). *See also* Fields
  accessor methods and, 11
  appleQnt text field, 129, 131–135

creditcard text field, 133
peachQnt text field, 129, 131, 134–135
pearQnt text field, 129, 131, 133–135
text field, 12–14
Total Cost field, 134
File access
  by applets, 55–57
  basic description of, 47–68
  code for, 61–68
  databases and, 69–87
  by servlets, 59
File class, 52
FileInputStream class, 49, 51–52
FileIO class, 48, 53, 55, 61–67, 70–74, 90–
  106, 108
FileIOAppl class, 55–58, 63–65
fileIO.html file, 57–58
FileIOServlet class, 59, 65–66
File class, 52
FileOutputStream class, 49, 51, 154
file.separator property, 52
FileUIAppl class, 57
finalize method, 116
finally block, 55, 155, 156
finally clause, 155, 156
final variable, 72–73
floating point values, 135
Foreign languages. *See* Internationalization
Forms, 38–40, 43, 59
Forward slash (/), 5
Frame(s)
  components, 26
  creating, with the main method, 32–33
  object-oriented programming and, 207–210
Frame class, 26
French. *See* Internationalization

German. *See* Internationalization
GET operation, 41
getContentPane method, 31, 33, 130
getData method, 91–92, 98, 100
  customer lists and, 157, 159, 160–161
  displaying data in a dialog box with, 160–
    161
getOrder method, 125, 154–156
getparameter method, 42

getString method, 177–178
getText method, 12–13, 16
Global variables, 213
Graphics class, 21, 23
Graphics context, 21
GridLayout layout manager, 130
GUI (graphical user interface), 19, 28

HashSet, 158–160
Hash tables, 158
<HEAD> tag, 44
Host machine, 95, 96, 97
Host names, 95, 96, 97
HTML (HyperText Markup Language), 6.
  See also HTML tags
  building servlets and, 37–46
  forms, 38–40, 43, 59
  HTTP and, 38
HTML tags. *See also* HTML (HyperText
  Markup Language)
  <APPLET> tag, 19, 201
  <BODY> tag, 44
  <HEAD> tag, 44
  <HTML> tag, 44
  <TITLE> tag, 44
HTTP (HyperText Transfer Protocol), 38,
  40–43, 89
  GET operation, 41
  POST operation, 41
HttpServlet class, 40–43

IllegalValueException, 54
Import statements, 23, 195
  basic description of, 26–28
  in SwingUI.java code, 26–27
index.html, 194, 201
Inheritance, 209–211, 214–215
init method, 20, 21
Installing, the Java platform, 3
Instance variables, 29–30, 49
  internationalization and, 175
  RMI and, 128–129
int data type, 134, 179
int primitive type, 157, 179
Integer class, 134, 157, 179

Interface(s). *See also* User interfaces
  ActionListener interface, 28–29, 31–32, 129
  Collection interface, 157
  List interface, 157
  Map interface, 157
  Runnable interface, 114
  Send interface, 125, 135, 156, 196, 222–225, 230–233, 249
  Serializable interface, 131
  Set interface, 157
  WindowListener interface, 33, 208
Internationalization
  basic description of, 169–191
  code for, 183–191
  creating keyword and value pair files for, 171–175
  identifying culturally-dependent data for, 170–171
  of numbers, 178–179
Internet Explorer browser, 4, 21, 38. *See also* Browsers
Interpreter, Java
  invoking, 4
  main method and, 11
  RMI and, 95, 97
intValue method, 134–135
Invalid Value error, 178
IOException class, 40, 42
IP (Internet Protocol) addresses, 76
Iterator object, 159
itotal variable, 133–134

JApplet class, 33
jar command, 200
JAR (Java Archive) file format, 193, 199–200, 220
java.applet package, 23
java.awt (Abstract Window Toolkit) package, 23, 26–29
  basic description of, 28
  import statements and, 26–27
  object-oriented programming and, 209–211
javac, 4, 93
javac command, 4
javadoc command, 7

javadoc tool, 5–7
Java interpreter
  invoking, 4
  main method and, 11
  RMI and, 95, 97
java.io.File.separatorChar variable, 52
java.io.IOException, 54, 155, 156
java.io package, 40, 52, 54, 155, 156
java.lang package, 24, 53, 215
  object-oriented programming and, 206, 209, 211, 213
  RMI and, 98, 134, 137
java.lang.RuntimeException, 53
Java Plug-in, 19, 58, 78, 182
java.policy policy file, 58, 78, 92, 194, 199, 202
java.rmi.security.policy property, 96, 97, 98
java.rmi.server.code.base property, 96, 97
java.rmi.server.hostname property, 96, 97
Java Software Development Kit (SDK), 7, 220
JavaServer Web Development Kit (JSWDK), 37
java.sql package, 71
java.util package, 175
Java VM (Java virtual machine)
  applets and, 17
  basic description of, 2
  compiling and, 3–4
  internationalization and, 182
  Java platform architecture and, 2–3
  RMI and, 93
  sockets communications and, 116
Java Web Server, 59, 78
Java Web site, 3, 7
javax.crypto package, 220–221, 229
javax.servlet.http package, 40
javax.servlet package, 40
JButton class, 29, 31, 178
JDBC, 69, 70–71, 74–78
JFrame class, 28, 29, 31, 130
  inheritance and, 209–210
  object-oriented programming and, 207, 209–210, 214
JLabel class, 178, 208
JPanel class, 30, 208
JPanel component, 130

JRE (Java Runtime Environment), 220
JSP (JavaServer Pages)
  basic description of, 43–45
  directives, 44
  scriptlets, 44
JTextArea.append method, 115
JTextArea class, 132

Keyword(s)
  internationalization and, 177–178
  pair files, 171–175

Languages, foreign. *See* Internationalization
LessonTwoA class, 12–14
LessonTwoB class, 12, 13–14, 17–19
LessonTwoC.java, 12
LessonTwoD class, 14–16
LessonTwoE class, 15–16
line object, 111
line variable, 114
listenSocket method, 111–112, 114
List interface, 157
listSocket method, 110–111
Locale class, 176
lookup method, 98, 100

main method, 10–11, 12, 16, 29
  basic description of, 32–33
  internationalization and, 175–177
  RMI and, 98, 100–102
Map interface, 157
Math class, 12
Memory, objects in, 208
message object, 176
MessagesBundle_de_DE.properties file, 176,
  194, 201
MessagesBundle_en_US.properties file, 194,
  201
MessagesBundle_fr_FR.properties file, 194,
  201
MessagesBundle parameter, 176
Method(s). *See also* Methods (listed by name)
  basic description of, 9, 10

nonstatic, 12–14
static, 12–14
Methods (listed by name). *See also* actionPerformed method
addActionListener method, 31
appendText method, 115
decrypt method, 227–229, 235–236
destroy method, 20, 22
doGet method, 43
doPost method, 41, 42, 43
doubleValue method, 135
DriverManager.getConnection method, 72
encrypt method, 218, 233–235
executeQuery method, 73
finalize method, 116
getContentPane method, 31, 33, 130
getData method, 91–92, 98, 100, 157, 159,
  160–161
getOrder method, 125, 154–156
getparameter method, 42
getString method, 177–178
getText method, 12–13, 16
init method, 20, 21
intValue method, 134–135
JTextArea.append method, 115
listenSocket method, 111–112, 114
listSocket method, 110–111
lookup method, 98, 100
main method, 10–11, 12, 16, 29, 32–33, 98,
  100–102, 175–177
paint method, 20, 22
println method, 11, 12, 159, 206
printStackTrace method, 54
rebind method, 98
run method, 114, 115
sendData method, 91–92, 98–100
sendOrder method, 154, 156
server.accept method, 110–111, 114
server.close method, 116
setBackground method, 21
setOrder method, 125
start method, 20–22
static method, 11
stop method, 20, 22
String.concat method, 206–207
synchronized method, 115

toString method, 54, 134, 137, 211
windowClosing method, 33
Multithreading, 108–109, 113–116

Netscape Navigator browser, 4, 21, 38.
    See also Browsers
NumberFormat class, 178–179
Numbers
    internationalization and, 178–179
    converting strings to, 134–135
    port, 94, 98, 110–111

Object class, 20
ObjectInputStream class, 156
Object-oriented programming. *See also*
    Objects
    basic description of, 206–216
    inheritance and, 209–211
    polymorphism and, 209–211
ObjectOutputFileStream class, 154
ObjectOutputStream class, 156
Objects. *See also* Object-oriented program-
    ming; Objects (listed by name); Classes
    (listed by name)
    sending, over networks, 132
    serialization of, 131–132
ODBC (Open DataBase Connectivity)
    basic description of, 76–78
    drivers, 74, 77, 78
Oracle, 70, 71–72
out.write call, 55

Package(s), 193–203, 220. *See also* Packages
    (listed by name)
    basic description of, 23–24
    declarations, 195
    fields, 213–214
    importing, 23, 26–28
    JAR file format and, 193–203
    public classes and, 195–196, 212
    setting up, 193–196
Packages (listed by name). *See also* Packages
    java.applet package, 23
    java.awt package, 23, 26–29, 209–211
    java.io package, 40, 52, 54, 155, 156

java.lang package, 24, 53, 98, 134, 137, 206,
    209, 211, 213, 215
java.sql package, 71
java.util package, 175
javax.crypto package, 220–221, 229
javax.servlet.http package, 40
javax.servlet package, 40
sun.jdbc.odbc package, 77
paint method, 20, 22
pair files, 171–175
Panel component, 19, 21–22, 31
Parameters
    ACTION parameter, 39, 43
    GET operation and, 41
    POST operation and, 41
    MessagesBundle parameter, 176
    passing, 41
Parent/child classes, 20, 209–211. *See also*
    Inheritance
peachQnt text field, 129, 131, 134–135
pearQnt text field, 129, 131, 133–135
Permissions
    for applets, 57–58
    basic description of, 47–68
    databases and, 69–87
    file access and, 57–58
    RMI and, 92
PKCS#1 standard, 229
Plug-in, Java, 19, 58, 78, 182
Plus sign (+), 73
Policy files
    creating, 57
    database access and, 74, 76, 77–78
    RMI and, 92
    running applets with, 57–58
Policy tool, 57, 76, 77
policytool command, 57
Polymorphism, 209–211
Port(s)
    numbers, 94, 98, 110–111
    sockets communications and, 110–111
    RMI and, 94, 98
POST operation, 41
Primitive data types, 134–135
println method, 11, 12, 159, 206
printStackTrace method, 54
PrintWriter class, 42, 111, 112
Private fields, 213–214

Private keys, 219–236
private variable, 72–73
Project Swing API, 26–29, 31, 33
    customer lists and, 157
    RMI and, 128–129, 130–131
Properties files, 172–173, 196
Protected fields, 213–214
Public classes, 195–196, 212
Public fields, 213–214
public_html directory, 92, 93, 95
Public keys, 221–236
Public keyword, 11
Purchase button, 125, 128–129, 131–132, 218

Reading
    basic description of, 48
    databases data, 73–74
    stack traces, 75–76
rebind method, 98
Registry, 93–95, 98, 100–101, 126–127, 180,
    197–198
RemoteException, 156
RemoteServer class, 93–106, 125, 135–136,
    153–155, 164–167, 222–225, 230–233,
    250–251
RemoteServer class, 92, 98, 99, 194
RemoteServer_skel.class, 199
RemoteServer_stub.class, 199
Remove button, 159
Request objects, 42
Reset button, 128, 129, 131
ResourceBundle variable, 176–178
Response objects, 42
ResultSet object, 55, 73
Return key, 124–125, 128, 138
RMI (Remote Method Invocation)
    API, 89–96, 107, 132, 135, 176
    basic description of, 89–106
    internationalization and, 176, 180, 182
    JavaBeans API and, 90
    Registry, 93–95, 98, 100–101, 126–127,
        180, 197–198
RMIClient1 class, 90–104, 124–151, 225–227,
    233–244
    encrypting symmetric keys with, 276–283
    exception handling and, 156–157

    internationalization and, 170–171, 175–178,
        180–181, 183–187
    JAR format and, 200–201
    packages and, 194–195, 200–201
    RMI and
        sending symmetric keys with, 265–271
    sendOrder method and, 155
RMICLient2 class, 90–105, 125–139, 143–
    146, 221–236, 245–249
    customer lists and, 157–160, 164–167
    encrypting symmetric keys with, 283–287
    exception handling and, 156–157
    getOrder method and, 155
    internationalization and, 170–171, 175–178,
        181, 187–191
    object-oriented programming and, 214–215
    packages and, 194–195, 198–199
    sending symmetric keys with, 271–276
rmiEapp.html file, 194, 201
RMIEnglishApp class, 194, 201, 260–264
rmiFapp.html file, 194, 201
rmiFrench.html file, 182
RMIFrenchApp class, 194, 201, 251–256
rmiGapp.html file, 194, 201
RMIGermanApp class, 194, 201, 256–260
rmiregistry command, 94
RMISecurityManager class, 98, 100, 101
RSA (Rivest, Shamir, and Adleman) algorithm,
    220–221, 229, 276–287
run method, 114, 115
Runnable interface, 114
Running
    applets, 19, 57–58
    introduction to, 1–7
    servlets, 39
    a simple program, 1–7
    socket communications examples, 110
RuntimePermission, 77

SDK (Java Software Development Kit), 7, 220
Send class, 93, 99, 106
sendData method, 91–92, 98–100
Send interface, 92, 125, 135, 156, 196, 222–
    225, 230–233, 249
sendOrder method, 154, 156
Serializable interface, 131
Serialization, 153–167, 229

server.accept method, 110–111, 114
server.close method, 116
ServerSocket object, 110–111
Servlet(s)
    building, 37–46
    database access by, 78
    file access by, 59
    JavaServer Pages and, 43–45
ServletException class, 40, 42
Session keys, 218–219, 222–223, 229–235
setBackground method, 21
SET CLASSPATH command, 6
Set interface, 157
setOrder method, 125
Sets
    accessing data in, 159–160
    creating, 158–159
SimpleApplet class, 19–20, 22–23
simpleApplet.html file, 19
skel class, 93, 94
Socket(s)
    basic description of, 107–122
    client-side behavior and, 109, 111–113
    multithreaded example for, 113–116
    server-side behavior and, 109–111
Socket class, 112
SocketClient class, 109, 111–112, 116–118
SocketServer class, 109–110, 118–120
SocketThrdServer class, 120–122
Solaris, 3, 76–77
SQL (Structure Query Language), 73–74
Stack traces
    database access and, 75–78
    reading, 75–76
    RMI and, 138
Start button, 6
start method, 20–22
Statement class, 55, 73
static keyword, 11
static method, 11
stop method, 20, 22
StoreData class, 11
StringBuffer class, 207
String class, 71, 73, 154, 157, 158, 179, 206,
    207, 211, 213
String.concat method, 206–207
Strings, converting numbers to, 134–135

stub class, 93, 94
sub.jdbc.odbc package, 77
Submit button, 38
SwingUI class, 28–31, 33, 48
Symmetric key encryption, 218–229
synchronized keyword, 115, 155
synchronized method, 115
sysedit command, 6
System class, 11–12, 24, 52, 206, 207
System.getProperty, 52
System properties, 52

Tab key, 133–134
Tables, creating, 70
Tags. *See also* HTML (HyperText Markup
        Language)
    <APPLET> tag, 19, 201
    <BODY> tag, 44
    <HEAD> tag, 44
    <HTML> tag, 44
    <TITLE> tag, 44
textArea component, 101, 111, 114, 115
Text editors, 3
textField object, 49, 51, 55, 112
Text fields
    appleQnt text field, 129, 131–135
    creditcard text field, 133
    peachQnt text field, 129, 131, 134–135
    pearQnt text field, 129, 131, 133–135
text.txt file, 57, 59
Thread(s)
    basic description of, 22, 108
    sockets communications and, 113–116
    start method and, 22
<TITLE> tag, 44
toString method, 54, 134, 137, 211
Total Cost field, 134
Translation, 172. *See also* Internationalization
try block, 53, 55, 72, 98, 154–156, 171

UnicastRemoteObject, 98
UNIX, 4, 97, 110
    file access and, 52, 58
    internationalization and, 179–181
    packages and, 197–198

RMI and, 92–95, 96, 126–127
URLs (Uniform Resource Locators)
   basic description of, 42
   database access and, 71–72
   GET operation and, 41–42
   RMI and, 89, 93
User names, 73
User interfaces, 25–35, 123–151. *See also*
     Interfaces

Value pair files, 171–175
Variables. *See also* Variables (listed by name)
   global, 213
   instance, 29–30, 49, 128–129, 175
Variables (listed by name). *See also* Variables
   CLASSPATH variable, 4, 6, 94, 95
   final variable, 72–73
   private variable, 72–73
View button, 158, 159
View Order command, 125
View order set, of files, 202
Visual Basic (Microsoft), 2–3
void keyword, 11

Web browser(s)
   destroy method and, 22
   doPost method and, 42

enabled for the Java 2 platform, 19
   JAR files and, 199
   policy files and, 58
   running applets and, 19, 58
   windows, top-level containers as, 26
Web Server, Java, 59, 78
WindowAdapter class, 33
windowClosing method, 33
WindowListener interface, 33, 208
Windows (Microsoft), 3,
   class path and, 6
   database access and, 76–77
   internationalization and, 180–181
   Java Plug-in and, 19, 58, 78, 182
   packages and, 197–199
   RMI and, 93–97, 126–127
Writing
   basic description of, 3, 48
   file access and, 48, 55
   databases data, 73–74

XML (eXtensible Markup Language), 43

ZIP file format, 199–200

ava™ Technology from Addison-Wesley

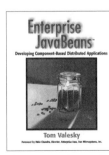

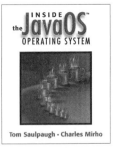

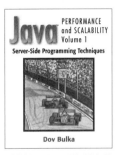

Addison-Wesley Professional

How to Register Your Book

Register this Book

Visit: **http://www.aw.com/cseng/register**

Enter the ISBN*

Then you will receive:

- Notices and reminders about upcoming author appearances, tradeshows, and online chats with special guests
- Advanced notice of forthcoming editions of your book
- Book recommendations
- Notification about special contests and promotions throughout the year

*The ISBN can be found on the copyright page of the book

Visit our Web site

http://www.aw.com/cseng

When you think you've read enough, there's always more content for you at Addison-Wesley's web site. Our web site contains a directory of complete product information including:

- Chapters
- Exclusive author interviews
- Links to authors' pages
- Tables of contents
- Source code

You can also discover what tradeshows and conferences Addison-Wesley will be attending, read what others are saying about our titles, and find out where and when you can meet our authors and have them sign your book.

We encourage you to patronize the many fine retailers who stock Addison-Wesley titles. Visit our online directory to find stores near you.

Contact Us via Email

cepubprof@awl.com

Ask general questions about our books.

Sign up for our electronic mailing lists.

Submit corrections for our web site.

mikeh@awl.com

Submit a book proposal.

Send errata for a book.

cepubpublicity@awl.com

Request a review copy for a member of the media interested in reviewing new titles.

registration@awl.com

Request information about book registration.

Addison-Wesley Professional

One Jacob Way, Reading, Massachusetts 01867 USA

TEL 781-944-3700 • FAX 781-942-3076